*The Trace of Judaism*

Northwestern University Press
Studies in Russian Literature and Theory

*Series Editors*
Robert Belknap
Caryl Emerson
Gary Saul Morson
William Mills Todd III
Andrew Wachtel

# The Trace of Judaism

DOSTOEVSKY, BABEL, MANDELSTAM, LEVINAS

*Val Vinokur*

NORTHWESTERN UNIVERSITY PRESS / EVANSTON, ILLINOIS

Northwestern University Press
www.nupress.northwestern.edu

Printed in the United States of America

10  9  8  7  6  5  4  3  2  1

Library of Congress Cataloging-in-Publication Data

Vinokur, Val.
    The trace of Judaism : Dostoevsky, Babel, Mandelstam, Levinas / Val Vinokur.
        p. cm. — (Northwestern University Press studies in Russian literature and
    theory)
    Includes bibliographical references and index.
    ISBN 978-0-8101-5208-3 (cloth : alk. paper)
    ISBN 978-0-8101-2585-8 (pbk. : alk. paper)
    1. Russian literature—History and criticism. 2. Lévinas, Emmanuel—Criticism
and interpretation. 3. Dostoyevsky, Fyodor, 1821–1881—Criticism and
interpretation. 4. Babel', I. (Isaak), 1894–1941—Criticism and interpretation.
5. Mandel'shtam, Osip, 1891–1938—Criticism and interpretation. 6. Ethics.
7. Judaism and literature. 8. Judaism in literature. 9. Aesthetics. I. Title.
II. Series: Studies in Russian literature and theory.
PG2987.E85V56 2008
891.709—dc22                                                    2008014825

*For Rose and Elia*

# Contents

# Acknowledgments

This book first emerged as a dissertation under the kindly and hyperactive direction of Caryl Emerson, who did for me only what she continues to do for most of her Ph.D. students—which is to say, far more than can be optimistically expected even from the best of mentors. As a comparative literature student at Princeton, my work also benefited—intellectually, materially, or morally—from the company and attention of Bob Gibbs, Olga Hasty, Leora Batnitzky, Jacob Meskin, Christine Hayes, Stanley Corngold, Thomas Trezise, Bob Fagles, Clarence Brown, Sandie Bermann, Judy Lewin, Gabriella Safran, Inessa Medzhibovskaya (later a colleague at the New School), Peter Gordon, Eileen Reeves, Claudia Brodsky, Thomas Pavel, April Alliston, the late Earl Miner, Elaine Showalter, Robert Fagles, Robert Wuthnow and the Center for the Study of Religion, Carol Szymanski, and Charlotte Zanidakis.

Beyond Princeton, I have been blessed with many thoughtful interlocutors and venues for my work. I am grateful to such readers as Harriet Murav, Bob Mandel, Gwen Walker, Harry Keyishian, Gary Rosenshield, Irene Masing-Delic and Kurt Schultz of the *Russian Review*, Jeff Perl of *Common Knowledge*, Brian Horowitz, Nancy Ruttenberg, Jim Rice, Sam Moyn, Janneke van de Stadt, Sasha Senderovich, Peter Atterton, Adam Newton, Sandor Goodheart, Paul Mendes-Flohr, Dale and Lorna Peterson, Stanley Rabinowitz, the Amherst Center for Russian Culture, and the Saul Z. Cohen Fund for Russian Jewish Culture.

My colleagues and students at Eugene Lang College/The New School for Liberal Arts have been great sources of encouragement and inspiration. I should thank Jonathan Veitch and Eliza Nichols—princes among academic administrators—for many things, the least of which was offering me an early sabbatical to complete my revisions. My departmental co-chairs Neil Gordon and Noah Isenberg supported me in every way as this book journeyed into print. Mark Larrimore, Tony Anemone, Julia Foulkes, Terri Gordon, and Virginia Jackson are only a few of the fellow teacher-scholars

*Acknowledgments*

at the New School who have moved my thinking about ethics and aesthetics over the years—as have such students as Jin Chang, Emma Jones, Frances Wood, Arthur Metcalf, Cole Larsen, Tracy Golden, Rebekah Smith, Jessica Glickman, Grace de la Aguilera, Liz Hynes, Emilija Guobyte, and many others. Carolyn Vega, my research assistant, deserves special praise for digging up elusive sources and cleaning up my citations.

I am grateful to Mike Levine, Saul Morson, Anne Gendler, Paul Fermin, and the anonymous readers at Northwestern University Press for welcoming this book with great alacrity and intellectual sympathy.

Thanks, always, to my mother, and to Ronnie Perelis, Sagi Kfir, Jules Chametzky, and Anne Halley (z'l).

Most of all I thank my wife (and colleague), Rose Réjouis, who helped me with countless versions of this project over fifteen years and whose love sustains me. I dedicate this book to her and to our son, Elia.

*V. V.*
*Brooklyn, 2008*

# Abbreviations

BK      Fyodor Dostoevsky, *The Brothers Karamazov*, trans. Richard Pevear
        and Larissa Volokhonsky (New York: Vintage, 1991)

CP      Paul Celan, *Collected Prose*, trans. Rosmarie Waldrop (Manchester,
        U.K.: Carcanet, 1986)

CPL     Osip Mandelstam, *Critical Prose and Letters*, trans. J. G. Harris and
        C. Link (Ann Arbor, Mich.: Ardis, 1990)

Demons  Fyodor Dostoevsky, *Demons*, trans. Richard Pevear and Larissa
        Volokhonsky (New York: Vintage Books, 1994)

Diary   Fyodor Dostoevsky, *The Diary of a Writer*, trans. Boris Brasol (New
        York: Charles Scribner, 1949)

EI      Emmanuel Levinas, *Ethics and Infinity*, trans. Richard A. Cohen
        (Pittsburgh: Duquesne University Press, 1985)

Idiot   Fyodor Dostoevsky, *The Idiot*, trans. Richard Pevear and Larissa
        Volokhonsky (New York: Vintage, 2003)

LR      Emmanuel Levinas, *The Levinas Reader*, ed. Sean Hand, trans.
        Alphonso Lingis (Oxford: Blackwell, 1992)

NT      Osip Mandelstam, *The Noise of Time and Other Prose Pieces*, trans.
        Clarence Brown (London: Quartet Books, 1988)

OM      Clare Cavanagh, *Osip Mandelstam and the Modernist Creation of
        Tradition* (Princeton, N.J.: Princeton University Press, 1995)

OTB     Emmanuel Levinas, *Otherwise Than Being, or Beyond Essence*,
        trans. Alphonso Lingis (Boston: Martinus Nijhoff, 1981)

PC      John Felstiner, *Paul Celan: Poet, Survivor, Jew* (New Haven, Conn.:
        Yale University Press, 1995)

PDP    Mikhail Bakhtin, *Problems of Dostoevsky's Poetics,* ed. and trans. Caryl Emerson (Minneapolis: University of Minnesota Press, 1989)

PN    Emmanuel Lévinas, *Proper Names,* trans. M. Smith (Stanford, Calif.: Stanford University Press, 1996)

PSS    Fyodor Dostoevsky, *Polnoe sobranie sochinenii v 30-ti tomakh* (Leningrad: Nauka, 1972)

SA    Vladimir Solovyov, *A Solovyov Anthology,* trans. Natalie Duddington (New York: Charles Scribner, 1950)

SDT    Osip Mandelstam, *Sochinenia v dvukh tomakh,* ed. Averintsev, Nerler, and Mikhailov (Moscow: Khudozhestvennaya Literatura, 1990)

SS    Isaac Babel, *Sobranie sochinenii v chetyrekh tomakh* (Moscow: Vremia, 2006)

SSCT    Osip Mandelstam, *Sobranie sochinenii v chetyrekh tomakh,* ed. Nerler, Nikitaev, and Sergeeva (Moscow: Art-Biznis-Tsentr, 1993)

TI    Emmanuel Lévinas, *Totality and Infinity,* trans. Alphonso Lingis (Pittsburgh: Duquesne University Press, 1961)

*The Trace of Judaism*

# Levinas and Russian Literature

> "I must confess," said Charlotte, "that when
> you speak of these wondrous entities as related
> they seem to me not so much blood relations
> as related in spirit and in the soul. In precisely
> this way true and important friendships
> may come about between people: opposing
> qualities make an intenser union possible. . . .
> Bringing things together is a harder task, and
> a worthier one. A man skilled in the art of
> bringing things together would be welcome
> in every walk of life."
> —Goethe, *Elective Affinities*

THE WORLD WANTS TO BE SEEN. It demands one's attention and response. This is an ethical demand and an aesthetic one. Nearly every artistic or literary manifesto claims to offer an aesthetic sensibility that will better "do justice" to the world. Wittgenstein's cryptic assertion that "ethics and aesthetics are one and the same" feels strangely intuitive either because it must be true or because we need it to be true.[1] But aesthetic perception has its limits; it can be reductive or essentialist, turning the other into more of the same. Then again, is it fair to ask literature or art generally—a human activity that nudges us beyond things mundane—to attend to this demanding world? After all, art in its otherworldliness not only reflects this world but discloses it—while being part of this world, another of its demanding constituents. All of which demands an "ethical criticism" that can address art without consigning creative works to the realm of philosophical illustration or anthropological corrective, and even more importantly, without suppressing the autonomous instincts that animate the best kinds of aesthetic activity. Unfortunately, the entire project of social criticism—in all its manifold richness, from Chernyshevsky to Foucault—does not satisfy this demand. On the one hand it offers too much—a system that accounts for the human condition, literary and otherwise, whether or not anyone needs such an accounting. On the other hand, in its tendency to overlook the strangeness of aesthetic detail, social criticism offers too little.

But these unwieldy concerns are better managed by way of a narrower intersection. In a 1984 interview Emmanuel Levinas, arguably the most important ethical philosopher of the late twentieth century, invokes a cultural stereotype that is pervasive in modern Jewish literature from Mendele Mokher Sforim and Isaac Babel to Henry Roth and Cynthia Ozick: the Jew as a creature at home more in books than in nature and history, and who discovers the world thanks to Christian authors. He explains this legacy, described by Franz Rosenzweig in the 1920s:

> Great art, that was non-Jewish art, accessible to Jews concretely by means of their coexistence with Christians. This is neither confusion nor syncretism; it is a symbiosis, which for Rosenzweig is profound and linked to the very structure of truth. It is as if there was a supplementary enrichment, an increase. The truth of Judaism would be the one which is given to a people already "near to" the Lord, but who do not see the world. Christianity would be the truth of the one who is on the road to the Eternal, traversing the world. But this experience of the road and the world is also given to Judaism, thanks to this neighborliness. A heretical theology? Or rather a possible understanding of destinies that are incontestably and essentially intertwined . . . And these are concrete things, because the state of Israel must cohabit with the Christian world, read Christian authors . . . all of Europe, which is irrecusable and which is Christian.[2]

This cultural symbiosis can be narrowed still further. Levinas recounts an anecdote about an Israeli academic, born in Eastern Europe, who paid him a visit in Paris. "Upon entering my house, he noticed that I had the complete works of Pushkin on the bookshelves: 'You can see right away,' he said, 'that this is a Jewish home.'"[3]

The investment in Russian authors by Jews of East European origin has always been especially striking. Beyond the historical circumstances of such an investment, the Russian and Jewish traditions share certain preoccupations. I believe these shared preoccupations are meaningful in ways that go beyond historical contingency. Both traditions, after all, are driven by ethical concerns, or, as Levinas puts it, the "philosophical problem understood as the meaning of the human, as the search for the famous 'meaning of life'— about which the Russian novelists ceaselessly wonder."[4] Furthermore, one finds in both a distinct trepidation about the ethics of aesthetic activity— from the biblical prohibition against graven images and the Jewish modernist critique of representational art, to Gogol and Tolstoy's repudiation of their own fiction (and indeed of any art unmoored from moral education) and Dostoevsky's anxiety about negative beauty (Dmitri Karamazov's talk of the "beauty of Sodom" and Ivan's of the "artistic cruelty" of Turkish soldiers in the Balkans).

Given such correlations, it seems surprising that, until recently, the topic of Judaism and Jews in Russian literature has been preoccupied with a fairly primitive test: Is this Russian author Judeophobic or Judeophilic? Or how did the author *really* feel about Jews? This book reflects the emergence of a relatively new effort to examine more deeply the interconnections between Russian and Jewish culture and thought, while avoiding the distortions of apologetics.[5] Unlike many of the scholars involved in this effort, I am less concerned with the construction of Jewish or Russian identity, per se, than I am with what these interconnections can teach us about ethics and aesthetics—two broad and tensely intertwined terms for how we make value and meaning as we engage with the world. More specifically, I argue here that such Russian writers as Fyodor Dostoevsky, Isaac Babel, and Osip Mandelstam are profoundly involved with an ethical vision central to Jewish thought. I focus this argument by selecting Levinas, the Lithuanian-born Franco-Jewish phenomenologist, as a philosophical evocation of this vision, not only because of his roots in Russian culture, but also because his idea of ethical nonreciprocity can claim partial Russian descent.[6] At the same time, an examination of Levinas alongside Russian literature seeks to address and see beyond the current revisionism in Levinas studies, in which scholars have been disappointed in their attempts to extrapolate a coherent politics from his ethics.[7] This book suggests that such incoherence may be understood in the context of the fundamental bipolarity in Russian culture—a tension between reality and utopia that is compellingly expressed in the authors considered here. Is it possible that Levinas's volatile mixture of philosophical messianism and Judaic moral realism, as Leora Batnitzky has described it, finds coherence not as theology, politics, or even philosophy but as literature—and particularly Russian literature, as a space in which the ethical and the aesthetic are so inextricably intertwined? If, according to Levinas, only the "I" (not institutions) can see "the tears that a civil servant cannot see: the tears of the Other,"[8] then we must consider literature's role in the construction of this kind of ethical subjectivity.[9] I wish to discover how the encounter with the other invokes responsibilities ethical and aesthetic: indeed, without aesthetic vision, ethics is blind and inert; without ethics, aesthetic activity reduces the other to an object of my pleasure or contemplation.

This book explores the intersection of several related questions: What are the ethical implications of genre? And how does this question acquire a spiritual orientation in these three writers? I argue that each of these authors grapples not only with Western or Russian Orthodox models but also with a Judaic remainder—a ghostly presence that can unsettle initial ethical and aesthetic preconceptions. Through my examination of a classic nineteenth-century Russian (Orthodox) novelist alongside two twentieth-century self-identified Russian writers (each a master of his genre) of differing Jewish backgrounds, I hope to achieve a complex range of responses to the "Russian-Jewish Question."[10] If the answer to this "Question" is neither simple opposition nor naive syncretism but messy symbiosis, what, indeed, is its "surplus"? I argue that, in Dostoevsky's case, this symbiotic surplus, concealed by his anti-Semitism, may have pushed him toward what has been called *The Brothers Karamazov*'s "practical Christianity"[11]—infused with the kinds of Western liberal, middle-class values he had derogatively associated with Jews in his nonfiction. The short stories of Isaac Babel and the prose and verse of Osip Mandelstam, on the other hand, more explicitly reveal the kind of symbiosis of which Rosenzweig and Levinas speak. In the case of Babel's literary profile, it is Russian literature (and his ambition to transform it) that casts him out of his cozy Jewish milieu and "on the road" of nature and history as he chronicles the 1920 Soviet-Polish War, while Mandelstam's poetic longing for (Christian) "world culture" ultimately leads him to a reappraisal of the "chaos of Judaism" that had alienated him growing up in an assimilated Petersburg Jewish household. Just as I ask how Levinas's thought, with its changing and layered views on art and writing, might help one think about this set of ethical, aesthetic, and religious questions, I also consider how readings of these writers might be used to adjust Levinas's ideas about literature and ethics. If, in his effort to critique the ontological bias of Western philosophy, Levinas borrows the anarchic compassion and aesthetic intensity found in Russian literature, does this reveal something enduring about his project?

The goal here is to offer a space for interaction between such questions and for a dialogue between Jewish and Christian ways of understanding the ethics of aesthetic sensibility. Of course, by my selection of authors I certainly do not mean to imply that there could be any single Russian or Jewish tradition, or that Judaism is anything but one of many lenses through which ethics may be passed. Instead, these choices reflect my understanding of Levinasian ethics as a valuable return on the Jewish investment in Russian letters. Drawing on Levinas allows me to productively examine the ways in which certain Russian authors pair the ethical and the aesthetic imagination. Although an influence study may recover "Levinas's Pushkin" or "Levinas's Dostoevsky," a close reading of Levinas actually suggests a different, intertextual path. Levinas reconfigures both the ethical and the Judaic. Careful attention to his writing therefore suggests new readings of the figuration of the Jewish value in Russian literature in particular as well as new ways of thinking about the ethical-aesthetic imagination in general.

Emmanuel Levinas (1906–95), born in Kovno, Lithuania, was led to philosophy by both the Hebrew Bible and the Russian literary classics, before leaving in 1923 for Strasbourg (and later the Freiburg im Breisgau of Husserl and Heidegger) to study the discipline in earnest. After the war, which he survived in a German camp for Jewish prisoners of war while his family of origin was murdered by the Nazis, Levinas became more involved in Jewish communal and intellectual life in France, studying the Talmud with the mysterious Shushani, who also instructed Elie Wiesel. Throughout his work, Levinas addresses the question (raised by both post-Enlightenment and post-Holocaust thought) of "whether we are not being duped by morality."[12] He displaces this question (which has dogged nearly every attempt at a philosophical or religious ethics) with the concept of the face. The face of the other—vulnerable and expressive, weak and demanding—transcends any moral economy or universal truth. The face does not ask me to follow a social contract or a categorical imperative; the face obligates simply because it needs me, even if only to see and acknowledge it.

According to Levinas, the source of this idea of facing is not specifically Judaic. Levinas does not draw the comparison, but a student of Russian culture will be reminded of the Orthodox theologian Pavel Florensky's 1922 essay "Iconostasis," which discusses the differences between the *litso* (face), *lik* (countenance), and *lichina* (a concealment, the opposite of countenance). The *litso* is what we see in ordinary life and may reveal nothing; the *lik* reminds us of holy imperatives; and the demonic "mug" is a *lichina,* a mask without a face, tempting us away from countenance. These concepts—the *lik* in particular—are central to Russian literature.[13]

Indeed, Levinas sees literary activity as a space for understanding and reimagining how we respond to faces: "Across all literature the human face speaks—or stammers, or gives itself a countenance, or struggles with its caricature" (*EI* 117). The concept of the face also motivates what Levinas calls the Saying and the Said. The Saying is the event of "addressing," like the eye contact that precedes a greeting, while the Said is the content or text. The Saying binds the narrator and audience in a dynamic of responsibility, a passionate and vertical relationship of generosity and entrapment. Literature tries to do justice to this relation between the addressing and the text (in which the human world inheres), just as laws and judges are addressed by and try to do justice to ethics. And an ethically attuned criticism, as the work of a growing number of scholars shows,[14] could examine the ways in which literature struggles to break out of its Said into a live Saying.

Just as his concept of the face transforms the ethical socially and artistically, Levinas also reformulates Judaism—even as he seeks to convey it—in a way that reveals specific discursive tensions. And just as I stress the prominence of a spiritually inflected moral-aesthetic tension in the Russian tradition, I rely on Levinas's emphasis that the rabbinic corpus is an expression of ethics over ontology. After all, Levinas's 1984 remarks about Judeo-Christian "symbiosis" evolve from earlier, more polemical commentary. In a 1955 radio homily, he argues that in Judaism spirituality is offered up not through a tangible substance, but through absence. God is real and concrete not through incarnation but through Law, and His greatness is not inspired by His sacred mystery. . . . Man can have confidence in an absent God and also be an adult who can judge his own sense of weakness. . . . This vigorous dialectic established equality between God and man at the very heart of their disproportion. This is a long way from a warm and almost tangible communion with the Divine and from the desperate pride of the atheist. It is a complete and austere humanism, linked to a difficult adoration. . . . A personal and unique God is not something revealed like an image in a dark room.[15]

In his emphasis on God's reality through Law (as revealed by rabbinic mediation) and through a "difficult adoration," and not through flesh and "tangible communion," Levinas seems to criticize the emphasis on incarnation in many forms of Christianity.

Elsewhere, however, he directs similar criticism at the basic assumptions of what he calls the "language of Greek philosophy," into which the "alternative . . . Judeo-Christian . . . approach to meaning and truth" has been incorporated. The key feature of this language "was its equation of truth with an *intelligibility of presence*, . . . an intelligibility that considers truth to be that which is present or copresent, that which can be gathered or synchronized into a totality that we would call the world or cosmos." The Greek equation of truth with presence presumes "that however different the two terms of a relation might appear (e.g., the Divine and the human) or however separated over time (e.g., into past and future), they can ultimately be rendered commensurate and simultaneous, the same." This totalization to presence, Levinas argues, can be applied to the interhuman realm. But the interhuman

can also be considered from another perspective—the ethical or biblical perspective that transcends the Greek language of intelligibility—as a theme of justice and concern for the other as other, as a theme of love and desire, which carries us beyond the infinite being of the world as presence. The interhuman is thus an interface: a double axis where what is "of the world" qua phenomenological intelligibility is juxtaposed with what is "not of the world" qua ethical responsibility.[16]

Ethical responsibility reflects my almost instinctive, nonreciprocal position of solicitousness to a person who is irreducibly not myself—and thus, in a sense, "not of this world."

What is striking here is that Levinas's "Jewish" discomfort with the idea of incarnation, central to Christian thought, draws partly on Greek skepticism (which he praises elsewhere and often in his work), while his critique of

Greek ontology mentions its co-optation of an "alternative Judeo-*Christian*" approach to truth. Likewise, his discussion of an "ethical or biblical perspective that transcends the Greek language of intelligibility" does not exclusively indicate the Hebrew Bible and does not preclude a Christian perspective. Such apparent inconsistencies reflect the manner in which Levinas straddles several contending and intertwined traditions. They also reflect the dual discourse—inclusive and oppositional—that characterizes his thought over time. This methodological dissonance suggests larger concerns: on the one hand, Levinas abhors the blinding generalizations (and, on occasion, outright tyranny) of all-inclusive universal values; on the other hand, he argues that "being toward the other" is a "non-allergic" condition, that sociality is generally good and not Sartre's hell of "other people."

These two concerns inform the laconic generosity of Levinas's involvement with Dostoevsky. Indeed, the philosopher locates his professional sound bite not in a verse in the Hebrew Bible or Talmud, but rather in the Elder Zosima's famous maxim from *The Brothers Karamazov:* "Each of us is guilty in everything before everyone, and I most of all."[17] This quote appears in easily half of Levinas's published works and in all of his interviews—more regularly and consistently than any single "Jewish" credo. This despite the fact that Levinas—a literary maven who published on Agnon, Celan, Leiris, and Blanchot, and who cited obscure details from a number of Dostoevsky's novels—did not write a single essay devoted to the classic Russian novelist.[18] For Levinas, Dostoevsky's maxim suggests that I always have one responsibility more than the other. The face of the other—in its nakedness and destitution and not in any conceived notions, images, personalities, or memories I may superimpose over it—makes me a hostage. Because real life does not support the anarchy of unmediated ethics, however, Levinas and his Judaic sources acknowledge the practical need for something more "of this world" than ethics, for institutions and laws, for an inherently approximate and imperfect justice, which is "the way in which I respond to the face [when] I am not alone in the world with the other."[19] If the other's face is unique, then the choice between two unique faces is a Solomonic agony, a violence without which ethics could not be enacted.[20] I argue that this unstable yet compelling dynamic between ethics and justice is the symbiotic product of a dangerously nonjudgmental, Christian (and Russian) incarnate aesthetic; an abstract Hebraic commitment to law; and a Talmudic inclination to interpret this law according to the demands of particular faces. And while it may be true that this product cannot attain coherence as theology, philosophy, or politics, I argue that it is comprehensible in (and as) literature—that amalgam of characters, narrative, and linguistic art that thrives on human incoherence.

Levinas's adaptation of Dostoevsky's ethical maximalism drives my contention that the novelist's Christian ambitions are subverted by the very dialogic novel form—with its almost Talmudic chattiness—that Bakhtin has associated with the novelist. This connection also allows the reader to further differentiate Alyosha Karamazov's practice of ethics from Zosima's ecstatically Christian credo and to appreciate more fully the moral failure of Dostoevsky's earlier attempt at a saintly hero, Prince Myshkin. My argument not only leads to a reappraisal of the relations between Dostoevsky's Christianity and anti-Semitism, but of his ethics and aesthetics.

*The Idiot* and *Demons,* respectively, show the ethical limitations of Christian rapture in the figure of Myshkin (who is ultimately unable to choose between "two unique faces"), and the moral emptiness of physical beauty in the figure of Stavrogin. My interpretation of *The Idiot* highlights Myshkin's tendency to remain transfixed by the face of the other—his ethics is quixotic, aesthetically generated, and unable to make the transition to justice. Critics tend to blame Myshkin's downfall on a corrupt world; few of them attend to Myshkin's realization at the end of the novel that "at that moment and for a long time past he was not saying what he should have been saying, not doing what he should have been doing." And, in *Demons,* written shortly after *The Idiot,* the charismatic model of incarnate redemption appears as a hollow, demonic parody in the figure of Stavrogin—an unresponsive, false *lik,* or *lichina,* a negative embodiment of Myshkin's quixotic and indecisive "positive beauty."

*The Brothers Karamazov,* on the other hand, introduces Alyosha, a hero who slowly evolves from a listener, an interpreter of faces and situations, into a *pravednik,* a righteous person, a teacher with the understanding, compassion, and strength to choose between faces and who can, by the novel's end, vigorously begin to manage the moral and emotional consequences of his brother Mitya's trial and elevate a group of schoolboys into "gentlemen." Unlike his predecessors in the two earlier novels, Alyosha attains a canny righteousness by the end of *The Brothers Karamazov,* when he declares that, if necessary, he himself would bribe the guards to free his brother Dmitri, despite the latter's classically Dostoevskyan conviction that Siberia will cleanse him spiritually of a crime he did not commit. Analyzing Alyosha's evolution, in light of Levinas and against the backdrop of the perennial "Dostoevsky and the Jewish Question," allows me to show the usefulness of distinguishing between a psychological guilt (which translates into chest-beating and self-punishment for most other Dostoevskyan characters and, indeed, for Dostoevsky himself) and an ethical guilt, a radical responsibility that requires a provisional and practical justice.

One implication of my efforts to "find" Levinas in Dostoevsky (and vice versa) has to do with what it means to "embody" an idea. For Dostoevsky, ideas are compelling only as "idea-feelings" (this is Dostoevsky's own term) in individuals;[21] for Levinas, ethics is expressed only in my solicitude for the other and never in any abstract concept. Accordingly, it may be more revealing to speak of covert, even ghostly, affinities between this Jew and that

Christian than between oppositional notions of Judaism and Christianity. My reading of Dostoevsky and Levinas begins to offer a description of an ethically and spiritually porous individuation, in which I may account for another without stripping away his or her difference—and in which the need for openness is balanced with the need to judge.

This porosity perhaps finds its most acute literary—and indeed, almost physical—expression in the short fiction of Isaac Babel. Babel inherited Dostoevsky's (and Tolstoy's) preoccupation with the aesthetics of political violence, as well as with its religious and ethical implications. Moreover, in Babel such porosity often appears as a defilement, which, bizarrely and brutally, may reveal an ethical horizon. Viktor Shklovsky wrote that Babel speaks "in the same voice of the stars and of gonorrhea."[22] But this is not just a decadent or ornamentalist aesthetic device. Perhaps the most radical example of its spiritual and ethical significance can be found in an invented apocryphal tale framed in "Pan Apolek," in which Jesus, before being baptized by John and contending with Satan in the wilderness, defiles Himself by laying with a humiliated bride who had vomited on her husband on their wedding night. Similarly, the saintly title character in "Sashka Christ" catches a venereal disease at the age of fourteen and (like Pan Apolek's Jesus) sleeps with women out of compassion and not desire. Yet Sashka Christ is authentically simple and good in spite (and according to some of the peasants, because) of such compromise and defilement—his saintliness has nothing to do with rule-bound purity, not unlike the Russian tradition of the holy fool.

This ethics of defilement finds resonance in both Russian and Jewish culture and thought. For example, Daniel Boyarin has emphasized the "carnality" of rabbinic ethics, while Dostoevsky takes this up in the theme of *Karamazovshchina* (a black smear, etymologically), the earthy "Karamazov force" that is shared not only by the impulsive Dmitri, the intellectual rebel Ivan, the murderous Smerdyakov, and the grotesque sensualist Fyodor, but also by Alyosha, the saintly acolyte. The Karamazov force is not original sin but a more general teeming, impure, subterranean life energy. One might say that it is the element that, according to Bruce Wilshire, provokes genocide and terrorism, that ultimate "anti-ecology" which is a "disgust and dread in the face of abounding, fecund, life itself—swarming, creeping, scurrying, unboundable, and uncontrollable."[23] Alyosha recognizes his own Karamazovism as an unpurgeable part of himself; and perhaps this is another reason why Levinas attributes to Alyosha the famous words of Markel, Father Zosima's dying brother, about being guilty "more than the others." This credo links Levinas's radical ethics to a recognition of the fundamental impurity of the self, an impurity that always makes the other (ontologically and often psychologically, if not always practically) my affair, whether this other likes me or not.

While I am suspicious of any ethics that seems to rely on transgression—

since transgression is often accompanied by self-absorption and insult and can lead to a cheaply aesthetic politics—I do argue for the moral significance of defilement in *Red Cavalry*. Like most prose fiction, Babel's is driven by a curiosity (his and ours) that risks collapsing the distinction between the self and others and thus risks the subjugation or effacement of these others. This risk also concerns Levinas, who insists on the irreducibility of other people. I argue that this concern is resolved, beautifully and generously, in many of Babel's stories, in which even the most integral and upright individuals are typically the most compromised and impure, contaminated by others and taking on their shame, while remaining themselves and helping others remain others. Defilement as moral revelation also characterizes Babel's narrator Liutov, just as it informs the book's orally marked or "speakerly" *skaz* narratives, in which the author's mimetic curiosity gives voice to an aesthetically exuberant depravity that implicates not only the brutal "folksy" narrators but Babel and his readers as well. I suggest that Babel's *skaz* reflects the larger artistic conception of ethics in his work, in which any good deed seems to require self-pollution: a "dirty ethics" that resembles and perhaps goes beyond Levinas's later invocation of an ethics of maternity.

Levinas's thought helps shed light on Babel's prose as an exquisitely uneasy intersection of brute ontology and literary ethos, of the good and evil of artistic witnessing. In *Red Cavalry*, prosaic curiosity is wedded to an intensely lyrical and poetically condensed sensibility. In this manner, the moral "direction" of dialogic fictional prose checks, and is checked by, the more static moral "stance" of poetry—a genre that so often metonymically signifies all of high literature if not art. It often seems that Levinasian ethics veers away from poetry in favor of prose, which is time-bound, like dialogue, a breaking of rhythm into action. Prose, like speech, presents the opportunity to argue, interrupt, criticize and self-criticize, to say and (to a limited extent) unsay something. The very shape of prose compiles words across time, and this diachrony seems to make prose more suitable than poetry for the redaction of complex and concrete ethical situations. Poetry, or rather, the ideal category of the poetic, is more temporally static.[24] At the heart of poetry is the author's *emission,* one that is emotional and even "physiological." A certain non-discursive self-centeredness abides in poetry. Prose, furthermore, is also driven by an other-directed curiosity. If poetry can be compared to an unmediated ethics, then prose approaches the language of justice. The chapter on Isaac Babel, however, seeks to complicate this view of prose by focusing on the *skaz* narratives in *Red Cavalry* in order to address the ethical ambiguities of prosaic curiosity and witnessing. I explore how the exuberant ventriloquism of the dialect narratives implicates both Babel and the reader in the depraved content of the Cossacks' tales.

This book progresses from prose to poetry—a progression that parallels the attempt to uncover the Saying in the Said and the ethical in the just.

In the dialogue between ethics and aesthetics, Babel's short, lyrical fiction serves as a bridge between Dostoevsky's novels and Osip Mandelstam's verse. The chapter on Mandelstam links existing scholarship about the poet's changing attitudes toward Judaism to a discussion of Levinas's complex view of the poetic both as evasiveness and, concurrently, an extreme exposure and sensibility to Otherness. One could frame the latter paradox in the following question: if poetry is indeed a supposedly less social genre, might the private sphere that it shapes actually serve a basic ethical function? In her trenchant defense of the lyrical sensibility, Clare Cavanagh writes:

> John Stuart Mill's claim that "poetry is not heard, but overheard"; T. S. Eliot's insistence that the poet "speaks only to himself—or to nobody"; Dickinson's letter to the world that "never wrote to me"; Mandelstam's solitary "reader in posterity"—all seem to place the poet at some remove from what a youthful Mandelstam called his "boring neighbors." But lyric poetry does not strive to set itself at an unbridgeable distance from the world of speaking beings that surrounds it. Rather it seeks to establish a little space between itself and the reader it nonetheless seeks to address. Or perhaps more precisely, it simply acknowledges, and works with, the space that necessarily separates us from any person with whom we hope to establish common ground . . . [We are invited] to consider whether "public" definitions are fully adequate to our private selves; perhaps true community . . . is best found at a little distance from the social selves we routinely inhabit. This commitment to the value of private selves and private space is in part what has permitted the poets of Eastern Europe to pay such eloquent tribute to all that was lost through its years of war, revolution, and Soviet oppression.[25]

Mandelstam develops into a poet who understands the ethically indispensable nature of his relation to his "boring neighbors," evolving from a certain youthful lyric preciousness into a more mature poetic ethos. At the same time, his attitude toward his Jewish origins gradually changes from self-loathing into an identification of Judaism with the spiritual roots of the poetic process.

Commentators often note Levinas's anti-aesthetic excesses—in which he lumps poetry together with the irresponsibility of pagan moods; and they have also noted Levinas's status as a literary maven and as someone whose philosophy often relies on poetic allusions and devices. Until recently, however, few have talked about the emergence of the word "poetry" in his later writing as an ethically central category, poetry not as the way being shows itself in language (à la Heidegger), but as the way tenderness, a breaking forth of a kind of private rectitude, rehumanizes a world that has been objectified by public discourse and public use.[26] The evolution of Levinas's views about poetry frames my examination of Mandelstam, who sees the poem as a message in a bottle, destined for a "secret addressee." For Mandelstam, poetry properly speaking refuses to imagine and objectify a concrete reader. These ideas were adopted by Paul Celan, and, eventually, through Celan, by Levinas himself. At the same time, I correlate the evolution of the Jewish theme in Mandelstam's work to a poetic negotiation between ethics and aesthetics. Between his early Judeophobic verse and his later prose and poetry, Mandelstam reclaims a customized version of his Jewish origins, a development in which the link between poetic ethics and Levinas's invocation of Judaism-as-ethics becomes evident. Mandelstam's early invocation of a Judaic chaos (a chaos that must be poetically overcome) becomes the "Judaic cares" of his later verse. These cares refer to the poetic process of breaking up the mundane order into creative disorder and then recomposing it as verse—a process mirrored by the ethical-aesthetic dynamics of Levinas's thought.

As I noted earlier, Levinas's postwar religious polemics against the Christian West mellowed into an expression of the symbiotic relations between the "Hebrew," "Greek," and "Christian" traditions. In this book, such symbiosis takes the form of a surprisingly almost crypto-Judaic trace in Dostoevsky; a tense interaction between Christian aesthetics and Jewish ethics in Babel; and the development of a "Jewish" ethical poetics in Mandelstam's later works—a poetics that emerges precisely from a "ghostly" Judaism likewise detectable in Dostoevsky. The Jewish-Christian symbiosis, in Levinas's view and to an extent in my readings here, is also an ethical-aesthetic one. In my conclusion I will consider the implications of such a model in the effort to reach an ethical criticism—for which Wittgenstein's intuition about the unity of ethics and aesthetics is not just a challenge but also a threat. After all, an all-consuming monism would certainly threaten criticism as much as the instrumentalism of the natural sciences would. The symbiotic model, on the other hand, may be richer and more organic than simple dualism or tolerance or syncretism: it suggests an ecology, in which difference and opposition (elective antipathies) are potential sources of mutual survival and enrichment (covert affinities)—and even, to paraphrase William Blake, of friendship.

14

## Chapter One

# Idiots and Demons: Dostoevsky's Aesthetic Perils

DOSTOEVSKY'S CHARACTERS tend toward vocal excess: excessive sincerity, insincerity, feeling, intellection, faith, doubt, and above all, excess speech. They talk too much. And their talk is typically charged with cosmic and practical questions of right and wrong—questions animated and muddled by the gales of human nature that Dostoevsky depicts so well.

Bakhtin was perhaps the first reader of Dostoevsky to appreciate the *aesthetics*, the artistic structure, of what I would call this vocal excess. Bakhtin argues that in Dostoevsky's mature prose, the novel reaches its apotheosis as a truly dialogic genre, that the vocal excesses are a kind of poetics. Bakhtin's *Problems of Dostoevsky's Poetics* leaves one with the sense that Dostoevsky's aesthetics—the formal structure of polyphony and multivalence that permeates his work—issues from an ethics of discourse that shuns monologic literature. In other words, while dialogue is often understood as an *ethically* positive category, Bakhtin turns it into something that is exemplary of a particular aesthetics.

In the process, Bakhtin offers a comprehensive way of understanding Dostoevsky's otherwise chaotic and emotionally contingent artistic form. Through Bakhtin, Dostoevsky's aesthetics make sense: he acquires a fitting, coherent poetics. This aesthetic approach does justice to Dostoevsky as a master craftsman and literary innovator. Such formal coherence, however, occasionally elides some of the more complex ethical problems in Dostoevsky's work, especially when these problems intersect with the aesthetic integrity of a given novel.

In this chapter, I seek to show how Levinas's idea of the face offers a deeper understanding of the ethical and aesthetic issues in *The Idiot* and *Demons*. Perhaps the face is a focal point to ambling prose the way poetic form is to poems: narratives and heroes turn toward the reader, pulling her along in time. And both of these novels specifically feature characters that respond to the human face in morally significant ways.[1] The textual thread binding this discussion will be something that Bakhtin elides: the meaning of death—or more precisely, the end of consciousness and the beginning of facelessness—in the two novels. First, I examine the connections and key differences between Prince Myshkin and Levinas's "ethics of the face." After considering how Myshkin's aesthetically saturated ethics cannot make the transition into worldly justice, the chapter turns to *Demons,* a novel which represents the total failure and perversion of the aesthetic model of redemption first tested in *The Idiot.* Contra Bakhtin, I argue that in Dostoevsky's world the end of consciousness (i.e., a character's death or lapse into insanity) underscores the immortality of the human voice less than it reminds us of the fragility of the human face.

Just as a stain allows the cell biologist to highlight the features of a tissue sample under a microscope, so too, for many readers, the fate of a novel's characters colors the meaning of the book. When a character dies, we take note; and the manner and context of this death are often significant in our ultimate sense of the work as a whole. In "Toward a Reworking of the Dostoevsky Book," however, Bakhtin proposes a theory about the *insignificance* of death in the dialogic novel. To be sure, he appreciates the fact that "characteristic for Dostoevsky's world are murders (portrayed from within the murderer's field of vision), suicides, and insanity"; but more important for Bakhtin is the fact that "normal deaths are rare in [Dostoevsky's] work, and [that] he usually notes them only in passing."[2] Unlike Tolstoy, whose narration frequents the minds of dying men, Dostoevsky holds that consciousness is ultimately as ignorant of its end as it is of its beginning:

> Dostoevsky *never* depicts death from within. . . . What matters here is not simply that one cannot spy upon death from within, cannot see it, just as one cannot see the back of one's head without resorting to a mirror. The back of one's head exists objectively and can be seen by others. But death from within, that is, one's own death consciously perceived, does not exist for anyone: not for the dying person, nor for others; it does not exist at all. . . . In Dostoevsky's world death finalizes nothing, because death does not affect the most important thing in this world—*consciousness for its own sake. (PDP* 290)

According to Bakhtin, it is essential that for Dostoevsky "to kill does not mean to refute" (*PDP* 290–91). Though, certainly, consciousness "dies objectively," it is likewise an "objective fact" that consciousness cannot perceive its own death; and herein lies its uniqueness, its peculiar independence from the material organism in which it existed (*PDP* 284). From this second objectivity, this concrete lack of information, metaphysics or religion (or literature, in its own fashion) is free to step in and eternalize the departed consciousness. It is in this sense, I would say, that Bakhtin stresses the insignificance of death in Dostoevsky's novels.[3]

The focus of my argument is different. I seek to examine the *signi-*

*ficance* of the end of consciousness in Dostoevsky and, more specifically, how its occurrence may indicate the novelist's awareness of a grand artistic failure. This failure is an ethical reaction—in Emmanuel Levinas's sense—to the morally ambivalent and aesthetically indulgent nature of consciousness-for-its-own sake and, indeed, perhaps even of Dostoevsky's religious faith in positive beauty. Straying from the dynamic of nihilism versus Christian morality that has often shaped Dostoevsky criticism, I will offer a critique of *The Idiot* on ethical grounds, a reading that sharpens the view that the novel's ending is a refutation of the author's beloved hero. Then I look at *Demons,* where death—Bakhtin notwithstanding—appears ubiquitously, as if to snuff out any glimmers of Christian redemption in this darkest of Dostoevsky's overcast novels. In these two books, the *end* of consciousness should give less rise to statements about the literary or spiritual immortality of consciousness and its supposed eternal dialogicity, but more to questions about the *ends* of consciousness, about its meaning and purpose—its ethical dimension.

Just as Dostoevsky had misgivings about a "science of Ethics," so too Levinas recognized goodness in the ability to respond to the face that turns toward me in need, prior to any moral code or utilitarian calculus. Dostoevsky's works have often been called theatrical, but one could be more precise in this regard: almost every one of his novels is really a series of face-to-face encounters (punctuated by the thoughts of individual characters on their way to meet someone) spread out over time (the medium of character development). Where Dostoevsky's characters embody the ethical dynamics of the response to the face, Levinas uses the prose of phenomenology to describe these dynamics in a more rigorous way: "ethics is an optics," but "it is a 'vision' without image" (*TI* 23). That is, ethics is a vision that has not yet objectified the other, subsuming her within preexisting categories. Imaging—aesthesis—may well be the most perfidious form of intellection, precisely because it is often so disingenuous, pretending to a noncerebral spontaneity. But as I noted earlier in my introduction, ethics arises not in any preconceived notions, images, personalities, or memories I may superimpose over the face of the other: ethics is, rather, my almost instinctive position of solicitousness to a person who is irreducibly not myself. (The fact that our facing someone makes us hostage, so to speak, is why we tend to avoid making eye contact with strangers.)

The obligation entailed by the other's face is transcendent—infinite. Such responsibility is indeed not of this world, and yet can and must be attempted only in this world. This paradox informs Levinas's idea of "the third,"[4] of the second other:

> The third must also have a face. If the third is also a face, one must know whom to speak to first. Who is the first face? And, in this sense, I am led to

compare the two faces, to compare the two people. Which is a terrible task. It is entirely different from speaking to the face. To compare them is to place them in the same genre. The other is unique, unique to such an extent that in speaking of the responsibility for the unique . . . I use the word "love." . . . What is a loved one? He is unique in the world. Now when there are two unique beings . . . [the] thought of comparison, of judgment, the attributes of the subject appear. . . . Justice is the way in which I respond to the face [the fact] that I am not alone in the world with the other.[5]

The fact that the third is also the other necessitates justice, which is unethical in the pure sense, doing violence to one of two parties, so to speak. Otherwise, ethics cannot be pursued in this world. As I indicated earlier, for Levinas, Zosima's pledge of superlative personal responsibility is moot without justice.

In *The Idiot* Dostoevsky intended to "portray a *positively* beautiful human being."[6] Prince Myshkin's virtue is linked to his regard for faces: he does not dispute Adelaida's remark that he is "an expert in faces."[7] But he isn't merely able to read faces; he is also transfixed by visages, whether in real life or representations—he is moved and obsessed by what they evoke, as Leslie Johnson has suggested.[8] He had "recognized a familiar face" (*PSS* 8:142; *Idiot* 168) in Nastasya's portrait, an image he associates with ingenuousness and holy suffering—with the cruel fate of the Swiss cowherd Marie, with the criminal facing execution, with Christ, or as Johnson notes, with "the projected image of himself as a child, orphaned and abused like Nastasya, almost out of his mind, trapped in the incommunicating chaos of a traumatized, autistic face."[9] Myshkin even quickly kisses the image, as one would an icon. In a way, the face of the other—here first encountered in and, one could argue, conditioned by its portrait—is validated by means of its core commonality with the face of the familiar, of the self, even; and this is precisely not the validation sought by Levinas's philosophy of the commandment that comes from the other *because he is other*. For Dostoevsky, according to his stated views and to commentators such as Robert Louis Jackson and Bakhtin (if we extrapolate his own ethical views from "Author and Hero in Aesthetic Activity"), the face is precious inasmuch as it is an incarnation: *litso* (face) as iconic *lik* (countenance). Not only was man created in God's image, but God even assumed human form as Christ. In this fact dwells Christian morality: "The main thing is the image of Christ from which comes . . . the thought that the chief acquisition and goal of mankind is achieved morality [; but] not Christ's morality, not his teaching will save the world, but precisely faith that the Word became flesh."[10] Dostoevsky's enthusiasm for icons and for icon veneration reflects this desire for divine incarnation.

Tolstoy's *Anna Karenina* provides an interesting foil here: Levin's introduction to Anna through Mikhailov's portrait, an encounter that is emblematic of his "intoxication" by Anna and by the idleness of city life during Kitty's pregnancy. Of course, unlike Levin, Myshkin does not recognize this aesthetic encounter as the beginning of what is, in fact, intoxication. Robin Feuer Miller describes "the overall tentativeness" of this passage in *The Idiot* as indicative of "the moment of perception before any analysis of it has occurred."[11] Analysis might reveal that Nastasya's portrait tells a story of abuse, despair, and corruption that the prince will never be able to overcome merely by perceiving and declaring her fundamental innocence. For Myshkin, however, she will remain what he first perceived in the portrait, reflecting an aesthetically conditioned ethics that ultimately helps no one in the novel.

The prince's relation to the face has more to do with emotions, with tears of sympathy, than with ethical deeds. (One could argue that even his attempt to marry Nastasya Filippovna manifests more pathos than ethos.) These emotions are provoked by the powerfully iconic clothing, the eager shroud of supreme mystery and pathos that covers the essential nakedness of the face in *The Idiot*. Myshkin echoes the Dostoevskyan need for a transcendently representative and Golgothic model of suffering, by which several familiarized faces blend into the supersaturated image (*obraz*), passive and timeless, and thus non-ethical. Levinas distinguishes ethics from imaging and divine incarnation, and thereby from aesthetics—as we saw above in his discussion of ethical seeing: "ethics is an optics," but "it is a 'vision' without image." Bakhtin, in "Author and Hero in Aesthetic Activity," makes a similar distinction between ethical and aesthetic activity, the latter being the "*excess of my seeing*, . . . the bud in which form slumbers, and whence form unfolds like a blossom."[12] Levinas's discussion, as one would imagine, is less concerned with aesthetics than with ethical activity, which is thwarted by this very excess of seeing:

> A God invisible means not only a God unimaginable, but a God accessible in justice. *Ethics is the spiritual optics.* . . . The ideal is not only a being superlatively being, a sublimation of the objective, or, in the solitude of love, a sublimation of the Thou. . . . *The Other is not the incarnation of God*, but precisely by his face, in which he is disincarnate, is the manifestation of the height in which God is revealed. (*TI* 78–79)

Levinas emphasizes here that the other's face is not the incarnation of *anything*—not God, not the other, and certainly not of any iconic image lent by an onlooker. Nothing—not cognition, ideology, nor aesthetic consummation—precedes my vision of the other's face, a face inadequate to its possessor and signifying only nakedness, vulnerability, destitution, a weakness that makes unreasonable demands upon me. This face, and the ethics it calls for from its unknowable and unreciprocal height, are not a foundation for anything ("pre-originary," as Levinas says).

For Dostoevsky, however, to put it in the bluntest Bakhtinian light, moral teaching comes less *from* another, from conversation, than somehow *because* of another—from the Christian model of incarnation, which is the possibility of ideal form, of "positive beauty." This beauty hopes for a non-temporal morality coming from a horizontal, side-by-side harmony, in which a community exists so long as it is bound by a common ideal (i.e., we are like Christ, are all one in Christ). This differs from a Levinasian ethics that comes from my vertical relation to the other in his height, an other who is not an image or ideal but a person. Levinas's God is accessible to justice partly because he is invisible and unimaginable: the other is wholly other, beyond image or generalization, and hence a specific alterity that demands a particular ethics.

Prince Myshkin's confusion between face and image leads him to fail another crucial moment in Levinasian ethics—the appearance of the third, of the second face before me. One should not, I think, disregard Dostoevsky's brutal intellectual and artistic honesty in his depiction of the ultimate failure, the collapse and psychiatric regression, of Myshkin, his favorite hero: the prince's demise is precisely a function of his inability to deal with the second face, to engage in the Solomonic agony of justice. This is why he is undone by the triangle he forms with Nastasya and Aglaya. Though it is possible (and common) to identify Myshkin's problems as the fault of the world, to do so is not to appreciate Dostoevsky's achievement fully. Myshkin is someone who only truly loves persons as manifestations of an iconic meta-face and not as concrete and individuated faces.

This confusion of goodness with beauty, face with icon, is logical given Dostoevsky's beliefs. Robert Louis Jackson notes:

> Christ came so that mankind might know that the human spirit can be in heavenly glory "in fact and in flesh, and not only in the dream and in the ideal." "Beauty will save the world," Dostoevsky observed in the notebooks to *The Idiot*. . . . The "utility" of a work (its moral element) is inseparable from the aesthetic element, from beauty incarnate, from form. . . . Myshkin's premonition of a higher life is a concrete aesthetic experience, a self-incarnation.[13]

The idea of the face offered by Levinas, on the other hand, breaks even beautiful forms. Naked faces are

> like those industrial cities where everything is adapted to a goal of production, but which, full of smoke, full of wastes and sadness, exist also for themselves. For a thing nudity is the surplus of its being over its finality. It is

its absurdity, its uselessness, which appears only relative to the form against which it contrasts and of which it is deficient. The thing is always an opacity, a resistance, an ugliness. . . . To disclose a thing by science and by art . . . is to clarify it by forms: to find a place for it in the whole by apperceiving its function or beauty. The work of language is entirely different: it consists in entering into relationship with a nudity disengaged from every form, but having meaning by itself, . . . signifying before we have projected light upon it, appearing not as a privation on the ground of an ambivalence of values (as good or evil, as beauty or ugliness), but as an *always positive value*. Such a nudity is the face. (*TI* 74)

Myshkin's love of the beautiful prevents him from seeing the face in its vulnerable nakedness, just as it stops him from the justice, the choosing between faces that ethics demands.

Of course, the prince has little choice—he is sick. "I can't marry anybody," Myshkin tells Ganya at the beginning of the novel, "I'm unwell" (*PSS* 8:32; *Idiot* 37). Accordingly, his solemn proposal to Nastasya is mostly a literary foil to the voyeuristic and vulgar spectacle of the auctioning of her hand in marriage: "Well, that's . . . out of some novel!" is how she responds to Myshkin (*PSS* 8:138; *Idiot* 163). His compassion is aesthetic. The way he behaves in that scandalous scene is, in a sense, "just beautiful"; it is Nastasya who is, arguably, the more ethical in her response. That is, even though she, too, "dreamed of someone . . . like [Myshkin], kind, honest, good . . . who would suddenly come and say 'You're not guilty, Nastasya Filippovna, and I adore you,'" she knows that she would "ruin" the prince, who "needs a nursemaid himself" (*PSS* 8:144; *Idiot* 170–71). In spite of his illness—and his obvious inability to understand what marriage means for a Russian prince—Myshkin takes up with Nastasya, later becomes engaged to Aglaya, and ruins this engagement, only to be abandoned by Nastasya at the altar. The confrontation between Nastasya, the prince, and his then-fiancée Aglaya is a perfect example of his disastrous response to more than one face:

"Here he is, look, my girl!" [Nastasya] cried to Aglaya. "If he doesn't come to me right now, if he doesn't take me and drop you, then you can have him, I give him up, I don't need him! . . ." Both she and Aglaya stopped as if in expectation, and they both gave him mad looks. But he may not have understood all the force of this challenge, even certainly did not, one may say. He only saw before him the desperate, insane face, because of which, as he had once let slip to Aglaya, "his heart was forever pierced." He could no longer bear it and with entreaty and reproach turned to Aglaya, pointing to Nastasya Filippovna: "It's not possible! She's . . . so unhappy!" But that was all he managed to say, going dumb under Aglaya's terrible look. That look expressed so much suffering, and at the same time such boundless hatred, that he clasped his hands, cried out, and rushed to her, but it was already too late! She could not bear even a moment of hesitation in him, covered her face with her hands, cried: "Oh, my God!"—and rushed out of the room . . . The prince also ran, but arms seized him on the threshold. Nastasya Filippovna's stricken, distorted face looked at him point-blank, and her blue lips moved, saying: "After her? After her? . . ." She fell unconscious in his arms. . . . Ten minutes later the prince was sitting beside Nastasya Filippovna, gazing at her without tearing his eyes away, and stroking her dear head and face with both hands, like a little child. He laughed when she laughed and was ready to weep at her tears. (*PSS* 8:474–75; *Idiot* 572)

He ruins both women through his almost comically democratic compassion. Marriage, like justice, is a socially binding decision to give one person somewhat more compassion than another. Yet even after Myshkin becomes engaged to Nastasya after this confrontation, he tells Evgeny Pavlovich that he wants to go to Aglaya, and that it "makes no difference that I'm getting married . . . [Nastasya] wants it; and so what if I'm getting married, I . . . Well, it makes no difference! Only [Nastasya] would have certainly died" with Rogozhin (*PSS* 8:483; *Idiot* 582). In other words, he is not marrying her to make him or her happy, but out of pity and fear. Even the prince does not disagree with Evgeny Pavlovich's analysis of this love triangle: "You know, my poor Prince, most likely you never loved either of them!" (*PSS* 8:484; *Idiot* 583)

Although the novel's loose plotting makes many things difficult to predict, the result of Myshkin's attempts to get married is not surprising. Myshkin begins (we are told) and ends up (we are shown) an "idiot," from the Greek *idiotes*, a private person.[14] From the idyllic Swiss privacy of Dr. Schneider's sanitarium, he sets loose—wide-eyed and coatless—upon the raw-rubbing public world of nineteenth-century Russia, a place full of madness, scandals, gross incongruities (social and otherwise), competing faces. Or as R. L. Jackson puts it, the "whole novel turns on the tragedy of the incomplete half-formed Myshkin who leaves his European aesthetic paradise and plunges unknowingly and with his premonitions of beatitude into the formless and disfigured hell of Russia."[15] And in this new context the prince-as-*idiotes* is inside-out; he becomes so porous and public that in the end his idiocy returns. He has just these two basic opposite modes, like a human on/off switch; and he can keep nothing, no image, out when he is turned on. Levinas explains that an "image marks a hold over us rather than our initiative, a fundamental passivity."[16] Indeed, the sensational madness of the world ultimately holds Myshkin in place: just as Myshkin earlier engages in a tearful, incoherent fusion with Nastasya after her disastrous confrontation with Aglaya, so, too, with Rogozhin over Nastasya's corpse, joining the murderer of his bride-to-have-been in a crazy all-night vigil.[17] At last the prince realizes then that "at that moment and for a long time past he was not saying what he should have been saying, not doing what he should have been doing, and that these [playing] cards he held in his hands, and which he had been so pleased to see, were no use now, no use at all" (*PPS* 8:506; *Idiot* 627). Perhaps the prince's random fidgeting with the playing cards is symbolic of his forced acquiescence to the amoral triviality of his new Russian milieu. Or maybe it represents Myshkin's failed attempts to compose an effective hand with the competing face cards at play in the novel. In any case, Myshkin's failure to say and do what he should have been saying and doing comes from the fact that he had not been seeing what he should have been seeing: that an ethical response to competing faces requires the mediation of judgment and not just the intensity of aesthetic perception. Understandably, a few hours later he suffers a breakdown.

This breakdown is the logical outcome of the rupture of a morality that stems from an image of Christian communality, of side-by-side harmony, rather than from an ethics that puts persons face-to-face in responsibility. In the context of such a schema, when murder disrupts the harmonious unity of human images, there is no ethical action that can be taken. Levinas, continuing his remarks on this "fundamental passivity," describes the absorbing condition of the aesthete:

> Possessed, inspired, an artist, we say, harkens to a muse. *An image is musical.* Its passivity is directly visible in magic, song, music, and poetry. . . . Such is a waking dream. . . . The particular character of a walk or a dance to music is a mode of being where nothing is unconscious, but where consciousness, paralyzed in its freedom, plays, totally absorbed in this playing. . . . An image is interesting, without the slightest sense of utility, interesting in the sense of *involving*, in the etymological sense—to be *among* things which should have had only the status of objects. . . . The subject is among things not only by virtue of its density of being, requiring a "here," a "somewhere," and retaining its freedom; it is among things as a thing, as part of the spectacle. . . . In imagination our gaze then always goes outward, but imagination modifies or neutralizes this gaze: the real world appears in it as it were between parentheses or quote marks.[18]

While much has been said about the amoral character of the neutral scientific gaze, here we glimpse the more general problem inherent in gazing at images. The aesthete behaves as if unaccountable to ethics—after all, he's *enthralled.* He is ecstatic, he emotes, he weeps for unity. He is indeed "guilty for all before all and more than the others," but on a tragic—passive, pathetic, emotional— level. The scene of the aforementioned vigil over Nastasya is telling:

> Now and then Rogozhin sometimes suddenly began to mutter, loudly, abruptly, and incoherently; began to exclaim and laugh; then the prince

would reach out his trembling hand to him and quietly touch his head, his hair, stroke it and stroke his cheeks . . . there was nothing more he could do! . . . Meanwhile it had grown quite light; he finally lay down on the pillows, as if quite strengthless now and in despair, and pressed his face to Rogozhin's pale motionless face; tears flowed from his eyes onto Rogozhin's cheeks, but perhaps he no longer felt his own tears and knew nothing about them. . . . When, after many hours, the doors opened and the people came in, [they found them], and each time . . . [Rogozhin] had a burst of shouting or raving, [Myshkin] quietly hastened to pass his trembling hand over his hair and cheeks, as if caressing and soothing him. But [Myshkin] no longer understood anything of what they asked him, and did not recognize the people who came in and surrounded him. (*PSS* 8:506–7; *Idiot* 611)

Unlike Levinas's concretely infinite "responsibility . . . for everyone else's responsibility,"[19] the prince yearns literally to merge with Rogozhin, crying the murderer's tears for him, and then physiologically abdicates from the judicial proceedings that follow.

The prince is simply profligate toward the face, and thus unable to live with the politics, the agony and violence of choosing between faces, that justice demands when I and the other are not alone in the world. Myshkin fails as a Christ-figure because, unlike Christ, he is not God with the power to perform miracles but, rather, a man who can become trapped in his own words, in a love triangle, and ultimately in the silence of his own subjectivity. One should not be too ready to fill in the blank of Dostoevsky's own expressed doubts about his Christian hero (see note 6 above) by insisting so wholeheartedly on Myshkin's potential. The world does not fail Myshkin. The world—notwithstanding Ivan Karamazov's rejection of any justification for its condition—*cannot fail.* Only the individual can fail against the resistance of the world. He can also, from time to time, unlike Myshkin, succeed.

*The Idiot* closes with the departure of Myshkin's consciousness, which in the schema of Bakhtin's "Toward a Reworking of the Dostoevsky Book" is an event equivalent to death. Hence Bakhtin mentions insanity in his discussion of murder, suicide, and normal death. In a dialogic novel, what matters is that both death and insanity (or idiocy) effect not an end but an evacuation of the speaking personality: "The person has departed, having spoken his word, but the word itself remains in open-ended dialogue" (*PDP* 300). This creates the possibility of understanding Dostoevsky's novels as works written "on the second day," so to speak, after the crucifixion and before the resurrection.[20] That is, the reader has the difficult task of keeping faith, of reviving the person's word departed and flying out of the text. In this sense, as many commentators suggest, maybe Myshkin is really somehow successful for the peculiar task Dostoevsky had in mind—as an aesthetic materialization of this tension between failure and rebirth. Bruce French argues that it makes no sense to judge or forgive Myshkin because "the aesthetic power of Dostoevsky's art in *The Idiot* lies in its revelation of the irrelevancy" of such assessments "when people relate to each other on a truly spiritual level."[21] In French's view, Myshkin remains a "morally beautiful human being" throughout the novel. Yet perhaps this conclusion, with which I agree, reveals the limitations of the aestheticized spirituality of an all-too-human and quixotic Christ-figure inside the diachronic world of the realist novel—limitations of which Dostoevsky himself was only too aware. The author understood that readers do judge novels and their heroes, and he was concerned that Myshkin (and consequently the novel) would be ill equipped to transcend the expectations of the genre. Moreover, one might argue that Dostoevsky actually respected these expectations: "The ending will decide everything" (*PSS* 28, part 2:330), he wrote in a December 1868 letter to Maikov. Miller suggests that while the dramatic final scene of *The Idiot*, Rogozhin and Myshkin's vigil over Nastasya's body, "could be described as a way of avoiding a resolution to the problems created . . . by the effects of the good man, Myshkin, upon others," Dostoevsky himself "would argue the reverse: he would find the predicament at the end of the novel to be the most extreme, most painful, but most fitting outcome of the dramatic situation."[22] In other words, to ignore the ending as somehow unimportant is not only perversely optimistic, but also ignores the significance of Dostoevsky's own doubts about an aesthetic approach to ethics and spirituality. To examine those doubts more fully, we must turn to Dostoevsky's subsequent novel.

*Demons*—where death banally cancels characters seemingly on the verge of redemption—makes the idea of Prince Myshkin's success seem more remote. Certainly, one can make the excuse that these lives are merely included, perhaps unfortunately, with the castaway sacrifice necessary to perform an exorcism, that they are precisely like the Gadarene swine in the verse from Luke 8:32 which precedes the novel: "Now a large herd of swine was feeding there on the hillside; and [the demons] begged [Jesus] to let them enter these. So he gave them leave. Then the demons came out of the man and entered the swine, and the herd rushed down the steep bank into the lake and were drowned."[23] Such an interpretation, however, overlooks the tortured humanity and goodness of a Kirillov or a Shatov wiped out in Dostoevsky's desire to release this new man. And who was to be this purified man, anyway? Nikolai Stavrogin? An impossible case to make, given that he is an essentially abortive main character, novelistically speaking, a disappointment.[24]

In the case of *Demons*, some literary observers would still privilege the "second day" idea. Among the most convincing is Harriet Murav, whose approach is largely sociohistorical. She reads Stepan Trofimovich's deathbed revelation—that he is perhaps the unwitting leader of the demoniac pigs that must die to heal a man—as if it were a pamphlet written by Dostoevsky:

This passage, and indeed the whole novel, suggests that all forms of civic life are riddled with the demonic. . . . Stepan Trofimovich recognizes for the first time that his civic role is implicated in the demonic possession that has overtaken Russia. It is only at the end of the novel that he attains to the interpretation of Russian history that Dostoevsky seeks to privilege: one according to which the demonic chaos of secular events is incorporated into a divinely intentioned sacred history. Dostoevsky . . . does not allow his devils to run free. The story that Luke tells reveals Jesus's power over the demons, who beg that they be allowed to enter the swine. Similarly, Stepan Trofimovich's figural interpretation of the events of the novel suggests that the crisis of Russian society is part of a divine plan, which will ultimately result in Russia's cure and restoration.[25]

But then, I would ask, who is to say which of the two is less banal: letting devils run amok or maintaining that everything is part of a divine plan? Neither addresses personal responsibility. At this point the currency of the pamphlet part of Dostoevsky's putative "novel-pamphlet," as he had first conceived *Demons,* seems to be undone by cumulative inflation. We are not interested in his political follies, when almost everything political looks like folly five or ten, much less one hundred, years down the road. The novel, however, is a product of Dostoevsky's genius, and if it is a product of the "second day" then this second day is every day of the week. Like Holbein's *Descent from the Cross* with its cadaverous Christ, *Demons* neither remembers the cathartic glories of the Via Dolorosa nor invokes the promise of a resurrection. The novel is a brutally honest reflection of Dostoevsky's profound aesthetic fixation with a painting whose disparaging effect on faith horrified him. Artistically, then, it makes sense that the inception of *Demons* followed *The Idiot,*[26] that the "second day," its hopes dashed by Myshkin's inherent failures, recedes in *Demons* into mere "day" in which the parentheses of revelation and redemption wither—leaving a bleak infinity of existence, an overcast chaos where the only amusements are grotesque. As these parentheses fall away, however, they uncover a remarkably moving novel.

Just after the spectacles orchestrated by Pyotr Stepanovich's crew and half-wittingly facilitated by Yulia Mikhailovna come together in flames, murder, and catastrophe, Shatov and Kirillov become the locus of an intense but doomed blossom of hope. After the flood—the fire. And now the prodigal wife—Marya Shatov—returns in a rainstorm, heavy with child. Fueling these proto-messianic evocations, the child is of course not her husband's. The whole episode shows both Shatov (a tortured caricature of Slavophilism) and Kirillov (his former bunk-mate in America, who does not sleep, lives on tea, employs a Martian syntax, and exists in the shadow of his self-willed impending suicide) fussing as if over Mary and the Unborn King. Even before she reveals her condition, we find here the conduct that perhaps most closely correlates Dostoevsky with Levinas, with an ethics in which I am in a position of insomnia, of hostage, toward the other whose vulnerably authoritative face resists any objectification:

> This strong and rough man [Shatov], his fur permanently bristling, was suddenly all softness and brightness. Something unusual, altogether unexpected, trembled in his soul. Three years of separation, three years of broken marriage, had dislodged nothing from his heart. . . . He was wildly chaste and modest, considered himself terribly ugly, hated his face and his character. . . . As a consequence of all that, he placed honesty above all things, and gave himself up to his convictions to the point of fanaticism, was gloomy, proud, irascible, and unloquacious. But now this sole being who had loved him for two weeks (he always, always believed that!)—a being he had always regarded as immeasurably above him, despite his perfectly sober understanding of her errors; a being to whom he could forgive everything, *everything* (there could be no question of that, but even somewhat the opposite, so that in his view it came out that he himself was guilty before her for everything), this woman, this Marya Shatov, was again suddenly in his house, was again before him . . . But when she gave him that worn-out look, he suddenly understood that this so beloved being was suffering, had perhaps been offended. . . . And he would hasten to look away, would hasten to get away, as if fearing the mere thought of seeing anything in her but an unfortunate, worn-out being in need of help—"what *hopes* could there be!" . . . And he went over yet again to look at her; her dress was turned back a little, and her right leg was half bared to the knee. He suddenly turned away, almost in fear, took off his warm coat, and, remaining in a wretched old jacket, covered the bare part, trying not to look at it. (*PSS* 10:434, 440; *Demons* 569, 576–77)

Shatov, unlike Myshkin, breaks out of his fear and reverie and rushes to hospitality, a concrete worship of the face of the other (and not an especially worthy other, this estranged wife pregnant with Stavrogin's child) in her height. In his Russian teenage years, Levinas would have encountered few moments in Western literature more fertile for his future ideas about the "vertical," nonreciprocal nature of ethical obligation. We see Shatov averting even his most arguably "legitimate" gaze, the mildly objectifying sexual glance of a husband at his wife: he will not turn her into the object of any of his hopes. He does not turn her face into an image, but simply reacts to its naked demands.

Shatov then runs for help to Kirillov across the hall—ironically, only two hours before Kirillov is visited by Verkhovensky and Liputin, who have come to ascertain his resolve to go through with his presuicidal deed for the revolution (that is, to "confess" to and thereby cover up Shatov's impending murder). Kirillov rises to the occasion:

> "If it's a wife, you need the samovar. . . . Take everything; take sugar; all of it. Bread . . . A lot of bread; all of it. There's veal. A rouble in cash. . . . Is this the wife who was in Switzerland? That's good. And that you ran in like that is also good."
>
> "Kirillov!" Shatov cried, . . . "If . . . if you could only renounce your terrible fantasies and drop your atheistic ravings . . . oh, what a man you'd be, Kirillov!"
>
> "One can see you love your wife after Switzerland. That's good if it's after Switzerland. When you need tea come again. Come all night, I don't sleep at all. There'll be a samovar. Take the rouble, here. Go to your wife, I'll stay and think about you and your wife." (*PSS* 10:436; *Demons* 570–71)

Here, too, Levinas may have found inspiration for his claim that ethics is a kind of insomnia, a rupture of self-satisfaction, that a "truly human life . . . is awakened by the other, . . . always getting sobered up" (*EI* 122). Indeed, the very fact that Kirillov is a man swallowed by his idea (as Pyotr Verkhovensky suggests) hints at the fundamentally infinite generosity of his nature. Kirillov, however, has already been digested, become disembodied, by his bizarre convictions, as he indicates when Marya reveals she is in labor: "It's a great pity that I don't know how to give birth, . . . that is, not that I don't know how to give birth, but that I don't know how to make birth happen . . . or . . . No, I don't know how to say it" (*PSS* 10:444; my translation).

Her labor strengthens the small and unlikely whirlwind of humanity around her, expanding it outside the house—prompting Shatov to think that "there's magnanimity in these people, too! . . . Convictions and the man—it seems they're two different things in many ways. Maybe in many ways I'm guilty before them! . . . We're all guilty, we're all guilty, and . . . if only we were all convinced of it!" (*PSS* 10:445–46; *Demons* 584) Even Lyamshin, Dostoevsky's crass Jewish stereotype, succumbs somewhat to the magnitude of this event that seems totally out of place in the world of this novel.

Shatov returns to find Kirillov one last time, and the latter, appropriately enough, tells him about his proto-epileptic religious ecstasies. And then: "Dawn broke. . . . In Arina Prokhorovna's hands a small, red, wrinkled being was crying and waving its tiny arms and legs, a terribly helpless being, like a speck of dust at the mercy of the first puff of wind, yet crying and proclaiming itself, as if it, too, somehow had the fullest right to life" (*PSS* 10:451; *Demons* 592). Even the midwife Arina Virginskaya's level-headed, if doctrinaire, materialism about "the further development of the organism" (*PSS* 10:452; *Demons* 593) cannot dampen Shatov's messianic awe:

"There were two, and suddenly there's a third human being, a new spirit, whole, finished, such as doesn't come from human hands; a new thought and a new love, it's even frightening . . . And there's nothing higher in the world! . . . Marie," he cried, holding the baby in his arms, "an end to the old delirium, disgrace, and carrion! Let us work, and on a new path, the three of us!" (PSS 10:452–53; Demons 593–94)

And now, Shatov goes as promised with Erkel to dig up the printing press in the park, an act which should release him from Verkhovensky's cell, "the very last step [before] the new path" (PSS 10:454; Demons 596). Neither Virginsky nor Lyamshin, both affected by the previous night's events and skeptical about Pyotr Stepanovich's claim that Shatov will denounce them to the authorities, can, however, sway Verkhovensky and the others from their gruesome plan.

Murder (Shatov's), insanity (Lyamshin's), suicide (Kirillov's), and normal death (that of Marya Shatov and her newborn son) follow. In each instance, we see the failure of consciousness—whether that of subject or onlooker—to take in these events. Virginsky and Lyamshin do not know how to witness Shatov's murder, despite the extent of premeditation. "This is not it, not it! No, this is not it all!" Virginsky cries (PSS 10:461; Demons 604), until Lyamshin convulsively grabs him from behind. Lyamshin's primordial shrieking strikes Verkhovensky as "very strange, [for he] had quite a different idea of him" (PSS 10:462; Demons 605). Likewise, Kirillov, though long convinced that in taking his own life he "will become God" (PSS 10:469; Demons 615), ultimately cannot glory in his peculiar raison d'être, yielding one of the most excruciating scenes in the novel. His body and soul—both lying beyond his intentionality—refuse to die with the dignity demanded of them by his idea. After a tortuous cat-and-mouse game with Verkhovensky (who is desperate for a useful suicide note), in

the corner formed by the wardrobe and the wall, Kirillov was standing . . . very strangely, . . . as if he wished to conceal and efface all of himself. By all tokens he was hiding, yet it was somehow not possible to believe it. . . . Then there occurred something so hideous and quick that afterwards Pyotr Stepanovich could never bring his recollections into any kind of order. . . . Kirillov . . . had leaned to him and bitten his finger. He finally tore the finger free and rushed headlong to get out of the house. . . . Terrible shouts came flying after him from the room: "Now, now, now, now . . . [Seichas, seichas, seichas, seichas . . .]" Ten times or so [and then] came a loud shot. (PSS 10: 475–76; Demons 624–25)[27]

In each case we see the inadequacy of consciousness—certainly of the subject and, one could make the case, even that of outsiders—in the face of death. Bakhtin understands that Dostoevsky is interested in murder, suicide, and insanity precisely because these are nodes of consciousness-negation in which consciousness plays a hand and which it unsuccessfully attempts to attend.[28] Hence within this depicted world, death literally does not finalize consciousness, because the latter, being the very element of the dialogic novel, cannot take in the former.

The deaths of Marya Shatov and her newborn son, however, should pointedly unsettle Bakhtin's notion about the inconsequentiality of the departure of a character's consciousness in Dostoevsky's work. To begin with, had both or even just the infant lived, the result might have been the novelist's most convincing hopeful ending—perhaps more powerful than Alyosha's eulogy at the end of *The Brothers Karamazov*. Their two deaths, precisely because they are almost afterthoughts, are the nails in the coffin of this fledgling redemption surrounded by catastrophe. These deaths, unlike the "abnormal" deaths above, have no intra-textual marker of consciousness, which, by failing to recognize them, disputes their ability to produce meaning. That is, the "unfinalizability of consciousness" seems irrelevant to these deaths, because nothing and no one is trying finalize them—not even the narrator, who mentions them casually and carelessly. This fact prompts the reader to look beyond Bakhtin's observation about the insignificance of "normal" death in Dostoevsky. Walter Benjamin writes that the genre of the novel is significant "not because it presents someone's fate to us, perhaps didactically, but because this stranger's fate by virtue of the flame which consumes it yields the warmth which we never draw from our own fate. What draws the reader to the novel is the hope of warming his shivering life with a death he reads about."[29] But these deaths in Dostoevsky should make us shiver. The brutality of Dostoevsky's artistic honesty does not relent even here when it seems feasible to do so. Bakhtin's "to kill does not mean to refute" sounds painfully disembodied in this case: Dostoevsky kills and thereby refutes.[30] The question is, who or what does he really refute?

If Myshkin is abortive because of a failed ethic, why do characters like Shatov—even when they approach a concretely "infinite" response to the other—suffer similar fates? It is ostensibly because, literally or figuratively, all of them—Shatov, Kirillov, Marya, and the newborn child—are the offspring of a chimeric fertility: Stavrogin. Contrary to the notion that Stavrogin is an antihero,[31] I think he is not even that much. He is an aesthetic error, and because the only criteria for his entrance are aesthetic, a failure quite simply. This claim and its importance require some explanation. Before we meet Stavrogin, the narrator window-dresses him without actually showing us any substance. All is in the realm of rumor or scandal: readers will recall the tantalizingly bizarre stories about this handsome and "remarkable" young man, his delightfully subversive nose-pulling and ear-biting antics, and his unspecified past "influence" over a wide assortment of the novel's primary and secondary characters. When he finally arrives—veiling himself in a kind of revisionist insensibility and aloof from his former "devotees"—the reader has certain aesthetic expectations of Stavrogin, of his capacity to give a center to the novel. These expectations psychologically parallel those of Marya Lebyadkina, Pyotr Verkhovensky, Darya, and Lise.

By the end of the novel, reader and characters alike are sorely disappointed. Even in the extracted "Tikhon" chapter (formerly "Part II, Chapter 9")—the only place where Stavrogin almost talks enough to live up to being a main character—he is a creature of transitory sensationalisms, engaged in a desperate and futile attempt to acquire narrative substance through his confession of a tabloid-style crime committed seemingly for no reason other than to confess it. Dostoevsky chose to leave well enough alone and did not reintegrate this episode (which would have required revising other chapters) after it was no longer suppressed by his editor. But this contingency may also reflect something fundamental about Stavrogin. Perhaps Dostoevsky felt ambiguous about Stavrogin's artistic status, which is why this character's only potential showcase remains a dangling appendix, take it or leave it.[32] Here, the non-hero exudes all of his banally portentous obscurity, only now under Tikhon's magnifying glass. This glass reveals it as little more than the self-consciously shallow agitation of a lukewarm soul craving for direction without accepting any. As Stavrogin himself admits in his suicide note, he is "not even [a force of] negation" (*PSS* 10:514; *Demons* 676). The flawless premeditation of his useless suicide (plagiarized from his victim Matryosha or perhaps from Judas) almost disqualifies him as a Dostoevskyan character: Stavrogin's consciousness, its turgid void, acknowledges itself at last, like darkness turning off the light. Unlike other Dostoevsky suicides, which may produce in the reader a feeling of horrified pity (in the case of Kirillov) or resentful disorientation (in the case of Smerdyakov in *The Brothers Karamazov*), one feels indifferent about Stavrogin's death.

I suggest that Dostoevsky had a provocative reason for casting this aesthetically questionable figure. Clearly, the expectation is that Stavrogin should be Luke's demoniac, given that (in Murav's words) "the novel ends not with an image of Russia's cure but with the medical autopsy which concludes that Stavrogin was not insane."[33] Of course, in Luke 8, the patient was not only ultimately "in his right mind" (*PSS* 10:5; *Demons* 3) but was also very much alive. Stavrogin, then, is not Luke's demoniac. Rather, Stavrogin represents the dark side of the idea of the Russian soul and soil, the notion of an accursed fertility. Because it can breed anything, its fecundity is boring and terrifying. Hence, Verkhovensky's obsession with Stavrogin is a lust for the omnipotent and dumb beauty of fat pastures: "Stavrogin, you are beautiful! . . . There's even simple-heartedness and naïveté in you. . . . I love beauty. I am a nihilist, but I love beauty. . . . You are a leader, you are a sun, and I am your worm. . . . It's you I need, you, without you I'm a zero. Without you I'm a fly, an idea in a bottle, Columbus without America" (*PSS* 10:323–24; *Demons* 419).

Stavrogin is potential personified (the prime number), and hence demons (zeroes) find him as inevitably as moths find and smother a flame. Beauty's downfall is in its emptiness that bestows content—dubious, even bad content. In effect, Dostoevsky does not deign to cure the very demonic possession of the Christian paradigm of redemption, the rich sentimental model of salvation. Beauty cannot save the world. And at its ready worst, beauty is manure for the devil. Stavrogin is the complete degeneration of Myshkin's full-bodied (if unsuccessful) "positive beauty"—degeneration not into negative beauty, but into empty, incoherent beauty. Stavrogin is Myshkin's grossly parodic foil: where the latter man is a definite presence afflicted with a fatal flaw, the former is a fatal flaw that seeks a definite presence. Myshkin's ethical gaze is hindered by his aesthetic emotionalism— more drawn to beauty and compassion than to responsibility and justice. Stavrogin has no gaze, nor can anyone look in his eyes without projecting his or her own expectations—expectations he himself has disowned—onto his fine figure. If Myshkin is paralyzed by the appearance of the third, as I have suggested, then Stavrogin's paralysis is less straightforward: every genuine other is his third, as it were, a third he cannot see because he is too busy trying (without success) to glimpse the second—which is *his own self,* or rather, a coherent reflection of himself. Stavrogin—a perfect example of Kierkegaard's definition of the demonic as a kind of "suddenness," as an "unfreedom [that] wills something, when in fact it has lost its will"—literally cannot find himself.[34]

Despite Stavrogin's demise, there is still a spiritual remainder in the novel. Richard Pevear notes that

> the artist's struggle for adequate formal expression is at the same time a process of awakening. The "healing" of the sick man is, however, barely adumbrated in the novel; the intensity of the demonic paroxysm all but overshadows it; yet awakening does come *in extremis* to Stepan Trofimovich, whose end is the antithesis of Stavrogin's, but equally exemplary. [Here appears] a broader laughter that saves, a comedy that is the embodiment of true freedom, in the portrait of Stepan Trofimovich, who, after standing as "reproach incarnate" for twenty years, finally begins to move.[35]

Indeed, Stepan—out of the ashes of a novelistic world in which everyone seemed to be, tried to be, or failed to become an "incarnation" of some abstract thing—breaks his own mold. This "broader laughter," however, is somewhat ironic, for Stepan's inspiration—though his "Last Peregrination" (*Poslednee stranstvovanie*) is most readily a loving parody of the Russian tradition of wandering and pilgrimage, of holiness through geographical "estrangement" (*strannichestvo*)—in fact predates this model of the Russian holy tramp (*strannik*). Stepan has an Ur-model, literally: Abram, the 75-year-old Hebrew getting up and setting forth from Charan to the place God will show him. Stepan is the sorry figure of Old Testament ethical monotheism, where redemption is sought not in the bewitching violence of apocalypse, rebirth, or aesthetic imperialism, but simply by moving someplace else.[36] (As always, Dostoevsky's generosity rests largely in his artistic refusal to congratulate himself in his own beliefs.)

Stepan Trofimovich recalls and augments his housekeeper's name-day wish for him: "'Live more' and try somehow not to be too bored" (*PSS* 10:377; *Demons* 491). This is not hedonism. As Stepan understands it, this is neither a wish for happiness nor for trouble, but simply for a kind of openness before the world and its faces—a questioning openness that is destroyed by the lazy cerebral excess Stepan calls boredom. Witness Stepan on the "high road" with the peasants: "and how they're studying me. . . . Strange, in a word, as if I were guilty before them, yet I'm not guilty of anything before them" (*PSS* 10:483; *Demons* 634). His revelation begins by frank observation, by his *seeing* for the first time. This leads—once he arrives at the country tavern where he will breathe his last—to the rebirth of other senses: warmth, taste, smell. By living more and trying not to be too bored, he realizes the simple generosity of the world, that (as Levinas suggests) the world is not mere sustenance but nourishment: "life is *love* of life" (*TI* 112). In Levinas's thought, this realization is necessary so that I then know when and how to *wake up* from this somnambulant enjoyment of the world outside me, to shake myself into the insomnia of infinite ethical obligation before the face of the other. But without this enjoyment, ethics turns into a numb and mechanical altruism.

I do not, however, wish to overstate the prominence of the quasi-Hebraic precipitant from this bleak and violent chemical reaction. Stepan Trofimovich is not simply an allegory; he has his own habits and continuities, retaining his silly, Frenchified manner of expression—all of which may undermine the truth, or at least the dignity, of his revelation in the reader's eyes. Indeed, his ecstasy here, together with the fact that the majestic ceremony of the final sacrament arouses his "artistic receptivity" (*PSS* 10:505; *Demons* 663),[37] somewhat muddles his spiritual transformation. Nevertheless, his consciousness, as it approaches its end, is clearly concerned not with persisting but with developing, with a search for purpose: he wishes "to live again . . . to see Petrusha . . . and all of them . . . and Shatov," to share with them the first "infinite . . . Great Thought" that abides even in them—that "love is higher than being" (*PSS* 10:505–6; *Demons* 663–64). This conclusion is all the more ironic and unexpected, given that the novel opens with the narrator's ridicule of Stepan Trofimovich as the emblem and implied root of Russian malaise, of a hopeless spiritual pettiness. In the penultimate chapter, however, the narrator steps aside and lets Stepan Trofimovich finally understand his own sickness as a self-centered inability to see: "I've been lying all my life. Even when I was telling the truth. I never spoke for the truth, but only for myself" (*PSS* 10:497; *Demons* 652). Because he avoided facing the other, his truth had merely been an expression of the lie that existence begins with the self. Stepan's last words, in which he also takes responsibility for Russia's malaise, echo Shatov's about his former comrades after his wife gives birth and before he is murdered: "Convictions and the man [are] two different things in many ways. Maybe in many ways I'm guilty before them!" These are awkward precursors to the ethical maxim introduced on Markel's deathbed (and adopted by Levinas) in *The Brothers Karamazov:* "Each of us is guilty in everything before everyone, and I most of all."

To say that consciousness for its own sake is the most important thing in Dostoevsky's novels would imply that the novelist really has little else new to communicate besides (and within) the innovative brackets of his dialogic form. Bakhtin himself avers, in "Author and Hero," that "only memory knows how to value . . . an already finished life."[38] That is, Dostoevsky most likely invites our evaluation of his characters, of their lives *and* their demise. Indeed, one could say that Dostoevsky's effort sustains a content—a fortunate conflation of literature, philosophy, and religious thought—which itself has profound formal impact. By allowing his fiction to transcend his stated dogma, he reveals the basic structure of revelation, prophecy, and inspiration—as described by Levinas: "For every man, assuming the responsibility for the Other is a way of testifying to the glory of the Infinite, and of being inspired. There is prophetism and inspiration in the man who answers for the Other, paradoxically, even before knowing what is concretely required of himself" (*EI* 113). Dostoevsky's art is prophetic precisely in the way it casts its ethical net ahead of the author himself, beyond his own fondness and prejudice—whether or not he is aware of it. For it is possible that, like Balaam, Dostoevsky blesses what he means to curse. And in this sense his novels are, as Levinas describes great works of literature, a "participation in Holy Scripture"—for "'God has spoken, who would not prophecy?' [Amos 3:8]" (*EI* 117, 113).

## Chapter Two

# "And I Most of All":

## Levinas in *The Brothers Karamazov*

"I'M LEADING YOU ALTERNATELY between belief and disbelief," the devil confesses to Ivan Karamazov, who is tormented because he is unable to sort out his responsibility in the murder of his father, Fyodor Pavlovich (*PSS* 15:80; *BK* 645). Nina Pelikan Straus notes a tonal kinship between Jacques Derrida and this shabby devil that Ivan hallucinates in *The Brothers Karamazov*.[1] She suggests that Derrida's late turn toward a "new self-submission . . . evoking both Augustinian penance and Jewish justice" comes from his newfound revulsion for this demonic aspect of disseminative undecidability. Deconstructive fatigue is demonic, she suggests, because it precludes both compassion and the recognition that truth may be based on faith. Derrida himself does not identify his "ethical turn" with Dostoevsky's evolution from (socialist) atheism to (Christian) faith—perhaps because of Dostoevsky's attitude toward Judaism and Jews. Still, according to Straus, "linking Derrida to Dostoevsky restores the significance of deconstruction's repression of metaphysical and ethical vocabularies in the 1970s, and invests their reinvention in the late 1990s with meaning."

The decision to read Dostoevsky alongside Derrida finds its justification in Levinas's influence on Derrida and in Dostoevsky's influence on Levinas. It is the latter influence—which connects a Christian anti-Semite with a post-Holocaust Talmudist—that requires further study. We need to trace, for one thing, how Dostoevsky depicts and tests his "ethic of self-restriction." Only then can we understand the relation between that ethic (invoked by a host of Jewish intellectuals besides Levinas) and Dostoevsky's Judeophobia. Neither Levinas nor his commentators attempt to bring the two together (and those readers who try too often tend toward apologetics or dramatic charges of hypocrisy). As a way of doing so, I would like to suggest that, if Derrida resembles Ivan Karamazov, then Levinas (at least in his notions of ethics and justice) evokes Alyosha.[2] What I am proposing, then, is not only that Levinas is in some ways "less Jewish" and "more Russian" than many assume, but, perhaps more provocatively, that

Dostoevsky may be "less Christian" and "more Jewish" than anyone has yet considered.[3]

Rabbi Hillel the Elder, when told by a gentile that he would convert if Hillel could teach him the whole Torah while standing on one foot, replied: "Whatever you do not want others to do to you, do not do to them. That is the whole of the Torah. The rest is commentary. Now go and learn" (Babylonian Talmud, Shabbos 31a). Hillel's at once clever, thoughtful, and impatient response evokes the rabbinic tendency to avoid essentialism through the process of interpretation (commentary), while recognizing that one is sometimes obliged to offer a sound bite.[4] It is a tendency emulated by Levinas, whose own counter-metaphysics—as expressed both in his philosophical works and in his "confessional" and exegetical writings—warns against the ethical dangers of reducing things and people to essences. Still, again like Hillel, Levinas had recourse to a slogan, borrowed from Dostoevsky. In numerous interviews and essays, he summarized his philosophy with the credo that Markel, Father Zosima's brother, utters during a deathbed confession in *The Brothers Karamazov:* "Each of us is guilty in everything before everyone, and I most of all" (*PSS* 14:262; *BK* 289). Levinas's formulation of his radical ethics, which was inspired in part by rabbinic Judaism, included reservations about Christianity. Dostoevsky was well known for his Russian Orthodox Slavophilism, as well as his occasional anti-Semitism. There is an obvious opposition between the ways in which the two thought about ethics. But there are also covert attractions and affinities.

The knowledge that Levinas was a close and avid reader of Dostoevsky makes his use of Markel's words especially odd and interesting, since Levinas was thus aware of their immediate context in *The Brothers Karamazov*— Father Zosima's hagiographic life narrative. Jill Robbins identifies Markel's credo as part of Zosima's articulation of a pietist and "ecstatic Franciscan spirituality, a universal responsibility that extends to the love of the earth, plants, and animals." She adds that this universalism is an "'aestheticized' religion,' and it occurs as an epiphany within the Christian matrix and worldview of a life of temptation, within a series of exemplary conversions, a stereotypical patterning of sin to redemption. This is the economy of personal salvation that Levinas calls 'egoistic,' . . . the life of temptation that is *itself* the temptation."[5] Levinas insists on the affinities between "aestheticized" religion and the Platonist tradition, because the former depends on the latter's will to know all. As he writes:

> In *The Republic,* after having drawn the ideal of a just but austere State, Plato is made to change his plan. A just and reasonable City is needed. But it must have everything. New needs must arise and proliferate in it. All temptations must be possible. . . . Christianity too is tempted by temptation, and

in this it is profoundly Western. It proclaims a dramatic life and a struggle with a tempter, but also an affinity with this intimate enemy. . . . Westerners, opposed to a limited and overly well defined existence, want to taste everything themselves, want to travel the universe. But there is no universe without the circles of Hell![6]

This drama of temptation reduces ethics to the service of knowledge: to be tempted by temptation is to experience "the ambiguity of a situation in which pleasure is still possible but in response to which the Ego keeps its liberty, has not yet given up its security, has kept its distance."[7] (Levinas's anti-Platonism is here explicitly anti-Christian and corresponds to his description of God as an *illeité*—beyond being, an absence that leaves its trace rather than an incarnated presence.) But ethics is not, for Levinas, a drama. He likens ethics to a process of sobering up: the face of the other presents me with an infinite obligation that, though it is a command without compulsion, I must meet. The face is not compelling; it is not beautiful. Much like the widow, the orphan, and the stranger whom the Hebrew Bible enjoins us to protect, the other is naked and vulnerable, requiring justice—a situation that paradoxically both limits and expresses my infinite responsibility. Levinas couples his concept of "the face" with a generally negative view of art and images, according to which mere things possess a "derisory . . . lifeless life."[8] (Levinas the anti-Platonist adopts a rather Platonic anti-aesthetic, iconoclastic stance.)

Then why, given this combination of distastes and preferences, does Levinas employ Dostoevsky—the exponent of a dramatic and aesthetic view of human conduct, not to mention a Christian capable of shrill anti-Semitism—to speak for his own, apparently Judaic ideas about radical ethics? Dostoevsky's abiding project was to reconcile beauty and goodness, a project motivated by the Christian model of incarnation. Judaism (the "yid idea," as he calls it in *The Diary of a Writer*) was for him guilty of stubbornly not transcending materialistic prudence; and he felt that the "simpler," more "innocent" Russian peasants were among its victims. Levinas's investment in the Russian classics and the Russian language, made during his gymnasium days in Lithuania, can only partly account for his intellectual identification with such a figure. In any case, the identification is tinged with self-mockery: Levinas chides his own and "our taste for pathos, a sensibility nourished on Christianity and Dostoevsky"—by which he means a sensibility that favors ecstatic generosity and violence over sober ethical engagement.[9] Elsewhere, Levinas notes that even though most Jews are still unresponsive to the person of Christ, "all Western Jews" are drawn by the dramatic life of temptations "which the Christian life is."[10] In other words, Levinas appears to approve and cite Markel's credo out of a (perhaps guilty) taste for its pathos, a taste shared in the West even by Jews.

I must concur, then, with Jill Robbins's assessment that "Levinas's intertextual relationship to Dostoevsky . . . complicates any simply Judeo-centered reading of Levinas's ethics."[11] But, as I began to indicate in the previous chapter, the reverse assessment—that Levinasian ethics complicates any simply Christian reading of Dostoevsky's fiction—may hold greater interest. It should repay the effort to complete or make explicit Levinas's reading of *The Brothers Karamazov* by examining it through the prism of his ethical thought, while considering the unresolved ambivalences in Dostoevsky's attitudes about Jews and Christianity. Doing so may suggest not only that Markel's credo is reoriented by Levinas's philosophy, but that this reorientation begins at the heart of the novel itself. The reorientation, accomplished through Alyosha Karamazov, shifts the meaning of Markel's ecstatic outburst away from the realm of the pathetic, beyond the psychology of guilt and salvation—and toward a practical notion of radical responsibility.

Setting aside the connection with Levinas, many commentators have observed a Jewish aspect in Dostoevsky's work. A few have suggested that Dostoevsky's Slavophile convictions, as well as his anti-Semitism, related to his own, somehow Judaic convictions about national chosenness and universal mission.[12] From another corner, Tolstoy apparently confided to Gorky that he thought there was "something Jewish in [Dostoevsky's] blood. He was mistrustful, vain, difficult, and unfortunate."[13] Arthur Cohen suggests that Dostoevsky's fictions seem "almost nonfictions," affording "them a curiously paradoxical allure for serious Jewish readers, who often regard the novel as a frivolous medium, suitable for distraction and relief, but not as replacement for philosophy or Talmud Torah."[14] But Cohen's effort at fleshing out a covert agreement between Dostoevsky's novels and aspects of Judaism may be just a more sophisticated way of saying that Dostoevsky's preoccupation with guilt and conscience is proverbially Jewish. Whatever the validity of this sentiment, it suggests one or another kind of prejudice.

Considering Dostoevsky's appeal for Jews by considering his appeal for Levinas is an approach offering more room for subtlety. A good place to begin might be the theatrical portrayal of human conduct in Dostoevsky's fiction. Almost all his novels comprise series of face-to-face encounters (punctuated by the thoughts of individuals en route to such encounters). Putting the point in Levinasian terms, Dostoevsky's characters respond to the other's face in ways demanded by proper ethical dynamics. Levinas employs the prose of phenomenology: "Ethics is an optics," he writes, "but it is a 'vision' without image" (*TI* 23). In other words, ethics is a vision that has not yet objectified the other and subsumed her under preexisting categories. The other's face takes us hostage, so to speak, and that is why we often avoid making eye contact with strangers. The obligation entailed by the other's face is not of this world, yet—as rabbinic ethics also insists—it must (and can only) be fulfilled in this world. That paradox informs Levinas's idea of "the third," of the second other whose appearance may force me to choose between unique faces. The third is also an other; and choosing between them, doing violence to one of the two, is unethical in the pure sense. But not choosing is unjust— and without justice, ethics cannot even be pursued in this world.

Where Levinas takes inspiration from the Hebrew Bible and the Talmud, Dostoevsky's notions of guilt and responsibility "toward the face" have Christian sources. Dostoevsky understood the veneration of icons, for instance, as a model for "facing." But compelled by the sectarian roots of the New Testament, he seemed haunted by Christianity's ghostly remainder— Jews and Judaism. It is difficult and probably unproductive to segregate ideas from emotions here: "Thought is born in the soul," he once wrote to his brother. Anti-Semitism was an "idea-feeling" that for Dostoevsky served intimate needs. One such need reflected his preoccupation with inherited paternal traits and circumstances. His father's family had originally belonged to the Lithuanian nobility around Pinsk, in a province that frequently changed hands between Orthodox Russia and Catholic Poland. By the eighteenth century, the Dostoevsky family, which had not abandoned Orthodoxy for Catholicism, was excluded from the nobility. In border areas with large Jewish populations, the feeling of being cheated out of one's station was often accompanied by anti-Semitism. Dostoevsky, who would have seen few Jews while growing up, may well have inherited his anti-Semitism from his paternal family's folklore. By most accounts, Dr. Dostoevsky was arrogant, irritable, strict, dutiful, and miserly. Felix Dreizin theorizes that, since miserliness "is also a proverbially 'Jewish' trait, Dostoevsky might not only have learned his anti-Semitism from his father, but also used it against his 'teacher.'"[15]

Dostoevsky's own gambling binges might have been a way to compensate for his miserly origins. In a November 1867 letter to his wife, Dostoevsky admits that he will "probably lose" at the tables, but swears he'll be "as prudent as a yid." Philistine "prudence" is a recognition that you are mortal, that the gods owe you nothing, that there probably are no gods. Money represents possibility, but possibility only in this world—lucre is filthy because it is earthbound. And it seems that Dostoevsky associated Jews not only with materialism and world domination, but with mortality and physical limitation, with poor circumstances and poor health—with banal carnality, a failure of transcendence. In a letter to his brother Mikhail, he writes: "I wish you health. As for me I cough like a yid" (*PSS* 30, part 1:54).

Dostoevsky's correspondence is full of financial preoccupations, but the anxieties are more than reflections of his poverty. Dostoevsky's bouts of acquisitiveness were ultimately the source of his privations: his spending was "neurotic, compulsive. . . . Expensive restaurants and gambling were means he used to get rid of his filthy lucre. Being poor and 'victimized' by usurers seemingly contributed to his psychological comfort."[16] He would feel obliged to purge his "philistine, kikish" bouts of miserliness with "noble, Russian" sprees. Saving money is an earthbound responsibility to this life, to one's own future and descendants; the spree is an act of faith in the life after death. While superficially, in other words, the motive of Dostoevsky's hedonism is *aesthetic,* at a more profound level it is paradoxically *ascetic:* an attempt to devalue the life of this world. He seems to have gone out of his way to place himself in the path of the indignities that went with compulsive gambling and spending—haggling at length, for example, with Jewish moneylenders. In the process, Dostoevsky's problem becomes a "Jewish" one.[17]

In April 1871, Dostoevsky went to Wiesbaden to play roulette. In a feverish midnight letter, he tells his wife what happened:

> I lost everything by half past nine and walked out in bewilderment; I suffered terribly, and ran to find a priest . . . I thought: he is God's pastor, and I won't talk with him as with a private person, I'll confess to him. But I got lost, and when I finally found a church that I took for a Russian one, they told me it was not Russian, but kikish. I felt as if I'd been doused with cold water. . . . Now this fantasy has ended forever. . . . I have been wholly reborn morally. . . . The hideous fantasy that has tormented me for almost ten years has vanished. Anya, trust that our resurrection has drawn near, and believe that from now on I'll attain my goal and bring you happiness. (*PSS* 29, part 1:98)

Konstantin Mochulsky, one of Dostoevsky's biographers, notes that this letter describes "some sort of mystical experience. From that day, Dostoevsky never gambled again in his life. The 'fantasy' had disappeared instantly and forever."[18] But what exactly *was* the fantasy? Perhaps it was simply the delusion that gambling could solve his emotional or financial problems. But given the peculiar way in which the fantasy was dispelled, it may well have had to do with his idea that "God's pastor" could absolve his sins. The notion that consciousness of sin (through the act of confession) is always a saving virtue played a significant role in Dostoevsky's gambling addiction. As Freud notes:

> Time and again [Dostoevsky] gave his young wife his . . . word of honor not to play . . . ; he almost always broke it. When his losses had reduced himself and her to the direst need, he derived a second pathological satisfaction from that. He could then scold and humiliate himself to her, invite her to despise him and to feel sorry that she had married such an old sinner; and when he had thus unburdened his conscience, the whole business was begun again the next day. His young wife accustomed herself to this cycle, for she had noticed that the one thing which offered any real hope of salvation—his literary produc-

tion—never went better than when they had lost everything and pawned their last possessions. . . . When his sense of guilt was satisfied by the punishments he had inflicted on himself, the inhibition upon work became less severe and he allowed himself to take a few steps along the road to success.[19]

It is, perhaps, the "fantasy" of this cycle that Dostoevsky finally confronts after mistaking a synagogue for a church.

The spiritual pathos of this cycle finds expression in Father Zosima's exhortation: "What you think is bad in you is purified for the sole reason that you have detected it in yourself." Dostoevsky's faith in the Russian peasant reflects that cycle as well: Edward Wasiolek argues that Dostoevsky saw "the peasants [as the] saviors of Russia because though they sin, they know they are sinning. And in knowing, they acknowledge a judgment and law beyond their judgment and law."[20] Common people thus possess a "positive openheartedness"—and wherever Dostoevsky saw this quality in the educated, "he considered it springing from those roots."[21] Positive open-heartedness (as opposed to Fyodor Pavlovich's decadent open-heartedness) relies on pity for human imperfection and on compassion for human nature. But human nature is like nature itself, full of generosity but also storms and quakes. Ethics is therefore *unnatural*: one avoids doing harm, not because one *cannot* do harm or has no reason to, but because one *should* not. As Levinas puts it, ethics is "*against nature* because it forbids the murderousness of my natural will to put my own existence first."[22] Compassion for human nature is the opposite of the Grand Inquisitor's tyrannical condescension, and such compassion is proper when directed at others; but it seems morally indulgent to direct it at oneself. Dostoevsky the gambling addict, xenophobe, and anti-Semite appears guilty of self-indulgent self-pity. Likewise Dmitri Karamazov, whom Dostoevsky associates—just as he wished, to a certain extent, to associate himself—spiritually with the common people. Andrei the coachman describes Dmitri as "just like a little child to us . . . The Lord will forgive you [on account of] your simple heart" (*PSS* 14:372; *BK* 412). Andrei assures him that hell is not meant for the likes of him, and Mitya frantically prays: "Lord, take me in all my lawlessness, but do not judge me. Let me pass without your judgment, for I have condemned myself; do not judge me for I love you, Lord! I am loathsome, but I love you" (ibid.).

Dmitri Karamazov's prayer embodies a stereotypically Russian religious sentiment. Wladimir Weidle (an unfriendly witness) lays out the common theme of Russian Orthodoxy's objections to the "juridical spirit" of Roman Catholicism, concluding:

Charity and compassion, in Russian eyes, not only transcend justice: they tend to abolish it altogether and render it superfluous. Such a view as this, applied to practical conduct, ends inevitably in rejecting what the West esteems highest: moral obligation and the sense of duty. If a Russian does good it is nine times out of ten out of love that he does it: out of sympathy, out of his instinct for charity, even out of caprice; but never out of duty. Even if it is simply a matter of work, he never performs it satisfactorily unless his heart happens to be in it; never if he is obliged.[23]

It is interesting how many of these emotive, anarchic stereotypes are involved with the Slavophile notion of *sobornost'*: the "free unity of Christian individuals based on the Russian Orthodox religion and sealed with the 'inner truth' manifested in the common people through their faith."[24] However, as Boris Shragin points out in his comparison of Jewish and Russian notions of national "chosenness," the anti-juridical bias in Russian culture and a corresponding "deficiency of personal responsibility were not a result but a cause. Russia failed to develop such a sense because of its slowness to discover individualism."[25] Slavophile *sobornost'* must therefore be understood as a "native" theological-philosophical concept that addressed Russia's sense of historical belatedness. And like many of the ideologies for social reorganization that flourished in Russia in the late nineteenth century, Slavophile thought was the fruit of (intensely idiosyncratic) individuals born into a culture in which the rights of the individual had never been enshrined.

The poignant anxiety of belatedness also informs much of the specific nature of Russian Judeophobia. In *The Diary of a Writer* of March 1877, Dostoevsky makes clear that for him the Jews emblemize all that stands ultimately in the way of this "great church *sobor*" of the Orthodox Slavs.[26] Under the banner of the Jews' exploitative "idea" coalesce all the foreign powers (Turks, Germans, English) as well as native elements (liberals, radicals, kulaks, capitalists) hostile to the Russian Orthodox vision. Although the peasants' suffering and sinfulness are, in a sense, qualities that make them Russia's saviors, the Jews—by taking "advantage of their [the peasants'] vices" (*PSS* 25:78; *Diary* 641)—impede a holy destiny. Dostoevsky deems this negative relationship inevitable, given the Jews' twenty centuries of life as a nation within other nations: a condition that leads not only to a drive for "self-preservation," but also to "alienation and estrangement in the matter of religious dogma; the impossibility of fusion; belief that in the world there exists but one national entity—the Jew, while, even though other nationalities exist, it should be presumed that they are . . . nonexistent" (*PSS* 25:81; *Diary* 646). This condition, while presumably based in religious dogma, seems to apply for Dostoevsky to any Jew, assimilated or otherwise: "We are here dealing with something of a pre-eminently religious character. Besides, it is impossible to conceive of a Jew without God. Moreover, I do not believe in the existence of atheists even among the educated Jews: they are all of the same substance!" (*PSS* 25:82; *Diary* 647). In Dostoevsky's caricature of Judaism, the commandment to serve God is subsumed in a spiritually intensified but basically secular and ethnic providence—a "firm material goal" toward which even Jewish atheists strive.[27]

Dostoevsky's young friend, the Slavophile philosopher Vladimir Soloviev—a Judeophile in certain respects and a student of the Talmud—rebuked and pitied the novelist for his prejudices. Soloviev too saw Judaism as a materialist idea, except that his thinking was not involved with anything like Dostoevsky's psychopathology; hence Soloviev makes an illuminating alter ego for our purposes. In "The Jews and the Christian Problem" (1884), Soloviev describes Judaism as a form of *religious* materialism, very different from either practical or scientific or philosophical materialism. (Dostoevsky's *Diary of a Writer* seems to accuse the Jews of all three.) Soloviev's argument is that a "Jew expects every idea and ideal to have a visible and tangible embodiment and produce beneficent results; he will not recognize an ideal that cannot subdue reality and be incarnate in it. . . . The religious materialism of the Jews springs not from the weakness but from the strength and energy of the human spirit which, unafraid of being defiled by matter, purifies it and uses it for its own ends."[28] Soloviev stresses that Jesus could have arisen only from this spiritually energetic people, indeed that he continued and developed its religious materialism: "The fundamental truth of Christianity—the incarnation of the divine Word—is a spiritually *sensible* fact. When Christ said 'he that has *seen* me has *seen* the Father,' He made the Deity more, and not less, accessible." Furthermore, the "Christians, like the Jews (in the prophets), strive not only for the renewal of the human spirit, but . . . hope for a new heaven and a new *earth* where righteousness dwells . . . [in other words, a] true *theocracy*" (SA 118).

Soloviev insists that Christians and Jews have the same religious goals—but, he writes:

> Christianity also reveals to us the *way* to this crown, and that way is the Cross. And it was just this way of the Cross that the Jewish people of the time were unable to understand; they sought after a sign, a direct manifestation of divine *power.* The Jews strove directly for the final conclusion; they wanted to obtain from without, by the formal way of testament, that which has to be gained through suffering, through a hard and complex process of inner division and moral struggle. (SA 118–19)

The Jews missed, according to Soloviev, the opportunity of renouncing their "national egoism and their attachment to earthly welfare." They ought to have welcomed the Chinese finger puzzle paradox of Christian asceticism: "To realize the Kingdom of God on earth, it is necessary, first, to *recede* from earth" (SA 119). And because the Jews refused to suffer then, Soloviev reasons, they suffer now.

Still, Soloviev condemned the persecution of the Jews, insisting that as long as the putatively Christian world remains pagan in character, it cannot expect them to rectify their error. Soloviev thus represents the Jewish Problem as a *Christian* problem, and in so doing he finesses a question that would continue to haunt Christian theologians. We find the same formula, for example, in Karl Barth's *Church Dogmatics* ("The Jewish Question . . . is really the Christian question").[29] And yet Barth, a fervent anti-Nazi (and in many respects a philo-Semite), also describes an un-Christianized Judaism as "a spectral form . . . a half-venerable, half-gruesome relic . . . [a] Synagogue of death."[30] Its existence "side by side with the Church is an ontological impossibility, a wound, a gaping hole in the body of Christ, something which is quite intolerable."[31] This ghastly, undead Judaism—a trope also adopted by many Zionist thinkers who sought to revive Israel's place among the nations—proved "intolerable" for Dostoevsky as well. His *Diary* becomes shrill on this point: "The Jews keep yelling that among them, too, there are good people. Oh God! Is this the point? Besides, we are speaking not about good or wicked people. . . . We are speaking about the whole and its idea; we are speaking about kikism [*o zhidovstve*] and about the kikish idea [*ob idee zhidovskoi*], which is overtaking the whole world, instead of 'unsuccessful' Christianity" (*PSS* 25:85; *Diary* 650–51). Where Soloviev sees the Jews' spiritual materialism as the wellspring of Christianity, as well as its greatest moral challenge, Dostoevsky sees only a threat—as if the Jews, in "the full armor of their organization and their segregation" (*PSS* 25:83; *Diary* 647), constitute a socioreligious technology that, if given the opportunity, would destroy the morally vulnerable, God-bearing Russian people (*narod*) along with the Slavic Orthodox *sobor*. Again, considering the Russian anxiety about belatedness, in the view of many *pochvenniki*—so-called people of the soil (*pochva*), intellectuals who wanted (in somewhat neo-pagan fashion) to reconnect to the rural essence of Russia—the Jews are akin to an overripe presence spoiling the underripe Russian earth.

It is significant that diatribes of this kind do not appear in Dostoevsky's fiction. There are indeed few Jews in Dostoevsky's novels after *The House of the Dead* (though the Catholic Church takes considerable abuse throughout the course of his work). Perhaps he thought the Jewish Question beneath the dignity of his literary creations. Dreizin offers a more interesting theory: Dostoevsky's "anti-Semitic diatribes were insincere. He needed to believe them, but without his novels they sound hollow. For some reason, Dostoevsky, in his later years, was afraid and ashamed of anything that could seem 'philo-Semitic.' He was a *compulsive,* rather than 'guilty,' anti-Semite."[32] David Goldstein, on the other hand, feels that Dostoevsky was insincere, not in his Judeophobia, but rather in his nominal support for Jewish civil rights: he "gives with one hand, [and] immediately takes back with the other."[33] (Dostoevsky's pronouncements on behalf of full rights for Russian Jews always take this form: I fully support Jewish rights, and pretty soon the Jews will take this country over and run it into the ground.) But Dreizin's idea of Dostoevsky as a "compulsive" anti-Semite raises another possible reading of this ambiguity. Perhaps Dostoevsky knew that his own prejudice was psycho-pathological and did not want his personal tirades to have real consequences. (Unfortunately, it is plausible that they did have consequences soon after he died, given that Crown Prince Alexander, who would preside over a golden age of pogroms when he became czar, was a great admirer of *The Diary of a Writer.*) In any case, it does appear that Dostoevsky did not want these tirades to mar the integrity of his art, and he probably valued his literary creations more than he did his own troublesome self.

But why was Dostoevsky in the 1870s "afraid and ashamed of anything that could seem philo-Semitic"? First, we must acknowledge that, unlike the more optimistic Soloviev, the anti-utopian Dostoevsky believed more in the *idea* of *sobornost'*—in the "'living unity' of all the psychological powers of man" in the Orthodox faithful[34]—than he believed in its concrete pos-sibility.[35] Dostoevsky's own psychology, not to mention his polyphonic depic-tions of the human personality, seems radically at odds with this Slavophile "wholeness." Soloviev insinuates as much when, seeking a rationalization for his friend's "terrible struggle" with faith and prejudice, he concludes that "in the realm of ideas [Dostoevsky] was more a sage and an artist than a strictly logical, consistent thinker."[36] As a "sage and artist," Dostoevsky was gifted with an uncanny ability to understand how and why people behave and interact the way they do, especially under stress—he practiced, in his own words, "a realism of a higher order." Hence he could never convincingly adopt Soloviev's theocratic optimism, the conviction that the humanist vision of Russian Orthodox redemption could come to pass. Dostoevsky knew in his heart that the problem underlying the Russian Problem was the Russians; his nuanced appreciation of human nature made him doubt the possibility of theocracy.[37] Perhaps Dostoevsky's anti-Semitic outbursts amount to over-compensation for his resistance to Christian utopianism.

Both Dostoevsky's and Soloviev's comments about the "Jewish idea" rely on an old polemical division between rabbinic Judaism and Christianity. Heinrich Graetz expressed the problem succinctly: Judaism *hears* God, whereas pagan-ism (and thus, some would say, Christianity) *sees* God.[38] "He that has seen me has seen the Father," Christ proclaims. Dostoevsky's fascination with icons, incarnation, and aesthetically rich hagiographies is certainly in keeping with Christianity's well-developed visual capacity. His understanding of Judaism as materialism relies on the idea of "Jews hearing God"—that is, Jewish materialism is the result of verbal and textual promises, covenants, laws, and is therefore a reflection of a Jewish propensity to hear, believe, and obey God while refusing to see Him in Christ. The "self-centered" refusal of Jews to "believe their eyes" has been particularly galling for Christians, especially because "holy and perfect" images can be so easily contaminated by doubtful gazes. The image of the Virgin can turn into a whore, and vice versa, in the blink of an eye. Dostoevsky's impatience with Judaism may have to do with his fear of the Jewish propensity to blink and thereby cause gentiles to blink as well. Indeed, Franz Rosenzweig suggests that the existence of Judaism perpetuates Christianity as a "not-yet," and thus as saved from itself. Judaism protects Christianity from vision, from an abuse of its propensity to sanctify sight. This relationship engenders Christian self-hatred, which, according to Rosenzweig, is what accounts for European anti-Semitism.[39]

This polemical issue centers on disagreement about what categories of sense perception and sensibility are corruptible and corrupting. Judaism accuses Christian reliance on sight of being pagan (paganism is arguably a spiritual materialism) and of being deceptive (because no image or incarnation can replace divine law). Christianity regards Jewish hearing as stubbornly materialist and contractualist and, finally—since Jews do not acknowledge the true meaning of words heard long ago—deceptive as well. It should be added that the understanding of Judaism as excessively contractualist has a specific resonance for Russian Orthodox culture. Yuri Lotman notes that, according to Orthodox tradition, a true "religious act has as its basis an unconditional act of self-giving, rather than an exchange."[40] The system of relationships that governed Russian *pagan* cults and magic, on the other hand, was characterized by reciprocal activity, compulsion, equivalence of exchange, and consensus (with its attendant casuistry). Historical circumstances lend even broader significance to this opposition, given that Russia's premodern isolation from the West fostered a culture that never quite granted moral authority to the contractualism of the Roman secular tradition. The contradictions in Dostoevsky's position on the Jewish Question seem more understandable in this context: however much he may *agree* with (and even act on) the principle that Jewish civil rights accord with Christ's law, Dostoevsky does not seem to *feel* that way. Emotionally embedded in the cultural opposition that Lotman describes, Dostoevsky probably found it difficult to consider Judaic reliance on hearing as anything but an old pagan (whether Russian or Roman) contractualism.[41]

This debate is fundamentally less about theology or epistemology than about ethics. Levinas makes explicit the ethical distinction, implicit in the debate, between vision as an opening to the other and the image as a closing off. The image fixes the other within a conceptual instant, hovering above the gritty world of time-bound responsibility. Judaism, according to Levinas, concerns itself precisely with this diachronic realm of response to the other, because it is less a religion of hearing than of interpretation. Unlike Russian Orthodoxy, Jewish tradition views legal wrangling as a holy activity. Sinai may have been an auditory experience, but rabbinic Judaism accepts the burden of interpreting what was heard there: even Moses saw only "God's back" on the mountaintop, or in another translation of Exodus 33:23, Moses caught a glimpse of *"what follows from [God's] existence."* What Levinas says follows from God's existence is not so much a contractual quid pro quo, a religiously materialistic covenant, as a manner of conduct for human beings to strive toward. Israel's holiness is an ambition, not a given. As Yeshayahu Leibowitz notes:

> The [early rabbis] comment that "the prophet only prophesies *what ought to be*" . . . If prophecy were a statement of what will happen, it would have no religious significance. What is the distinction between the meteorological forecast and a prophetic oracle about tomorrow's weather? Both of them oblige me to do nothing, they are irrelevant to the service of God.[42]

The notion that God is approached less through hearing than through interpretation appears most vividly in the well-known Talmudic midrash in which even a voice from heaven fails to trump the accepted procedures of rabbinical jurisprudence.[43] At the end of that midrash, God is said to smile and declare, "My children have overruled me." Hearing, strictly speaking, is still pre-ethical—hearing is simply about being open to the other. Interpretation, however, is response and interaction: interpretation is the beginning of ethics, of the decision-making process of justice. Response to the other, which goes beyond openness and hearing, is according to Levinas what defines and sustains rabbinic Judaism.

As Levinas understands the orientations of Judaism and Christianity, the difference between them is even more radical than one based on the distinction between hearing and seeing. And an iconicism like Dostoevsky's presents its own set of ethical complications. Often his characters self-consciously humiliate or harm themselves and others just for the beauty of it—the negative beauty. There are few awful or petty misdeeds that Dostoevsky could not associate with beauty. Yet he yearned to link beauty with goodness: "Only that is moral which coincides with your feeling of beauty and with the ideal in which you embody it."[44] Perhaps he simply could not accept evil's fat share of beauty and therefore insisted that the good has likewise to be beautiful.

Indeed, *The Brothers Karamazov* abounds with dark views of aesthetic sensibility. Early in the novel, Fyodor Pavlovich declares that "all my life I've been getting offended for the pleasure of it, for the aesthetics of it, because it's not only a pleasure, sometimes it's beautiful to be offended" (*PSS* 14:41; *BK* 44). In the same vein, Ivan theorizes that it is our "artistic" cruelty that sets us apart from other animals; and he seems to relish tormenting Aloysha with propaganda about Turkish atrocities in the Balkans: "The baby laughs gleefully, reaches out its little hands to grab the pistol, and suddenly the artist pulls the trigger right in its face and shatters its little head . . . Artistic, isn't it? By the way, they say the Turks are very fond of sweets" (*PSS* 14:217;

*BK* 239). Finally, we encounter Dmitri's feeling that "beauty is a fearful and terrible thing! Fearful because it's undefinable." Dmitri "can't bear it if some man, even with a lofty heart and the highest mind, should start from the ideal of the Madonna and end with the ideal of Sodom . . . What's shame for the mind is beauty all over for the heart. Can there be beauty in Sodom? . . . For the vast majority . . . that's just where beauty lies" (*PSS* 14:100; *BK* 108).

As Dmitri's anxiety about the instability of beauty suggests, an insistence that the moral should also be beautiful subjects goodness to the vagaries of aesthetics. In Levinas's view, the face of the other—an "always positive value"—transcends beauty and ugliness: for him, it is language and interpretation (rather than aesthetic disclosure) that respond to the other and commence the work of ethics (*TI* 74). But in Dostoevsky's world, aesthetic flaws in the good are potential sources of humiliation and shame (the ideal of Madonna giving way to the ideal of Sodom), and these are among the roots of human sin. When "the positively beautiful" is blemished, the good is disfigured and becomes a *bezobrazie* (literally, "without-image"), a disgrace. Mortality and carnality are likewise humiliations—scandals that feed scandalous reactions. Many scholars identify *bezobrazie* in the novels as a disfigurement that can be healed only by an iconic ethics (a sacred *obraz*), but few appreciate (as Dmitri seems to) that the former can arise from the latter.

Much of the famous intensity of Dostoevsky's work derives from just this avalanche of disfigurement, of withered smiles and sweetness turning into sneering. Witness Grushenka's first meeting with Katerina Ivanovna or the scene in which Alyosha tries to deliver money to Captain Snegiryov. Dostoevsky clearly appreciated the disfiguring, even demonic, risks of an iconic ethics, an ethics driven by aesthetics. A peculiar sort of disfigurement—the *nadryv*, the laceration or strain—is especially involved in the scandals of *The Brothers Karamazov*. The *nadryv* is, in that novel, a self-destructiveness that harms others. Ivan's diagnosis of Katerina Ivanovna's obsession with Mitya makes a nice summation: "The more he insults you, the more you love him. That is your strain [*nadryv*]" (*PSS* 14:174; *BK* 192). The *nadryvy* of most Dostoevsky characters have to do with what René Girard calls their addiction to obstacles.[45] With few exceptions, the suffering sought after by Dostoevsky's characters is seldom expiatory, since it is usually achieved by making others suffer first. His characters torment themselves by hurting others in order to feel violent shame. It is especially tempting to evade this realization, since goodness would be easy if all one had to do was accept suffering.

Levinas, too, evades this truth about Dostoevsky's characters when he mentions them as an example of "the expiatory suffering of the just suffering for others, the suffering that illuminates."[46] Their self-lacerations often wound those closest to them or render them useless to others. Raskolnikov's transgression and redemption make for an obvious case, but then so does Zosima's conversion from callow hussar to pious monk after he beats his defenseless manservant Afanasy. Prince Myshkin, who does not actively seek suffering and humiliation but rather seems to fall into both, arrives at disaster in his quixotic and naive quest to be impartially generous to all: Aglaya is crushed, Nastasya is murdered by Rogozhin, the prince himself relapses into autism. Indeed, my suffering, even if it is the result of well-intentioned moral risk-taking, is seldom just my own affair. This dynamic connection between my suffering and that of the other is also revealed when Alyosha seeks suffering after his mentor Zosima's death by going to Grushenka, thereby making ungenerous assumptions about her. Grushenka, in turn, had been planning to debase herself by corrupting Alyosha. But once she learns of the Elder's death, she is mortified and spares the young disciple. Her gesture restores Alyosha's soul: "I came here looking for a wicked soul—I was drawn to that because I was low and wicked myself, but I found a true sister, I found a treasure—a loving soul" (PSS 14:318; BK 351). In turn, Alyosha's confession arouses Grushenka's dormant sense of ethical agency. That is to say, moral illumination comes only when both of them discard their masochistic goals, retreating from their cruel projects of personal suffering.

We must also recall that Alyosha's willingness "to suffer" (PSS 14:221; BK 242) through the torments of Ivan's challenges to his faith in the "Rebellion" chapter, during their encounter at the tavern, distracts him from his mission to find Dmitri: "Several times, later in life, in great perplexity, he wondered how he could suddenly, after parting with his brother Ivan, so completely forget about his brother Dmitri, when he had resolved that morning, only a few hours earlier that he must find him, and would not leave until he did" (PSS 14:241; BK 264). We seldom suffer alone. And while Nietzsche's condemnation of holy suffering is essentially aesthetic, the Levinasian objection would have to do with justice—which requires not my suffering per se, but rather that I actually be available for the other. (A parent wants nothing better than to suffer or even die for her ailing child; but this will accomplish nothing for the child, who usually gets better only to call upon the parent's remaining strength later down the road.)

It seems odd, then, that Levinas should mention Dostoevsky's characters without qualification here. Then again, one also recalls Levinas's assertion that "all Western Jews" are drawn by the dramatic life of temptations "which the Christian life is," a "taste for pathos, a sensibility nourished on Christianity and Dostoevsky"—by which he means a sensibility that favors ecstatic generosity and violence over sober ethical engagement. My sense is that Levinas found it difficult to draw a neat distinction between my "meaningful" suffering for the sake of the other (a result of my subjection to his demands) and the Western taste for pathos—for suffering-as-temptation. In other words, there is always the danger that my suffering for the other might become more meaningful to me than the other as other. The drama of the sinner-saint narrative is aesthetically attractive: it is not just spiritually or ethically compelling; it is, after all, sexy.

It is the project of suffering, however, that forms the initial context, and the context of subsequent development, for what would become Levinas's basic ethical maxim. Zosima's born-again yet dying brother Markel, in a condition his doctor calls madness, is the first to declare that "each of us is guilty in everything before everyone, and I most of all." But Markel continues: "Dear mother, my joy, I am weeping from gladness, not from grief; I want to be guilty before them, only I cannot explain it to you, for I do not even know how to love them. Let me be sinful before everyone, but so that everyone will forgive me, and that is paradise" (*PSS* 14:262–63; *BK* 289–90). The way that Markel's words resurface in Zosima's life narrative seems to extend this emotionally indulgent context. Some years after his brother's death, the young Zosima, having goaded someone into a duel, comes home and strikes his servant Afanasy in the face. The following dawn, Zosima's soul is pierced by his own cruelty, and it is then that he recalls his dead brother's words and undergoes his own conversion. Jacques Rolland notes that the Afanasy story underscores what would become a central Levinasian notion—that the naked face of the other inspires both murder and the commandment *Thou shalt not kill*.[47] Of course, a distinction between psychology and ontology is required here: Levinas would not concede that bloodying the other's face must precede the realization that to do so is wrong. "Without ever having done anything, I have always been under accusation: I am persecuted."[48] By using the present perfect, Levinas stresses that I am always *already* accused by the other—I don't actually need to beat him up, and doing so is usually a misguided response to this fundamental "persecution," a response that might or more likely might not awaken my conscience. Levinas invokes the "*insatiable* compassion" of Sonya Marmeladova in *Crime and Punishment* in order to emphasize the possibility of an ethical hunger for the other that is neither sadistic nor masochistic.[49] This insatiable compassion—which, significantly for Levinas, is *not* inexhaustible—is something Levinas elsewhere calls "*glory*, . . . a debt that increases in the measure that it is paid" (*OTB* 12). This is a very different idea of obsession and persecution. Yet many of Dostoevsky's characters—who share certain impulsive and compulsive traits with their creator—behave as though the realization of an infinite ethical obligation can only succeed a wicked act.

Typically, Dostoevsky's characters are careless about the distinction between *feeling* and *being* guilty. If the face inspires both murder and generosity, one is tempted to hover between the two. But this hovering "temptation of temptation" comes from a misunderstanding of the nature of the difficult gift of freedom with which, according to Ivan's Grand Inquisitor, human beings are burdened. If I am always already responsible, then—as

Levinas makes explicit and as Dostoevsky implies—ethics precedes freedom: Ivan's absolute notion of freedom is an illusion. We have partial freedom of action—partial because everyone is constrained by contingency, by having been born into a world that already exists—but the ethical obligation before the face is an authority without compulsion. Ivan loses his grip on consciousness because he cannot separate responsibility (which is nonvoluntary) from justice and ethical activity (which require me to make choices). Ivan's inability to understand the meaning of human freedom also explains the two stumbling blocks (*skandala*) set to test him in *The Brothers Karamazov*. To be sure, there is Ivan's petty devil, who comes to torment him with metaphysical undecidability: either the devil is real and therefore God (probably!) exists and then human freedom is not absolute; or the devil is Ivan's hallucinated projection and everything is permitted. But the devil is not the only *skandalon* here.[50] There is also the drunk peasant, into whom Ivan literally stumbles twice—first, roughly knocking him down on the way to the final meeting with Smerdyakov (who will confess to their father's murder), and then, on his way back, picking the little peasant up out of the snow and sparing no expense in arranging for his care. There is something pretentious and whimsical about Ivan's "magnanimity" with the peasant—he does not acknowledge that he had been the one who pushed the peasant into the snow in the first place, instead acting the benefactor and lingering much longer than necessary. Instead of simply following through on his responsibility in this case, Ivan seems to be trying to prove (to himself? witnesses? God?) that, though he feels guilty (over his father, over the peasant) and feels the need to do some compensatory good deed, he still retains his total freedom throughout. Ironically, his ostentatious concern for the peasant distracts Ivan from his suspicion that Smerdyakov might soon commit suicide and make it impossible to clear Dmitri. Moreover, Ivan's sudden sense of responsibility is displaced and discharged by saving the drunk instead of saving his brother. Even doing the right thing (or in this case, ostentatiously righting something you did wrong) can be a *skandalon*. The most difficult thing about ethics is the just decisions it requires.

But while Ivan, Markel, the young Zosima, Dmitri, and Dostoevsky himself all seem drawn to the temptation of temptation, Alyosha is not. And Levinas's appropriation of the novel's credo is what makes Alyosha's significance finally clear. As Levinas reads them, Markel's words express the understanding that "I can substitute myself for everyone, but no one can substitute himself for me" (*EI* 101). Levinas elaborates:

> I am responsible for the Other without waiting for his reciprocity. . . . Reciprocity is *his* affair. . . . It is I who support all . . . [as in] that sentence in Dostoevsky: "*We are all guilty of all and for all men before all, and I more than the others.*" This is not owing to such or such a guilt which is really mine,

or to offenses that I would have committed; but because I am responsible for a total responsibility, which answers for all the others and for all in the others, even for their responsibility. I always have one responsibility *more* than the others.[51]

In other words: I have one more responsibility, not because of guilt, but because my commitment does not reflect or depend on that of the collective. Dostoevsky scholars rarely quote the second part of this famous statement, since most see "I more than the others" as a flourish, an overpersonalization of a grand moral principle. For Levinas, on the other hand, this flourish is the heart of the matter:

> If I say that "virtue is its own reward" I can only say so *for myself;* as soon as I make this a standard for the other I exploit him. That would be like the story of the Czar's mother who goes to the hospital and says to the dying soldier: "You must be very happy to die for your country." Alyosha Karamazov says: "We are all responsible for everyone else—but I am more responsible than all the others." And he does not mean that every "I" is more responsible than all the others, for that would be to generalize the law for everyone else—to demand as much from the other as I do from myself.[52]

For Levinas, the maxim (very tellingly attributed to Alyosha, who is "merely" transcribing Zosima's life narrative) is precisely not a "formula of unity,"[53] but rather an expression of the responsibility that arises in my *separateness* from, my *nonidentification* with, the other. It is this ethical separation that is also, significantly, linked here to a rejection of theodicy ("You must be very happy to die for *X*"). This, indeed, is Alyosha and Levinas's answer to Ivan's anti-theodicy: the only meaningful response to the other's suffering is not an egoistic rejection of the world that makes it possible (as though the world could care!), but the realization that, in this world where God may be dead or hidden, "I am more responsible than the others."

Of course, my overflowing obligation to the other must be contained in vessels of justice. Levinas thus qualifies his reading of Markel's words: "These are extreme formulas which must not be detached from their context. In the concrete, many other considerations intervene and require justice even for me. Practically, the laws set certain consequences out of their way. But justice only has meaning if it retains the spirit of disinterestedness which animates the idea of responsibility for the other man" (*EI* 99).

In "Judaism and Revolution," Levinas interprets Talmudic labor law (Baba Metsia 83a–83b) to suggest this dynamic between ethics and justice in two basic ways: (1) the employer's obligation to his workers is infinite, and therefore he must quickly strike a contract with them (at dawn, before they are fully awake!) that would make wage labor possible in the first place; and

(2) the employer must understand the letter of the contract generously, loyal to the spirit of the ethical obligation that precedes it—and toward which it must strive without hope of fulfillment.[54] In other words, Levinas understands Dostoevsky's sentence not in its practical or legal sense, but rather as the expression of an ontological relation: I am never done with the other. It is also important to note that this is not the same as a lacerative psychological condition for Levinas, for whom "psychological 'accidents' are the ways in which ontological relations show themselves" (*EI* 70). That is, the pursuit or acceptance of unwarranted self-punishment may seem like a valid reaction to the ontological relation of nonreciprocal responsibility for the other, but there is nothing normative about it. In the real world—where I am involved in a complex web of associations and circumstances beyond my control, where "I am not alone with the other"—such self-punishment is a psychological manifestation, a passion play, and not an actualization of ethics. In the real world, there is generally someone who needs my help and not my show of self-punishment; and it is exactly this that Alyosha realizes over the course of the novel.

Unlike Mitya, Markel, and Zosima, Alyosha does not need to sin and suffer to be righteous. Zosima admits that he loves Alyosha because his face (or more precisely, *lik* or countenance) and spirituality remind him of Markel, but on the next page Zosima describes his brother as having been "hot-tempered and irritable by nature" (*PSS* 14:260; *BK* 287), not at all like Alyosha. As Michael Holquist notes, with the scandal caused by the stench of the Elder's body, Dostoevsky seems to be abandoning the structure of Zosima's life narrative "as a possible paradigm for the life of his hero Alyosha, whose progression will not be that from sinner to saint."[55] At the wake, Father Iosif insists that "it is not bodily incorruptibility that is regarded as the main sign of the glorification of the saved, but the color of their bones after their bodies have lain in the ground many years and even decayed in it" (*PSS* 14:300; *BK* 332). Zosima's life and teaching will not be Alyosha's models so much as they will be transformed in his own life and teaching.[56]

Perhaps Alyosha's *lik* evokes Markel's in the way that, for Levinas, justice arises from ethics. Levinas uses the manic, neurotic, obsessive, and indeed otherworldly overtones of Markel's declaration to suggest a phenomenological description of ethics that is not a matter of who is to blame (which is the standard Western idea of ethics as a way of being above reproach) but of "what am I to do?"[57] It is important to remember that unlike Markel and Zosima, who are both on their deathbed in the layered narrative context of this ethical credo, Alyosha is the one left to put these words into action: so what is he to do, in this world full of contending others? Like the rest of us, Alyosha must compromise in order to strive toward a just world that is more ethical than not. Short of murder, there is no simple formula for escaping the "persecution" of ethics—only provisional negotiations and contracts, the stuff of Jews and Jesuits, and scorned by Mitya and Ivan.

The "Odor of Corruption" chapter of *The Brothers Karamazov* is, perhaps like the Talmudic parable cited earlier, about the transformation of piety into agency by the realization that God's way is shaped and enacted only on earth. As Dostoevsky himself implies in his satirical treatment of the superstitious fanatic Father Ferapont, divine displays are irrelevant and unnecessary: righteousness is not about seeing or even hearing God per se, but about interpreting and following his commandments, especially the basic interdiction against murder that is expressed in the face of the other. "My children have overruled me," God proclaims, smiling, in the Talmudic story. Alyosha likewise defeats Zosima, as well as the Elder's sinner-saint paradigm—a context in which Levinas's idea of paternity comes to mind: "The ego can become other to itself . . . only . . . through paternity. Paternity is the relationship with a stranger who, entirely while being Other, is myself, the relationship of the ego with a myself who is nonetheless a stranger to me. The son, in effect, is not simply my work, like a poem or an artifact, neither is he my property. . . . I do not *have* my child; I *am* in some way my child."[58] In 1878, shortly after Dostoevsky started working on *The Brothers Karamazov*—with Alexei Fyodorovich Karamazov as its "unheroic" hero—his own three-year-old son, Alexei Fyodorovich, died. And in a sense, Alyosha Karamazov *is* Dostoevsky (though also completely other). Alyosha transcends Dostoevskyan psychology: he listens more than he talks, and he lives through and eventually untangles some of the contradictions he witnesses. When his early efforts at well-meant intervention go awry (with Captain Snegiryov, with Ivan and Katerina Ivanovna), he scolds himself, retreats, takes stock, and vows to listen more carefully in order to make wiser judgments and decisions. The novel traces his slow evolution from an interpreter of faces and situations into a righteous man, a teacher who has the understanding, compassion, and strength to elevate a bunch of stormy but well-meaning boys into "gentlemen."[59]

The relation between Mitya and Alyosha likewise offers an important study in contrasts. Mitya's secret neck pouch, in which he had hidden half of Katya's 3,000 rubles, is a richly symbolic item (*PSS* 14:144; *BK* 156). Simple, sincere, openhearted, noble, priapic Mitya secretly takes half the money and sews it up in an amulet made from his landlady's old bonnet. Mitya does this for Grushenka, apparently—in case she should change her mind and "choose the son over the father" (they would then have the means to elope). But Mitya also sews up the money because, as long as he had half the rubles, he could still do the right thing, he could still say to himself, "No, Dmitri Fyodorovich, perhaps you're not yet a thief. Why? Precisely because you can go tomorrow and give the fifteen hundred back to Katya" (*PSS* 14:444; *BK* 493). Returning it, however, would have revealed that, like his vile father, Mitya possesses a calculating prudence—a pagan trait according to Lotman, and probably a "kikish" one for the author of *The Diary of a Writer*—that stands in stark contrast to Mitya's Russian maximalism: "I set it aside out of baseness—that is, out of calculation, because calculation in this case is baseness" (*PSS* 14:443; *BK* 492). And so, justice, "doing the right thing" and returning the rest of the money, would painfully reflect the fact that human weakness, cruelty, and circumstances turn moral decisions into unseemly (indeed, disgraceful, *bezobraznye*) compromises.

As the prosecutor insists, the "real" Mitya, the impulsive and open-hearted Russian, could never have saved the 1,500 rubles (*PSS* 15:130–31; *BK* 700–701). Not only did he save it, however, he wore it around his neck, against his bare chest—a badge of shame as well as an unused key to his recovery. Like the guilty philo-Semitism that Dostoevsky may have obscured with his compulsive anti-Semitism, Mitya's amulet leaves no traces that could exculpate and save him from being falsely convicted of his father's murder. Since Mitya's pouch remains his shameful secret until it is too late, the prosecutor and the jury condemn him to suffer for his Russianness: "Our peasants stood up for themselves . . . and finished off our Mitenka" (*PSS* 15:178; *BK* 753). Because "our Mitenka" would have used up all of Katya's 3,000 long before, the rubles that Mitya spent on his last spree in Mokroye must have been Fyodor Pavlovich's. Neither the jury nor the innkeeper believes that Mitya could have had the prudence to spend only half of Katya's money that night in Mokroye.

Mitya, however, wishes to bear the cross of this false condemnation. His desire emanates from his dream about the *dit'jo*, the "wee one": "Why is the wee one poor? It was a prophecy to me at that moment! It's for the wee one that I will go. Because everyone is guilty for everyone else. For all the wee ones, because there are little children and big children. All people are wee ones. And I'll go for all of them, because there must be someone who will go for all of them" (*PSS* 15:31; *BK* 591). Mitya is transfixed by the deep pity evoked by the word *dit'jo*—a pity that refutes the Grand Inquisitor's patronizing contempt for God's weak children. Jacques Rolland and Alain Toumayan suggest that Mitya's revelation of his guilt toward the *dit'jo* resembles the kind of infinite responsibility for the other that Levinas discusses.[60] Mitya wants to go to Siberia, not to atone for the parricide he did not commit, but to help the wee one, the helpless other imperiled by the simple fact of my being. But we must remember Levinas's caveat: "Extreme formulas . . . must not be detached from their context . . . [where] many other considerations intervene and require justice even for me." Alyosha, however, seems to be aware that, without this provision, ethics can rarely be enacted in this world—that without it, ethics is a hyperbole in the service of aesthetics or emotional fulfillment, but not in the service of people. Mitya is so afraid "that this risen man not depart from [him]" (*PSS* 15:31; *BK* 591) that he takes an ontological relation (responsibility for the absolutely needy other) as a pretext to assume the punishment meted out for a specific crime that is not his but Smerdyakov's. This move has more of a psychological than an ethical motivation; and it is the kind of costly, ostentatious, dubiously effective form of self-therapy for which Dostoevsky, too, had a penchant. In 1849, the young Dostoevsky's death sentence for belonging to a secret utopian society was commuted to what amounted to a decade of imprisonment and exile in Siberia. And while Dostoevsky describes the depths of his mental and physical torment in *House of the Dead* and in letters, and although he would on occasion show the scars left by the shackles on his legs,[61] he also tended to see his punishment as a penance for his "spiritual degeneration."

Self-humbling in the absence of concrete crimes is a métier that Mitya shares with Dostoevsky. Significantly, however, Alyosha goes beyond Mitya's romantic and indulgent babble and helps arrange plans for his brother's escape. As he tells Mitya: "Heavy burdens are not for everyone, 'for some they are impossible. . . . Of course, bribery is dishonest even in this case, but I wouldn't make myself a judge here for anything, since, as a matter of fact, if Ivan and Katya asked me to take charge of it for you . . . I would go and bribe [the guards myself]" (*PSS* 15:185; *BK* 764). Likewise, when Kolya declares that he envies Mitya's martyrdom and his "sacrifice for truth," Alyosha exclaims: "What do you mean? How can you be? And why? . . . But not for such a cause, not with such disgrace, not with such horror!" (*PSS* 15:190; *BK* 768) This response comes from the same conviction that prompts Alyosha's puzzling statement to Ivan that it was "not you . . . not you" who killed their father Fyodor Pavlovich (*PSS* 15:40; *BK* 602). Gary Saul Morson suggests that what Alyosha means is that Ivan is responsible only in the realm of possibility.[62] But perhaps this idea of "side-shadowing" unnecessarily complicates the issue: it is easy to blame Ivan for this murder, but his responsibility for it (shared by many others in the novel, including Alyosha) should not obscure the fact that Ivan did not kill Fyodor and that (as Alyosha understands) blaming Ivan is not what needs to be done. Alyosha's strange, and almost inarticulate, insistence conveys this rather unliterary truth.

Such a reading would suggest that the "Karamazov force" is not some genre of original sin, but a more general teeming, impure, subterranean life energy. Alyosha recognizes his own Karamazovism as an unpurgeable part of himself; and perhaps this is yet another reason why Levinas attributes Markel's credo to Alyosha. This credo links Levinas's ethics to a recognition of the fundamental impurity of the self, an impurity that always makes the other (ethically, if not always practically) my affair, whether this other likes me or not. This impurity of the self means that feeling guilty is not enough and may be too much: more important is the ability to decide, with wisdom and probity, when and how to be responsible to whom.

I suggest that it was the emergence in Dostoevsky of this practical ethics (so central to rabbinic thought), in addition to a Dostoevskyan (and Christian) "taste for pathos," that inspired Levinas since his days reading the

Russian classics in his father's bookstore in Kovno. By the end of *The Brothers Karamazov*, Dostoevsky's avowedly Christian vision seems tempered by what can perhaps be described as a "proto-Levinasian" ethical sensibility. If Dostoevsky's novels are, as George Clay writes, about "the most that can happen," it is quite appropriate that Levinas's hyperbolic notion of infinite responsibility sprouted from their fertile soil.[63] But where Zosima exhorts his followers to "water the earth with tears of your joy, and love those tears" (*PSS* 14:292, 328; *BK* 322, 362), Levinas makes a subtle but crucial adjustment: I am "called on the *brink* of tears and laughter to responsibility" (*OTB* 18; emphasis added).[64] In other words, neither Myshkin's nor Zosima's tears of oceanic fusion can actually respond to the needs of others. Alyosha's version of Zosima's tears, however, is ethically transformative: "He fell to the earth a weak youth and rose up a fighter, steadfast for the rest of his life. . . . Three days later he left the monastery . . . 'to sojourn in the world'" (*PSS* 14:328; *BK* 363). Levinas's at times self-mocking attachment to Dostoevsky suggests that the former's thought is, in part, a distillation of the ethical spirit of the latter's work—a distillation that relies on but checks pathos and hysteria, and that includes a more explicit and sober notion of justice. There is perhaps no ethics without pathos; but there is also no ethics when pathos overwhelms everything else—hence the significance of *remaining* on the brink. Despite his repeated use of Markel's credo, Levinas never wrote even a few pages on Dostoevsky, conceivably because so much of Levinas's philosophical writing was in any case a tacit reading and extension of *The Brothers Karamazov*.

In these last two chapters, I have examined the significance of Levinas's proto-philosophical encounter with Dostoevsky's novels. My project has been to show, by way of a kind of "subterranean Judaic discourse," how Dostoevsky's artistic and philosophical originality dwells in something beyond Bakhtinian polyphony, on the one hand, and overwrought pamphleteering, on the other. That is, Dostoevsky's artistic genius is philosophical less because of his actual views or how these views find expression in his fiction, but rather in the fact that his obsession with truth refuses to successfully mythify even the impulses and sentiments he loves. In his quest for the deepest human truths—truths that pure philosophy cannot readily depict, partly because they are attached not only to ideas but to idea-*feelings*—Dostoevsky leaves no stone unturned; and each stone reveals its dank, too-fertile underside. At the same time, Dostoevsky dreams of an ethical center to arise from the very midst of all these overturned stones—for the true to give over to the good. His novels are, in this sense, aesthetic investigations into a question Levinas makes explicit philosophically: "A philosopher seeks, and expresses, truth. Truth, before characterizing a statement or a judgment, consists in the exhibition of being. *But what shows itself in truth, under the name of being? And who looks?*" (*OTB* 24) Or, to paraphrase Stepan Trofimovich at the end of *Demons: How can I be certain that I'm not lying even when I tell the truth?*

The Levinas-Dostoevsky connection has several implications for the humanities. First, it suggests that Levinas bridges Derrida's deconstructionist indeterminacy and Dostoevsky's onto-theology. If, as Straus writes, "Dostoevsky's supposedly 'unfinalized discourse' . . . functioned for literary theory as a kind of transitional object between deconstruction's quasi-erasure and dialogism's quasi-preservation of a religious sensibility," then Levinas may occupy a satisfying middle ground between Derrida and Bakhtin. Levinas is a religious philosopher of selfless ethics, suspicious of moralism and formulas; he is also a skeptic for whom the dialogic process of questioning is more valuable than its Socratic, negationist "results." If the challenge of contemporary thought is how to negotiate between the need to be open and the need to judge, then Levinas's ideas about ethics and justice, along with his acknowledgment that it is perhaps unethical to preach a "piety without reward," become increasingly relevant.[65]

Unlike Derrida's triumphalist, guilty, and somewhat negligible "Judaic turn," Levinas's serious engagement with the rabbinic tradition (serious, whether or not one agrees with his reading of the Talmud) incorporates Dostoevsky's aesthetic and moral (Christian) insights as well as his secular skepticism. And this is also true in places where Levinas's thought seems weak and incoherent, as it does in his peculiar turn to religious Zionism in 1951, when he suggested that what "genuinely matters about the State of Israel is not that it fulfills an ancient promise, or heralds a new age of material security . . . but that it finally offers the opportunity to carry out Judaism's social law."[66] A strange thing to say, for someone who looked to Judaism as a source for anti-utopian morality. And yet, it sounds so similar to Dostoevsky's exhortations in *The Diary of a Writer* for the "reconquest" of Constantinople as a way of achieving pan-Orthodox *sobornost'* in history (*PSS* 25:74) and to Ivan Karamazov's ironic (yet serious?) article that seems to argue in favor of the expansion of ecclesiastic law into the secular legal system. Perhaps there is something characteristically Russian about both Levinas and Dostoevsky's bursts of theo-political impatience—even as Soloviev might argue that such "spiritual materialism" is in fact Judaic.

Such political impatience may be read as a naive response to the radical ethical immediacy that interests Levinas and which he and others have characterized as "Russian." In a 1985 interview, Levinas describes a scene from the end of the Battle of Stalingrad in Vasily Grossman's novel *Life and Fate,* in which German soldiers are removing bodies from a cellar before a hostile Russian crowd. When they bring out the body of an adolescent girl, a woman runs to the body, straightening out her hair. Filled with hatred, she picks up a brick and approaches a German officer, intending to bash his skull. Instead:

Not understanding what was happening to her, governed by a power she had just now seemed to control, she felt in the pocket of her jacket for a piece of bread that had been given to her the evening before . . . She held it out to the German officer and said: "There, have something to eat." Afterwards, she was unable to understand what had happened to her, why she had done this. Her life was to be full of moments of humiliation, helplessness and anger, full of petty cruelties that made her lie awake at night, full of brooding resentment. . . . At one such moment, lying on her bed, full of bitterness, she was to remember that winter morning outside the cellar and think: "I was a fool then, and I'm still a fool now."[67]

In Levinas's description of this "foolish" woman, he adds that "this is a type that exists in Russia. It is *The Idiot* of Dostoevsky . . . The human pierces the crust of being."[68] This suggests that Levinas looked to Russian literature and culture—full of unmediated extremes—for examples of radical ethics in its raw form, so to speak. Then again, as we have seen, Dostoevsky's Alyosha may also resemble one of the canny sages from Levinas's reading of Talmudic labor law as much as he resembles Myshkin, "the Russian type." This mirroring suggests that the relation between the Russian and Jewish traditions is most revealing neither as fusion (a double chosenness) nor as opposition (two competing forms of chosenness), but as two intertwined, mutually sustaining modes of spiritual election—an election that can be only ethical, not ethnic. Such symbiosis suggests that Dostoevsky borrows a "Judaic" spiritual middle for Alyosha's "practical Christianity," just as Levinas adopts the compassion typical of Russian literature in his critique of Western ontology.

Perhaps there is another implication of this effort to "find" Levinas in Dostoevsky and vice versa. For both Dostoevsky and Levinas, an idea is most meaningful—most itself—when it is not systematic but embodied. For Dostoevsky, ideas are real and interesting only as "idea-feelings" in individuals; for Levinas, ethics is expressed only in my solicitude for the other and never in any abstract concept. Accordingly, it seems more meaningful to speak of covert affinities between this Jew and that Christian than between syncretistic or oppositional notions of Judaism and Christianity. Yeshayahu Leibowitz held that, while there can and should be dialogue between Christians and Jews, no dialogue is possible between Judaism and Christianity. And yet connecting Levinas and Dostoevsky blurs Leibowitz's distinction, because a dialogue (good or bad) between two faiths can only happen between individuals.

## Chapter Three

# Isaac Babel's Dirty Ethics

> I'm not surprised that the audience would
> applaud the violence, because I wanted them
> to be complicit in it. I wanted them to be
> involved in it. Because I guess you have to
> ask them after the movie's over how they feel
> about their complicity in those violent acts;
> because if it's done in such a way that the
> audience is repulsed and held outside the
> movie, then I've actually lost the opportunity
> to deliver to them the paradox of enjoying
> something that you find morally reprehensible.
> —David Cronenberg on his film *A History of*
> *Violence,* Cannes Film Festival, May 2005

IT SEEMS COUNTERINTUITIVE to make the leap
from Dostoevsky to Isaac Babel. If anything, Babel, who wanted to write at
least as well as Tolstoy and Maupassant, nominally sought to distance himself
from Dostoevsky.[1] In his cheerfully wry 1916 manifesto, "Odessa," a 22-year-
old Babel calls for a "Literary Messiah" to bring southern sunshine to Russian
literature, citing Dostoevsky as the emblem of that dark Petersburg tradition
that overcame the warm Ukrainian light of a younger Gogol:

> With Dostoevsky you can feel the uneven grey carriageway along which
> Karamazov walks to the tavern, the mysterious and heavy fog of Petersburg.
> The grey roads and the shrouds of fog stifle people and, stifling them, distort
> them in a manner amusing and terrible, giving birth to a rumble and jumble
> [*chad i smrad*] of passions and making the usual human bustle that much
> more frantic.[2]

An oddly parataxic image of Dostoevsky's literary universe. Which Karamazov
is walking to which tavern?—Alyosha on his way to meet Ivan and his tale of
the Grand Inquisitor? Dmitri on his way to the tavern where Grushenka has
gone to meet the Polish lover who had abandoned her? Or is Babel conflat-

ing the Karamazovs with Raskolnikov, who would be the one to walk to a tavern in the Petersburg fog? This is, to be sure, a carefully studied carelessness on Babel's part. It is a kind of prose poem distilled from Dostoevsky, in which the novelist's atmospherics return us to the "welter and waste" of the human condition (the alliteration of *chad i smrad* recalls the *tohu va-vohu* of Genesis 1:2). The implication is that it falls to a "Literary Messiah, awaited so long and so fruitlessly, [who] will come . . . from the sunny steppes drenched by the sea" (*SS* 1:48) to let there be light (Genesis 1:3).

At face value, Babel's reading of Dostoevsky's fiction in "Odessa" seems by turns absurdly and glibly aesthetic, moralistic, and theological. Like Proust, whom Levinas chides for focusing on the aesthetic details and not the spiritual struggles in Dostoevsky's fiction, Babel first reduces Dostoevsky to roads and fogs.[3] He then accuses these roads and fogs of "stifling people" (all people? characters? readers? perhaps only Russian readers?). He concludes with a literary-theological solution for this "stifling" situation: "People feel the need for new blood. It's stifling. A Literary Messiah . . . will come." This prophecy reflects a restoration of Russia's southerly roots and yearnings—not only in Gogol's Ukraine and in Kievan Rus, but in "the cross of the Holy Sophia" (*SS* 1:48), that is, in the Hagia Sophia of Constantinople, the formerly Byzantine, now Turkish capital so coveted by Dostoevsky and other Russian nationalists as a base from which the light of Orthodox Christianity would radiate through Europe and Asia in historical time.

It is not just the flippant tone of "Odessa" that makes it impossible to read this echo of Dostoevsky's Russian messianism at anything like face value. There are also the obvious and orientalized Jewishness of its author, who signs this and a few other early publications as "Bab-El,'" and his characterization of this messianic city as specifically Jewish:

> Half of the population consists of Jews, and Jews are a people who have figured out a few very simple things. They get married so they won't be lonely, they love so as to live through the ages, hoard money so they can have homes and give their wives astrakhan jackets, love the kids because—well, after all, it's very good and even necessary to love your children. These poor Odessa Jews get very confused by officials and regulations, but it isn't easy to get them to budge from their positions, their fixed and ancient positions. Budge they will not, and much can be learned from them. To a great extent it's because of them that Odessa has this light and easygoing atmosphere. (*SS* 1:43)

This teasing, loving stereotype (of what Jewish intellectuals such as Hannah Arendt would dismiss as "parvenus")[4] recalls the idea of a Jewish "spiritual materialism"—attempted in the Talmud and caricatured by Slavophile thought. According to Babel, the Russian striving toward the southern steppes and toward the Hagia Sophia of Constantinople ends in the Jewish ghetto of Odessa, from whence will issue the savior of Russian literature. With his talent for partial travesty, Babel makes explicit what I have argued was implicit in Dostoevsky's later novels.

But we may pose the same question prompted by Ivan Karamazov's various essays and "poems": is Babel only joking? At the beginning of this book, I suggested that literary manifestos are moved by an ethical urgency—even, perhaps, such a one as this, whose style, as Janneke van de Stadt argues, consists of a parodic deflation of other manifestos.[5] What then is the ethos of Babel's strangely ironic essay?—which, after all, begins by telling his reader that "Odessa is a nasty town. As everybody knows" (SS 1:43). If anything, Babel—whose main device, in Shklovsky's memorable description, "is to speak in the same voice of the stars and of gonorrhea"—would seem to be the bard of the beauty of Sodom, of the "artistic cruelty" that Dostoevsky understood so well and so wished to overcome with "positive beauty," the "ideal of the Madonna." Any reader will be struck by Babel's Homeric "lyric joy in the midst of violence," sex, and excrement.[6] All the less reason, it would seem, to examine Babel after Dostoevsky and Levinas's ethical urgency and their anxieties about beauty.

In this chapter, however, I argue that Isaac Babel's style—its lyrical ambiguities and excesses typically characterized as grotesque, decadent, or ornamentalist—reveals a specific ethical horizon. This is partly an elaboration on Lionel Trilling's comment that the "apparent denial of immediate pathos is a condition of the ultimate pathos [Babel] conceives." Trilling suggests that this ultimate pathos is established because the writer's "intense concern with the hard aesthetic surface of the story . . . [ is] cognate with the universe, representative of its nature, of the unyielding circumstance in which the human fact exists."[7] In my view this aesthetic surface is actually quite soft and porous. The ethical porosity that is revealed in Levinas's thought and in Dostoevsky's novels finds perhaps its most demanding form in the bizarre moments of sexual, physical, verbal, and even moral defilement in Babel's *Red Cavalry* tales. The most righteous figures in these stories are often the most compromised and impure, contaminated by others and taking on their shame, while remaining themselves and helping others remain others. Defilement as moral revelation also characterizes the fate of Babel's narrator Liutov, just as it informs the book's orally inflected *skaz* narratives, in which the author's mimetic curiosity gives voice to an aesthetically exuberant depravity, implicating not only the brutal "folksy" narrators but Babel and his readers as well. What's striking about the *skaz* pieces in *Red Cavalry* is that even though their narrators are typically vicious, obtusely self-righteous braggarts, Babel infuses their narratives with the peculiar aesthetic and writerly elements that we associate with Babel or Liutov. I will linger considerably on such *skaz* for two main reasons: (1) because it evokes a Levinasian preference for "sound over semantics," which is to say, "the presence of others making themselves felt in advance of what is said";[8] and (2) because it suggests an "ultimate pathos" that goes beyond a moral evaluation of literary *content* (that is, of characters or events) and reflects a broader literary ethics or an art-as-ethics that is revealed in self-pollution: a dirty ethics, so to speak, with roots in both Russian and Jewish culture.

Shklovsky was far from the only admirer or critic to have described Babel's vision as an ornamentalist mingling of the sacred and the profane. The Red Cavalry general Semyon Budenny himself accused Babel of *babizm* (a bad pun on the author's name and the Russian word for *wench*)—of a cowardly, pornographic, effeminizing libel upon the honor and history of his Red Cavalry Army.[9] Budenny's response was crude, but not surprising. Judith Deutsch Kornblatt, echoing Victor Terras, explains that

> Babel creates a world that knows no barriers, a type of permanent liminality. Things and people transgress the restrictions normally imposed by gravity, the march of time, or the distinction between discrete objects. Heaven is juxtaposed with earth, beautiful with sordid, incredible with real, and thus Babel creates a picture of a mythical realm.[10]

In this reading, *Red Cavalry* becomes an *Iliad,* with Babel as its wandering bard. Of course, as Budenny sensed, Babel's epic also contains its own mock-epic, best embodied in the authorial alter ego and narrator Kirill Liutov and his pathetic, halfhearted attempts to fit in with the Cossacks: he kills a goose in "My First Goose"; in "After the Battle," he scratches someone's cheek, and later knocks down an invalid who was taunting him for being a "Molokan" (a milk-drinking, pacifist schismatic) riding into battle with an unloaded gun; and in "Argamak," the anticlimactic final story of one version of the collection, he finally picks up the rudiments of the Cossack style of riding and the soldiers finally ignore him when he's on horseback.

The partial *1920 Diary,* which includes much of the raw material for these stories, does not contain anything like the intensity of this self-parody and mock-epic, even though Babel really did try to conceal his Jewishness (without great success) by adopting the overly Russian nom de guerre of Kirill Liutov ("Cyril Savage") when he rode with the Red Cavalry as a propagandist for its broadsheet. Nor is the epic mythical dimension to be found in the *Diary,* which makes palpable Babel's disgust with the Cossacks as they kill prisoners and rape and plunder Jews and Poles alike. Given the clear moral outrage in Babel's *Diary,* how to account for the transformation of its material into a transgressive mixture of myth and parody, in which the savagery of the Cossacks is Homeric and in which Homer is a Jew-in-Cossack-cloak who has renamed himself a Savage? Critics usually talk about this mixture as a distinctive marker of Babel's style and aesthetics—described as ornamentalist, modernist, decadent, naturalist, surrealist, and/or Nietzschean, depending on the critic.

To be sure, apart from Trilling's abbreviated insight, others have made arguments about the ethics of Babel's writing, but too often these either rely on his *Diary* to apologize for his "adventurous" running with naughty commissars (see Cynthia Ozick) or else simply use the *Diary* as a magic key to unlock the "real ethics," that is, the moral outrage, locked up in the stories. Lee Siegel, for example, writes that "Babel transforms the he-men Cossacks into sexually repressed men who sublimate their desire to fuck other men into acts of atrocity."[11] (This recalls the attempts to attribute Nazi atrocities to sublimated homosexuality, which does the neat trick of simultaneously insulting homosexuals and fascist war criminals.) Such a reading asks us to treat every mythic description of Cossack appearance and every clinical account of Cossack violence in *Red Cavalry* as elaborate and ironic jokes. Critics like Ozick and Siegel basically take the ambivalence in *Red Cavalry* about Jews and Cossacks and proceed to make Babel's mind up for him. But more significantly, they still leave Babel's mixed-up aesthetics, the stars and the gonorrhea, on the cutting-room floor. After all, if all he wanted to do was mock the Cossacks, he wouldn't need such aesthetic complexity and ambivalence. And such complexity and ambivalence are considerably more interesting (and as I hope to show, more ethical) than mocking Cossacks (who don't really exist as Cossacks anymore, outside of folk dance ensembles) or Communists (also moribund).

This urge to make Babel take sides reflects our basic anxiety about great art, an anxiety shared, with cruel irony, by the tyrants who execute the likes of Babel. Even Trilling confessed to feeling threatened by *Red Cavalry*'s ability to disclose—and thereby, as it were, "make"—a world:

> I was afraid of its terrible intensities, ironies, and ambiguities. If this was what I really felt, I can't say that I am now wholly ashamed of my cowardice. If we stop to think of the museum knowingness about art which we are likely to acquire with maturity, of our consumer's pride in buying only the very best spiritual commodities, the ones which are sure to give satisfaction, there may possibly be a grace in those moments when we lack the courage to confront, or the strength to endure, some particular work of art or kind of art.[12]

This fear—noble when confessed by a discerning critic, deadly when it moves a dictator—arguably acquires a special potency in prose fiction. Curiosity drives prose. Where poetic truth may be revealed through loose connections that go beyond a word's immediate context (metaphor), prose generally moves forward through metonymy, which operates by way of a more causal relation between words.[13] And curiosity is animated by the promise of learning causes, what makes things tick. Passages are curious things, drawing the reader forward in time and knowledge, because there is a presumption that something about the world itself—and not just a metaphoric impression of the world—will be revealed.

Curiosity—as the self-centered quest for knowledge and power that Levinas warns against—can be ethically troublesome. And this is something to keep in mind in probing Babel's urge in his *1920 Diary* to do aesthetic justice to the war that would be the subject of *Red Cavalry:* "What is Kiperman? . . . Describe this evening . . . Describe this Khast . . . Who and what is Zholnarkevich? . . . Describe the origins of these units . . . Describe our soldiers . . . Describe our supply system . . ." As Elif Batuman points out, there is something almost clerk-like about these reminders; and at times Babel, the exacting literary clerk, is overwhelmed and revolted by his task: "Must penetrate the soul of the fighting man, I'm penetrating, it's all horrible, wild beasts with principles" (SS 2:301), he confesses in his *Diary*.[14] So how does Babel's "penetrating clerkship" unfold in the collection of short stories that would make up *Red Cavalry*? What is the ethical dimension of his curious aesthetics? Does the fiction present an aesthetic suspension of the ethical— or its intensification?

The first story in *Red Cavalry* shatters the idea that incuriosity is the answer to curiosity's ethical problems, by throwing a challenge in the face of the narrator, author, and reader. And I would also suggest that this story be read in light of an ethics of defilement. In "Crossing the Zbruch," Liutov is lodged with a pillaged Jewish household, the floor littered with broken Passover dishes and human excrement. Throughout the story, Liutov is oblivious and contemptuous of his hosts: "'Clear this up,' I said to the woman. 'What a filthy way to live.'" He compares them to monkeys and "Japs in a circus." Only at the end of the story does he realize that as he slept, dreaming of Cossacks and military dispatches, he had been spooning the butchered corpse of the father of the pregnant woman of the house, who wakes Liutov and concludes the story:

> *"Panie,"* said the Jewess, shaking up the featherbed, "the Poles slaughtered him, and he begged them: 'kill me in the backyard so my daughter won't see how I die.' But they did as they needed—he passed away in this room thinking of me . . . And now I want to know," the woman said suddenly with terrible force, "I want to know, where else in the whole world will you find such a father like my father?" (SS 2:45)

In this, the first story of the collection, the daughter's outburst undoes Liutov's project, his desire to be accepted by the Cossacks and to conceal his own Jewish background. Liutov, the half-hearted representative of a revolution that was to bring justice, peace, and bread, is a mean substitute for the dead father. Like the anti-theodicies in Dostoevsky and Levinas, the woman's question is unforgiving. No one can pick up the gauntlet. We can't go on. And yet we do, for another thirty-four stories.[15] What is one to make of this paradox? This first story invokes the perennial issues of religion and identity, as the covertly Jewish narrator's Oedipal concealment is undone. The ghost of the murdered Jewish father, conjured by the lips of a vulnerable, demanding other (the pregnant daughter), is a caesura, a rupture that would preclude narrative redemption. And it is Liutov's defilement by proximity to human feces and death itself (a source of ritual impurity for the priestly line in Jewish tradition) that sets up the daughter's ethical revelation—an ethical revelation that shows Liutov his own capacity for cruel incuriosity. Accordingly, the stories that follow tend to mock and punish the narrator for his original sin, the initial indifference of his mean, uncomprehending entrance into Poland. The campaign "pries his eyes open," to borrow the revolutionary slogan he tepidly offers Gedali, the blind Jewish shopkeeper and "founder of an impossible International" of kindness (*SS* 2:72–74).

The narrator's incuriosity in "Crossing the Zbruch" is all the more striking because of the nature of the author's curiosity. Nadezhda Mandelstam recalls that

> everything about Babel gave an impression of all-consuming curiosity—the way he held his head, his mouth and chin, and particularly his eyes. It is not often that one sees such undisguised curiosity in the eyes of a grown-up. I had the feeling that Babel's main driving force was the unbridled curiosity with which he scrutinized life and people. . . . [Osip Mandelstam] asked him why he was so drawn to [drinking with agents of the Cheka]: was it a desire to see what it was like in the exclusive store where the merchandise was death? Did he just want to touch it with his fingers? "No," Babel replied, "I don't want to touch it with my fingers—I just like to have a sniff and see what it smells like."[16]

Nadezhda Mandelstam's sketch casts Babel as a bit of a dauntless Faustian, as if to suggest that incuriosity is a form of cowardice. She also implies that Babel's inquisitiveness was childlike because it was undisguised; most adults have learned to be more circumspect. After all, unbridled curiosity is unseemly—a breach of the other's privacy and a display of naïveté. But curiosity also carries a moral imperative, one that Babel seems to appreciate and live by as an artist.

An unfinished childhood story from 1915 called "At Grandmother's"— arguably the most accurate of Babel's "autobiographical" pieces[17]—suggests a kind of genealogy of the writer's ethics of knowledge:

> "Your grandfather . . . was a great one for telling stories. He didn't believe in anything, but he trusted people. He gave away all his money to his friends,

but when he came to them for help they threw him downstairs, and that made him a little queer in the head." . . . He was a big man with a sharp tongue, wrote essays at night, and knew all languages. He was ruled by an insatiable thirst for knowledge and life. . . . All grandmother had left was my father and me. Everything else was gone. For her, day was slowly turning into night and death was coming slowly. . . . "Study!" she suddenly said with great vehemence. "Study and you will have everything . . . ! You must know *everything*. The whole world will fall at your feet and grovel before you. . . . Do not trust people. Do not have friends. Do not lend them money. Do not give them your heart!" (*SS* 1:181)[18]

Here the need to "know everything" is presented both as a Faustian will to power and emancipation (the unlettered Jewish grandmother's crude, assimilationist injunction) and as the desire to love (the grandfather's joie de vivre). The latter type of knowledge is a love of experience, as the etymology of the Russian word for curiosity (*lubopytnost'*) suggests. But this is a love of experience less for the sake of power (a kind of circling homeward in the manner of Odysseus) than for the sake of glimpsing the world as something other than what can be assimilated. While Babel may not quite have his grandfather's pathological trust of others, neither does he acquire his grandmother's pathological distrust of the outside world.[19]

Babel's is not an all-consuming curiosity devoid of immediate moral considerations. It is a liturgical attentiveness, made difficult in a defensive reaction to life's creeping cruelties: first, the erudition and wisdom of this curiosity make it witty, then cynical, and finally morbid. Throughout, however, the world in its capacity for evil is "sniffed," its beauty taken in with bemusement and fascination, but as far as possible never quite touched in participation. This is Babel's balancing act, his response, as it were, to what the athletic proofreader Smolich says to the "scribbling" ghetto-boy hero of "Awakening": "A man who doesn't live in nature, as a stone does or an animal, will never in his whole life write two worthwhile lines" (*SS* 1:201). Babel follows the proofreader's advice to acquire a feeling for (and a knowledge of) nature, but the hero of *Red Cavalry* never successfully manages to "live in nature as a stone or an animal"—Cossack indifference and cruelty never seem to fit him, no matter how he tries.

Such is the basic juxtaposition of the Cossacks' violence and Liutov's pacifism in *Red Cavalry*. One should also say—and Levinas is again helpful here—that this is a juxtaposition of two visceral reactions to the face, to the vulnerability and nakedness of a person's eyes: (1) Kill; and (2) Thou shalt not kill. The other's vulnerability provokes either contempt or sympathy. And as a man of both overwhelming curiosity and sympathy, Liutov, the Jew who rides into battle with an unloaded gun, is aesthetically drawn to the knowledge that violence makes available. In his *skaz* narrative, the Red general

Pavlichenko equates killing with getting "to know life, such as it is with us," and torture with getting at a man's soul, "where it is in a person and how it shows itself" (*SS* 2:108). One hopes such knowledge is false, but it will in any case ultimately be inaccessible to someone like Babel, who reads "*Thou shalt not kill*" in the eyes of the other. The Haskalah encouraged Jews to contemplate not just the flora and fauna mentioned in the Talmud, but the nature around them. The scribbling Jew—the archetype of a people who have filtered reality through a book—has already learned the names of the birds and the trees, but he has yet to know what it is to kill a man.

As for the self-loathing, self-concealing, "scribbling Jew" in "Zbruch," one should pause to consider the possible figuration of the pregnant Jewish orphan as Babel's "reader." In a 1937 interview, Babel declared that it is "good to read a story only to a very intelligent woman, because this half of the human race, in its best specimens, sometimes possesses an impeccable taste . . . Thus, if I were to choose for myself a reader, then I would think about how best to deceive and to knock this intelligent reader . . . unconscious" (*SS* 3:402–3). In "Zbruch," however, it is not the woman but the narrator and the reader who are stunned. Of course, the fictional prototype for this reader is not in *Red Cavalry* but in Babel's "My First Fee" and "Answer to an Inquiry"—the good-hearted prostitute Vera.

In these two versions of the same metafiction, Babel's twenty-year-old narrator, an aspiring writer employed as a proofreader, seeking "love" spiritual and carnal, earns his "first honorarium" from Vera, when—suddenly repelled (and perhaps made impotent) by the prospect of clinical sex for hire—he stalls and deflects by inventing a tale about his sexual slavery as a "boy with the Armenians." Vera's heart swells with compassion for this "little sister," who gets his heart's desire:

> Have you ever seen a village carpenter helping a fellow carpenter to build his cottage? Have you seen how thick and quick and gay the shavings fly as they plane a beam together? That night this thirty-year-old woman taught me her science. That night I learned secrets you will never learn, I experienced a love which you will never experience, I heard the words that one woman says to another. I have forgotten them. We are not supposed to remember them. (*SS* 1:223)

Alexander Zholkovsky notes that "Babel's theme, along with literary and sexual initiation as such, is the conceit 'literature = prostitution,' involving a carnivalesque glorification of both and at the same time, a subversion of Russian and Soviet literature's spiritual/official pieties."[20] Elsewhere Zholkovsky writes that both versions of Babel's story respond to Dostoevsky's *Notes from the Underground*, in which, as in Babel, "the motifs of 'redemption' and 'literariness' form part of the general 'prostitute' paradigm."[21]

The story's "Oriental" setting of Tiflis, Georgia, underscores other parallels: (1) the hero as Scheherazade, recast as a male neophyte writer; (2) overtones of the New Testament, given the references to a saintly prostitute (compared to the figure of the Virgin Mary), to carpenters, and to the gold coins that Vera refuses at the end of the story—the author's first and most precious literary fee; and (3) "a boy with the Armenians," which evokes the tradition of the Turkic minstrel or *ashik*, often Armenian and sometimes under pederastic patronage, the best known—having entered Russian literature by way of Lermontov—being Ashik Kerib of Tiflis, who begins his journeys with worldly love and attains wisdom before becoming a saint. More than *Notes from the Underground* (Dostoevsky's response to the prostitute-themed Chernyshevsky's *What Is to Be Done?*), such allusions suggest that, throughout Babel's carnivalesque subversiveness, the idea of good fiction as life-sustaining, even "life-creational (*zhiznetvorcheskie*)," triumphs.[22] That is to say, if a "Literary Messiah" from Odessa is a far-fetched conceit, the workings of a messianic literature, as sketched by this Odessan writer, are decidedly not. Babel's metaphoric and gnomic (or perhaps Gnostic) description of his hero's physical and spiritual communion with Vera (Russian for *faith*) is utterly messianic.

Indeed, I would argue that Babel's hero spins his tale out of a sense of ethical obligation—because he doesn't want to offend the prostitute with his sudden disgust. After Vera, "like a surgeon getting ready for an operation" (SS 1:219), prepares her contraceptive enema bag and undresses,

> a large woman with drooping shoulders and crumpled stomach stood before me. Her flabby nipples pointed blindly sideways. "The water's getting ready," said my beloved, "so get over here, boychik." I didn't move. I was numb with despair. Why had I exchanged my loneliness for this sordid den, for these dying flies and three-legged furniture? O Gods of my youth! How different this was, this dreary business, from the love of my neighbors on the other side of the wall, their long, drawn-out squeals. (SS 1:219)[23]

After the hero moves Vera with his elaborate tale of woe, her body appears to undergo a transformation: "My head shook against her breasts which welled freely above me. The taut nipples nudged at my cheeks. Opening their moist eyelids, they nudged, like calves" (SS 1:223). The earlier "blindness" and "flabbiness" are now wide-eyed and taut—and it is impossible to tease apart what is hallucinatory, physiological, or spiritual about this change. After all, the hero is not looking for sex but for "love," or at least something that could compete with his newlywed landlords, who, "crazed with love, turned and twisted like two large fish stuffed in a jar," their tails thrashing against the wall (SS 1:214). The transformation of Vera (Faith) by the light of a "radiant artistic lie"[24] proves the narrator's claim that a "well made-up story needn't try to resemble real life. Life tries as hard as it can to resemble a well made-up story" (*SS* 1:220). As Zholkovsky puts it, in the "tandem of art and life, the driving wheel for Babel is that of art."[25]

This art-driven descent into the underground is a commentary on Dostoevsky's ethics and aesthetics in more ways than one. Vera's room, in which "flies were dying in a phial filled with a milky fluid," recalls Dmitri's recitation of Schiller's "To Joy," apropos the Karamazovism: "To insects—sensuality!" (*PSS* 14:98; *BK* 108). After Babel's Armenian tale, the sensuality of insects gives way to the sensuality of fish, those symbols of Christian abundance introduced by the Georgian newlyweds. (And not only Christian: the image of fish thrashing about indoors also evokes the days before refrigeration, when Jewish grandmothers would have kept live carp in the bathtub until Sabbath eve to make gefilte fish.) Dostoevsky's dark, sordid, and "stifling" underground is then transformed by the hero's kindly act of inspired, fictional self-abasement: after his story is finished, the first thing Vera does is throw "the shutters wide open" as the sun begins to rise over the mountains (*SS* 1:223).

One could even argue that this is not so much a transformation as it is a revelation. Vera, that Beauty of Sodom, had *always* been a Madonna as well, sailing "ahead of the apelike throng as the Mother of God rides the prow of a fishing boat," pausing in front of the doors of the "Sympathia" tavern, when the hero solicits her with his garbled "To what Palestines . . . Where is God taking you?" (*SS* 1:216). Her earthy compassion is evident as she drags the narrator along on various errands before their "appointment." After passionately and unsuccessfully trying to convince a stubborn bar-owner to move his business to a better location,[26] she helps a friend pack:

> "We've just said goodbye to Feodosya Mavrikekeyvna," she said. "She was just like a mother to us, you know. She traveling all alone, the old woman, she's got nobody to go with her." Vera sat down on the bed with her knees apart. Her eyes were far away, roaming in the pure realms of her care and friendship for the old woman. Then she saw me in my double-breasted jacket. "You're tired of waiting, I bet . . ." (*SS* 1:218–19)

This is the woman the narrator does not wish to insult, the woman who will refuse his coins because he defiles his life story with a compelling and convincing lie.

To return to *Red Cavalry*, Babel's "reader" in "Crossing the Zbruch"—unlike Vera, who is so conspicuously Russian, blatantly revealing and revealed—is Jewish and concealed, a ghost that suddenly rises to shatter and (at least temporarily) silence Liutov's blind and flabby account of entering Poland. Furthermore, if Vera is Babel's ideal reader, who does not rival the writer in his particular art, the woman in "Zbruch" may well be a competing author: not only does she bring Liutov up short, she is also heavy with child. Interestingly, Levinas elevates the maternal body as a key simile for ethics in *Otherwise Than Being*, in that a mother is bodily and morally responsible for her child, even for the child's responsibilities, without any reciprocity; in that pregnancy involves sharing one's own body and its finite resources while composing a new being that is always becoming absolutely other.[27] This idea recalls what Gedali tells Liutov in "The Rebbe":

> "All is mortal. Only the mother is destined to immortality. And when the mother is no longer among the living, she leaves a remembrance which none yet has dared to sully. The memory of the mother nourishes in us a compassion that is like the ocean, and the measureless ocean feeds the rivers that dissect the universe. . . . The passionate edifice of Hasidism has had its doors and windows burst open, but it is as immortal as the soul of the mother. With oozing orbits Hasidism still stands at the crossroads of the turbulent winds of history." (*SS* 2:79)

Gedali's image of immortal maternity is wounded, physically compromised, like the Hassidic world of eastern Poland—and yet it still has the power to nourish an oceanic, insatiable compassion. This image also recalls the bereaved and pillaged expectant mother at the end of "Zbruch." Babel, for whom art had value only as something life-creational, does not try to compete with such "authorship" directly.

The literary skills of "My First Fee" give way to a failed authorial narcissism and seem useless in war-torn Novograd. Another metafiction is needed. Accordingly, the daughter's ethical revelation—which shows Liutov his own potential for incuriosity and cruelty—will find its corresponding gospel in "Pan Apolek," a story that fuses the richness of aesthetic attention and curiosity with a forgiving ethics of impurity.

In "Pan Apolek," the specific ethical dimension of Babel's aesthetics of myth, parody, liminality, and defilement is especially prominent. Accompanied by a blind organ grinder named Gottfried, Apolek is an itinerant Polish painter (perhaps, like Gottfried, of German origin) who draws from the local population (rich and poor, Christian and Jew) to create religious paintings deemed sacrilegious by the church hierarchy:

> Gray-haired Josephs with partings down the middle, pomaded Jesuses, village Marys with knees apart, mothers already of many children; all these icons hung in the corners reserved for holy images . . . "He has made saints of you in your lifetime," cried the Vicar of Dubno, in response to the crowd's defense of Apolek. "He has surrounded you with the ineffable attributes of holiness, you who have thrice fallen into the sin of disobedience, distillers of brandy in secret, merciless usurers, makers of false weights, and dealers

in your own daughters' innocence" . . . "Your Holiness," replied the limping Vitold, buyer of stolen goods and cemetery keeper, "who is to tell the ignorant folk where the all-merciful Pan God sees truth? And isn't there more truthfulness in the pictures of Pan Apolek, who finds our dignity, than in your words, full of blame and lordly wrath?" The cries of the multitude put the vicar to flight. (SS 2:62)

Vitold's response to the vicar points to the ethos of Apolek's aesthetics, which, like Babel's, mingles the earthly and the holy (or mythic) in ways that trouble the authorities—be they clerical in Apolek's case, or secular (Budenny, and eventually and fatally, Stalin) in Babel's. This is especially significant in light of what the narrator declares at the beginning of this story:

The wise and wonderful life of Pan Apolek hit my head like an old wine. In Novograd-Volynsk . . . fate threw at my feet a Gospel hidden from the world . . . I then made my vow to follow Pan Apolek's example. And the sweetness of meditated rancor, the bitter scorn for the curs and swine of humankind, the fire of silent and intoxicating revenge—all this I sacrificed to my new vow. (SS 2:56–57)

One would guess that Babel is sacrificing the meditated rancor—about his comrades and about the war—that one finds in his *Diary* to his vow to follow Apolek's example. If we understand this at face value, and we probably should, then even someone he loathed in his *Diary* like Apanasenko (a braggart and narcissist who kills prisoners, seduces nurses, and hates intellectuals) gets to present his life story as "Pavlichenko, Matvei Rodionych," like a "pomaded Jesus," in a *skaz* narrative modeled on Russian legend, or *bylina,* and hagiography.

I will return to Pavlichenko in my discussion of *skaz* later in this chapter, but for now, I will focus on "Pan Apolek." Liutov's vow makes reference to a hidden gospel—which at first seems like a vague attempt to turn Apolek into an artistic evangelist, until we recall that near the end of the story Apolek tells Liutov a blasphemous story. According to Apolek, Jesus attends the wedding of a young maid, Deborah, who was so nervous when her husband approached to consummate the marriage that she vomited all the food she had eaten at the feast.

Shame fell on Deborah . . . and her kin. Her bridegroom left her, mocking, and summoned all the guests. Then Jesus, seeing the anguish of the woman who thirsted for her husband and feared him, placed upon himself the bridegroom's apparel and, full of compassion, was joined with Deborah, who lay in vomit. Then she went forth to her guests, noisily triumphant . . . And only

Jesus stood aloof. A deathly perspiration had broken out on his body; the bee of sorrow had stung his heart. Unnoticed, he departed from the banquet hall and made his way to the wilderness east of Judea, where John awaited him. And Deborah bore her first child, [who would be] hidden by the priests [*popy*]. (*SS* 2:65)

According to Apolek, before Jesus is baptized by John, before he contends with Satan in the wilderness, he defiles Himself, that is, defiles the very body of God in vomit and in adultery, out of compassion for a humiliated bride. James Falen notes, in his inspired Nietzschean reading, that in Apolek's apocryphal tale, Babel suggests that Jesus and Dionysus have "a common origin . . . In taking pity upon the forsaken Deborah and becoming her lover, Jesus resembles the Dionysus who similarly consoled Ariadne after Theseus had abandoned her. In Jesus's siring of a son . . . there is the promise of a natural alternative to the Christian concept of immortality—the regenerative powers of nature." The postscript about John in the wilderness means, however, that "purity triumphs in Apolek's tale":

> The child . . . is hidden away by the priests, for the Church has no need for renewing its myths. Having adopted Jesus as the eternal Son of God, the Church must deny his fatherhood, for this would imply an unacceptable recurrence, a chain of replacements and transferences . . . Thus in the Christian era the worship of the ascetic Jesus has supplanted that of Dionysus, and Babel, clearly preferring the latter as a symbol of life and resurrection, regards the change as an impoverishment.[28]

In other words, according to Falen, Apolek's pagan nature-gospel of art is ultimately idle and escapist and thus insufficient for Babel, "with his unquenchable hope for progress," as his narrator returns to "spend the night at home with my plundered Jews" (*SS* 2:66)—the same billet as in "Crossing the Zbruch." But surely, the fact that Babel goes back to his shit-stained and death-defiled new "home" suggests another interpretation of Apolek's tale— "an old wine" that Babel pours into an old skin.

In the Gospels, after all, Christ is the Sinless One. His baptism by John is only a confirmation of this; and his sinlessness is what enables him to contend with Satan in the wilderness and—through healing and exorcism— in the world at large. Apolek's gospel, however, offers a different background. Which is not to say, as Falen seems to, that this is a pagan, Dionysian Christ, unburdened by conventional morality—a Gnostic Jesus, who would be Christ in no meaningful sense. Rather, this Jesus seems ashamed and nervous— "the bee of sorrow had stung his heart." By this Babel is suggesting that the godliness of Jesus is his willingness to compromise himself physically and morally out of an "insatiable compassion." If anything, this is Christ as

Sonya Marmeladova, the saintly prostitute in *Crime and Punishment*. And as with Sonya, Apolek's gospel presents a thoroughly human godliness: Jesus's "deathly perspiration" hints at his mortality. Furthermore, Apolek offers to paint Liutov as Saint Francis, who ministered to the birds: "He was a simple saint, Pan Francis. And if you, Pan writer [*pisar* means *writer* in Polish, *clerk* in Russian], have a bride in Russia. . . . Women love the Blessed Francis, though indeed not all women, Pan" (*SS* 2:64). Notwithstanding the wonderfully funny caveat, it is telling that, for Apolek, the proof of Francis's saintliness is the fact that he was loved by women, that he was a saint who appealed to and was appealing to the earthly senses.

"Pan Apolek" is not the only story in *Red Cavalry* to associate sexual defilement and moral compromise with a radical ethics. The saintly title character in "Sashka Christ" catches syphilis from a wandering beggar at the age of fourteen and, like Apolek's Jesus, sleeps with women out of pity. Perhaps more shocking, Sashka permits his likewise syphilitic father to sleep with his "pure" mother in exchange for allowing him to become the village shepherd. Yet Sashka Christ, a carpenter's son, is authentically gentle and good in spite (and according to some of the peasants, because) of such compromise and defilement—his saintliness has nothing to do with rule-bound purity, not unlike the Russian tradition of the Holy Fool.

The connection between perilous sexual transgression and ethical revelation is, of course, older than Dostoevsky and the Russian tradition of holy foolishness. The Deborah in Apolek's gospel recalls Deborah the judge of Israel in Judges 4–5, who prophesies and later sings the praises of Yael's (implied) seduction and brutal assassination of Sisera, the Canaanite general fleeing his army's defeat at the hands of Barak.[29] Like Apolek's Deborah, the prophetess, too, is "noisily triumphant" in her song, in which she calls herself—somewhat presumptuously—a "mother of Israel," and in which Yael, notwithstanding her breach of hospitality in knocking a tent stake through Sisera's head, is "blessed . . . above women in the tent" (Judges 5:24). Yael's "praiseworthy" and arguably sexual deception recalls the even more apposite story of Judah and his daughter-in-law Tamar, who disguises herself as a ritual prostitute and lies with him:

> About three months later Judah was told, "Your daughter-in-law Tamar is guilty of prostitution, and as a result she is now pregnant." Judah said, "Bring her out so she may be burned to death!" As she was being brought out, she sent a message to her father-in-law. "I am pregnant by the man who owns these," she said. And she added, "See if you recognize whose seal and cord and staff these are." Judah recognized them and said, "She is more righteous than I, since I wouldn't give her to my son Shelah." And he did not sleep with her again. (Genesis 38:24–26)

Tamar prompts Judah's ethical maturation in the wake of his role selling Joseph into slavery, a maturation that prepares him for the moral leadership he assumes during the brothers' confrontation with Joseph in Egypt, during which Judah will offer himself as hostage in Benjamin's stead: "How can I go back to my father if the boy is not with me? No! Do not let me see the misery that would come upon my father" (Genesis 44:34).[30] It is Judah's words that finally convince Joseph of his brothers' contrition and prompt him to reveal his true identity. The other remarkable thing about this story is that Perez, one of the twins Tamar bears from Judah, is the ancestor of King David and his messianic line. Babel's Jewish education and later thematic predilections would have made him intimately familiar with such biblical plots; and no doubt they figure in his own ambitions to be a southerly—cosmopolitan Odessan, Greek (Hagia Sophia), and Judean (Davidic)—"Literary Messiah."

This intertwining of sex and redemption does not simply represent a pagan fusion in nature. In Babel—as in the Hebrew Bible and Dostoevsky—the more righteous figures are often the more compromised and impure, contaminated by others and taking on their shame, while remaining themselves and helping others remain others. This complex dynamic between impurity and ethical individuation is perhaps most apparent in *Red Cavalry*'s orally marked *skaz* narratives, partly because these are the only stories in the book in which Liutov seems to recede almost entirely and which introduce not just Cossack characters but Cossack narrators. In such stories as "Salt" and "The Life Story of Pavlichenko, Matvei Rodionych," Babel's mimetic curiosity gives voice to an aesthetically exuberant depravity, implicating not only the brutal "folksy" narrators but Babel and his readers as well. I will now consider such *skaz* at length, in the hope of fleshing out Babel's broader art as ethics or ethics as art, one that is revealed in self-pollution—revealed not just through a didactic analysis of characters and plot, but through aesthetic form as well. I suggest that Babel's use of *skaz* narrative can be understood as the pursuit of a literary ethics through a deliberate aesthetic pollution of the authorial narrative voice. In other words, Babel sullies Liutov's lyricism (and his own) by lending it to a narrator like Pavlichenko. But such a gesture is at the heart of the vow Liutov makes to follow Apolek's example.

Sometimes only particular voices can reveal particular truths. Imitation can be a most profound and rigorous form of succumbing to curiosity, of attending to and honoring that which is compelling. *Skaz* is mimesis and ventriloquism, a form of vocally embodied inquiry. Since fate never grants Liutov that "simplest of abilities—the ability to kill a person" (*SS* 2:188), he settles for being the transcriber of murderers.

In my view, Babel does not use *skaz*—in its strictest sense—to dwell on the victims and survivors in *Red Cavalry*. The outburst of the bereaved daughter in Novograd and the laconic tombstones of Kozin are far more eloquent than any extended, embodied testimony: "O death, O covetous one, O greedy thief, why could you not have spared us just once?" ("Cemetery at Kozin," SS 2:109). And the more "talkative" Hassidic- and Yiddish-flavored *skaz*-style dialogues one finds in such stories as "Gedali," "The Rebbe," and "The Rebbe's Son" are always framed by Liutov, whose ironic distance toward his fellow Jews becomes gradually strained until it gives way altogether in the last of these, in which the narrator buries his "brother" Ilya Bratslavsky, Red Army commander and "the last prince" of his Hassidic line (SS 2:93).[31] The collapse of such distance accords with the *1920 Diary*, in which Babel describes how he would seek refuge from the Cossack campaign with "my people," eating and even praying with them.

*Skaz*, in its crudest form, is a genre of typecasting. And Babel certainly reveled in literary stereotypes. His tough Odessa Jews, for example, are an extension of an older Russian and Russian-Jewish literary type: Jew as smuggler, Jew as criminal.[32] Babel revels in caricature, types, cliché, and parodic cadence; but he also uses disjunction and exaggeration to point to their inadequacy. Such a method evokes Stephen Schwarzschild's "theology of the slashed nose," by which Jewish artists would deliberately introduce imperfection into their representation of the human figures so it could not be mistaken for idolatry.[33] As in "My First Fee," Babel uses fictional tropes like building blocks, not to achieve realism but to allow "real life" to resemble the story it would want to tell. The "Jewish *skaz*," if there is such a thing in *Red Cavalry*, functions in this manner—the authorial narrator is always explicitly present, showily peeking from behind his mask, never forcing others onstage, while lovingly stitching the clichés together in a way that renders them unfamiliar and mysterious.[34] Because of this disruption of typecasting, the Jewish stories in *Red Cavalry* may use *skaz* dialogue but are *not* freestanding *skaz* tales. The Cossack *skaz* tales are different animals: the typecasting remains intact here; and with the exception of the frame around "A Letter," Liutov is not present in them, even though, as I will discuss, they are infused with his lyrical sensibility.

Babel understood that a victim is, in essence, muffled—not mute, but unable to express exhaustively the depths of suffering and loss, and inspiring stunned silence or compassion in the witness. This is why, unlike the sharp-tongued Jewish gangsters of the *Odessa Tales*, the Jewish victims of *Red Cavalry* do not need extended, hyper-expressive, freestanding *skaz* narratives. If, in the *Odessa Tales*, *skaz* is attached to the people of the book only when they take up the gun, in *Red Cavalry* it is primarily the language of the people of the saber, the Cossacks.

In this sense, while Babel admired and translated the stories of Sholom Aleichem, he largely did not choose to emulate the Yiddish master's tendency toward comical victim-narrators. The moral context of Babel's *skaz*, then, distinguishes it from the origins and typical characteristics of the genre. And at this point *skaz* should be discussed more generally.

*Skaz* is narrative written in language marked not as the author's own—and especially in language of a more popular and oral register than the author's. The development of *skaz* and its non-Russian equivalents across other national literatures is linked with the rise of the modern age, a response to modernity's tendency to view Language as written language and spoken language as ethnographic fodder. Since the mid-nineteenth century, orally marked narratives have constituted a modernist prose genre in the sense that they are more than mere devices, more than just putative transcripts of oral narratives: rather, they are also about transcription itself, about writing paying attention to its "poorer" (yet freer and more fresh) spoken cousin.

In the wake of the industrial revolution, Romanticism, Grimm, Herder, and the birth of modern anthropology, *skaz* offers the somewhat utopian idea of folk orality as a response, if not an antidote, to outmoded Enlightenment and classicist literary traditions that are unable to account for an increasingly heteronymous world. At the same time, there is an element of reactionary conservatism in the notion that culture and literature can be revived by a return to (or at least an appreciation of) the spoken roots of human language. In any case, the restitution of oral culture—and consequently, of the role of the storyteller—is a concern that can be encountered among figures as diverse as James Joyce, Walter Benjamin, Zora Neale Hurston, and more recently, Patrick Chamoiseau.[35]

In Russian literature, classic *skaz* of the realist period is associated with Nikolai Leskov. In his signature tale in this form, "Levsha" or "Lefty" (1881), *skaz* injects a social critique of the established (written) order into the unwitting mouths of illiterate narrators. The "native" storyteller's colorful malapropisms reveal the poverty of meaning and value behind the facade of "educated" bureaucratism by hinting—under cover of clumsy respect— at the national establishment's estrangement from national wisdom, its lack of common sense. In the final section of "Lefty," this critique ceases to be comic and delivers a withering, estranged indictment of official society. Leskov's Tula gunsmith, though poignantly comical throughout, ends up a hapless martyr for a Russian fatherland that exploits and mistreats its subjects. Here the author, concealed behind a markedly folksy and politically unsophisticated voice, constructs events so as to manipulate the reader's civic sentiments, so that by the last chapter Leskov's folksiness gives way to brutal reportage.

Among the most important features that distinguish Babel's *skaz* is his inversion of the sociopolitical dynamic in "Levsha," with folksy Red Cossack narrators voicing the unbridled power put at their disposal by Revolutionary excess. In this sense, Babel's oral narratives evoke some of the issues raised by one of Leskov's earlier pieces, a work of "proto-*skaz*" called "Lady Macbeth of the Mtsensk District" (1865). In "Lady Macbeth" a folksy, though thoroughly skillful and omniscient, narrator[36] tells the story of Katerina Lvovna, the young childless wife of Zinovy Izmailov, a wealthy provincial merchant. Desperate to preserve her affair with her husband's new clerk, Sergey, Katerina murders her father-in-law, her husband, and her little nephew (the other heir to the Izmailov fortune). Katerina and Sergey are caught smothering the boy and are sent off to Siberia. On the convict caravan, Sergey loses interest in her and takes up with other women. After he and one of his new lovers taunt and humiliate Katerina, she pounces on her rival, pushes her into the river, and both drown.

The narrator's ethical and aesthetic position is complicated here. The third-person account is full of ornamental asides coupled with evil acts. For instance, right after Katerina and Sergey kill her husband, they return "to the bedroom [just as] a thin ruddy streak of sunrise cut across the sky in the east and, lightly gilding the flower-dressed apple tree, peered through the green trellis bars into Katerina's room."[37] Such lyricism coolly distracts the reader from what has just taken place, while offering just a hint of symbolism. Also peculiar is the narrator's coy description of the first murder, that of the father-in-law:

> The old man had mushrooms with buckwheat porridge for supper and this gave him heartburn; suddenly he was seized with a cramp . . . , began vomiting, and died towards morning, just like the rats in his granaries. Katerina, to take care of the rats, had always prepared with her own hands a special kind of meal mixed with a dangerous white powder that had been entrusted to her.[38]

It almost sounds like the narrator is winking at the cover-up, or is perhaps trying to entertain the reader by also offering an opportunity for a conspiratorial wink. If Leskov meant for this narrative to lend moral drama to the classic rural crime story, the result is not especially encouraging.

At the same time, the narrator does evoke sympathy for some of the figures in this "folk drama": the hapless nephew is portrayed as a complete innocent; and by the time Katerina commits suicide, the reader cannot help but see her cold-bloodedness as something that had been motivated by her self-destructive passion for the callow Sergey. The trait that marks this Lady Macbeth as Russian rather than Shakespearean is "the absence of any dramatic maturation, or of anything like a conscience. The horror is induced in the audience, not on stage, and whatever inner voice the heroine might have had is undeveloped or silenced."[39] For Leskov, "straight *skaz*"—as embodied by the hero of "Levsha," whose decency is made possible by his naïveté—was more ethically clearheaded than the position of the folksy and educated hybrid narrator of "Lady Macbeth." Babel, however, seems to inject this hybrid story-teller's lyrical and morally ambiguous style into his own "straight *skaz*."

Babel's *1920 Diary* makes clear his true feelings about the "beasts with principles" (*SS* 2:301) who would become his *skaz* narrators in *Red Cavalry*. So then what is one to make of the high lyricism that is lent to these illiterate or semiliterate narrators? Clearly, their performances are supposed to be enjoyed, despite their moral grimness. Babel's method draws attention not only to the ability of common folk to commit uncommon evil, but also to the ethical complicity of writers and readers whose aesthetic location permits them to savor the linguistic spectacles that ensue.

Babel's *skaz* in this collection must also be understood as a variant of the so-called ornamentalist trend of modernist Russian prose. Nikolai Stepanov explains that such writing involved two main tendencies:

> (1) An attempt to introduce poetic principles into prose (the use of rhythm, poetry's relation to the word), or (2) stylization and *skaz*, which made it possible to color and stress the lexical and syntactic aspects of the prose. Babel demonstrated that he was the vanguard of this wave. In his short stories he simultaneously united and distorted both of these tendencies.[40]

Babel's *skaz* is by no means formally pure, assuming it is possible to define "pure" *skaz*; rather, it has equal standing among other devices in his aesthetic arsenal. Unlike, say, Zoshchenko, Babel was committed to the perfect short story, and *skaz* was the means, not the end. (This was perhaps one of the reasons why he couldn't cross over to socialist realism, which writers such as Zoshchenko were able to feign by embracing the genre requirements of *skaz* more rigidly.)

*Skaz* served Babel well in his effort to portray the ruptures that occur when peasant traditionalism mingles with Revolutionary "futurism." Commenting on this sociohistorical background, Efraim Sicher writes that the

> post-Revolutionary decade saw changes in the function of slang, argot, and dialect expressions as the masses gained social mobility and slowly absorbed educated or borrowed forms in the standard language and in the political terminology of Bolshevik propaganda. . . . From his work on the propaganda newssheet *Krasnyi kavalerist,* at the forefront of the literacy campaign, Babel saw in the distorted hybrids of Cossack and peasant speakers an imperfect comprehension of the Revolution but also a stylistic device to create a nar-ratorial voice distinct from the primary intellectual narrator.[41]

With this device Babel reveals the Cossacks' deluded conviction that Revo-lutionary justice should coincide with their own seemingly personal and immediate, though culturally codified, sense of what ought to be, that Revolutionary dynamism is identical to a kind of virile mania.

In "The Story of a Horse" and its "Continuation," Squadron Commander Khlebnikov's white stallion is requisitioned by Savitsky, his superior. In a written declaration of protest (a good example of *skaz*), Khlebnikov expects the Revolution to understand the profundity of his attachment to white stallions, especially to the one he claims to have rehabilitated: "Such stallions feel my hand, and I can feel his unspoken wants too . . . , but the unrighteous raven-black mare is unnecessary to me" (SS 2:71; 113). When Savitsky, pursuing his own "revolutionary justice," ignores the official document that rescinds the requisition (a piece of paper obtained by Khlebnikov with great effort and against the grain of his Cossack nature), Khlebnikov breaks down and tries to quit the Party.

Likewise, in "Treason" the narrator Balmashev, defending his rowdiness at a rear-guard military hospital in a letter to an investigator, also invokes a Cossack's understanding of the Revolution. These Red cavalrymen, whose "souls burn and rip with fire the prison of the body" (SS 2:178), cannot abide sitting around in hospital robes along with regular wounded infantry, those "long-curled comrades, their monstrous bellies swollen with food, so that they play at night like machine guns . . . [and who seem to have already] thrown in the towel" (SS 2:177). Balmashev and his buddies see blatant treason in the lack of military vigilance and enthusiasm in the civilian town of Kozin—the town where Liutov transcribes the death-weary tombstone in the Jewish cemetery. The reader can appreciate the laughter of the civilian Jews at the pitiful sight of Cossacks in hospital robes, uniforms confiscated, hollering for justice and waving revolvers in the town square.

In "Salt," however, the casualties of Balmashev's fervor exceed a few broken windows. A black marketeer has taken advantage of his Cossack ethos: Balmashev had vouched for an apparent mother with "infant" (a bundled-up slab of salt), sparing her a pro forma wartime gang rape. When the woman is unrepentant about her deception and insults the Communist Party, Balmashev's soul has no peace until he throws her off the moving train and shoots her in the back. Despite the loathsomeness of the event, which he recounts in purely heroic terms in his letter to the editor of *Red Cavalryman*,[42] Balmashev's prose is amusing and even felicitously poetic: "I am only going to write to you about what my eyes seen with their own hands" ("Opishu vam tol'ko za to, chto moi glaza sobstvennoruchno videli") (SS 2:123).

A typical attribute of *skaz* narratives is, to borrow Édouard Glissant's term, their opacity. There is a tendency (one that varies according to an author's level of political commitment) among many writers who use or invent oral narratives to include words and idioms that are incomprehensible to the average educated reader, as a way of demonstrating the gap between official written culture and an oral subculture. Babel's *skaz*, however, is readable—mimetic but legible. Indeed, *Red Cavalry*'s oral narratives are probably not the best illustrations of what Boris Eichenbaum—who declared in 1918 that "the written is a kind of museum"[43]—meant by an inherently valuable and rejuvenative orality. The reader's understanding of the meaning of what is being expressed (its ethical charge) is more valuable for Babel than any celebration of the spoken word for its own sake. Carol Luplow, among others,[44] notes this legibly mimetic quality of Babel's *skaz*. She also helps place this feature in the context of the book as a whole:

> Although Babel authentically reproduces the speech patterns and lexicon of the Cossacks, he incorporates them into a standard Russian base. In order to recognize the Cossack speech in *Red Cavalry* as a stylized replica, one need only turn to other writers of the time who, in producing regional speech, created dialog which was at least in part incomprehensible to the reader. Furthermore, many of the dialogs as a whole are stylized to produce particular artistic effects. Although dialog is partly individualized, it is also worked into the general stylistic system of the cycle, containing figurative imagery and rhetorical devices, rhythmic devices, and repetitions. Thus the Cossack speech elements function not merely to create realistic character speech, but as another aspect of the verbal design of *Red Cavalry*, . . . [its] rich stylistic mosaic.[45]

Babel's *skaz* narrators are not only Liutov's foils. Their voices are actually refracted through Liutov's and through Babel's own aesthetics.

Even though Babel's curiosity may have led him to take up the ventriloquism of *skaz* in the first place, he ultimately privileges readability over a more "accurate" mimesis. He does this because he understands that the content of the *skaz* stories has to be clear enough to be perceived in all of its ethical difficulty by an audience that no longer simply hears but reads. Marc Schreurs makes a good point when he notes that "A Letter," the first *skaz* story in *Red Cavalry*, may be a "key" to the interpretation of those that follow, inasmuch as it is framed by the "narrator's distinctly negative evaluative stance": Liutov's subjective description of the Kurdyukov family photo.[46]

In introducing the letter, Liutov notes that "it does not deserve forgetting" ("ono ne zasluzhivaet zabveniia") (*SS* 2:48); and it might be worth pausing to consider the meaning of this apparent throwaway comment. That is, the content of the letter (which describes counterrevolutionary filicide avenged by revolutionary parricide), as well as what Victor Terras calls the stylistic, structural, and emotional "wrong accents"[47] in how this content is conveyed, are the kinds of things that actually seem to deserve forgetting, that make one "want to go and cover [one's] eyes" (*SS* 2:187), as Sasha the nurse puts it in "After the Battle." But Babel wants us to remember this letter not only because he found it compelling, but also because it is the only *skaz* narrative that Liutov explicitly claims is reproduced unembellished. His evaluation of the letter's content (and of the Kurdyukovs) as brainless, brutish, terrifying, and pathetic is meant to set the tone for the more autonomous and more embellished *skaz* in the rest of the book. This "key" to the oral narratives frames them as ethical investigations above all else—certainly above being celebrations of the spoken word. Instead, *skaz* speech in *Red Cavalry* tends to be crooked: the savage inner impulse takes on the outside phrase (misappropriated from Revolutionary jargon or elsewhere) and justifies itself through it.

There is also another type of "outside source" present in the *skaz* stories, one that is not so much crooked as ambivalent: authorial lyricism. Having established his moral touchstone in the first *skaz* tale, Babel interjects his primary narrator's distinct aesthetic voice and sensibility into nearly all of the *skaz* narratives that follow "A Letter." In addition to the preponderance of mock-epic and mock-biblical rhetorical structures,[48] we find the Cossack narrators uttering strikingly Babelian lyricisms and metaphors. In his eponymous narrative, Konkin describes his prisoner's wounded stallion collapsing under him "like a bride" and notes the defeated Polish general's "white tears, human milk" (SS 2:117). After the Pole, unable to surrender to a Communist, "breaks his sword and lights two lamps in his eyes, two lanterns over the dark steppe" (SS 2:118), Konkin ends up killing him because fatigue prevents him from guarding the prisoner.

At least Konkin seems to express mild remorse in his farcical and somewhat poeticized narrative. When asked if he killed the prisoner, Konkin replies, "'Fraid so" ("Byl grekh") (SS 2:119), literally, "Was a sin"—an expression of the thematic kernel of *Red Cavalry*. Balmashev and Pavlichenko, on the other hand, have absolutely no ethical misgivings as they recount their sadistic and berserk conduct in perhaps the most lyricized *skaz* in the collection:

> And the nice little night pitched its tent. And in that tent there were star-lanterns. And the men remembered the Kuban night and the green Kuban star. And a tune flew up like a bird. While the wheels clattered and clattered. . . . Time passed, and when the night changed its guard and the red drummers welcomed the dawn on their red drums . . . I got up from my resting place where sleep had run off like a wolf from a pack of nasty hounds. ("Salt," SS 2:125)

> Open space around me in the fields, the grass rustling through all the world, the heavens above me unfolding like a multikeyboard accordion. ("Pavlichenko," SS 2:102)

Shortly before Pavlichenko leisurely beats his former master to death in an act of ontological inquiry, the Red general notices that old Nikitinsky "suddenly has no eyes, only balls standing in the middle of his face, as if they had rolled these balls into position under his forehead, and with these crystal balls he was blinking at me cheerful-like, but very horrible" (SS 2:106). (Eyeballs and eye sockets seem to be a staple motif for Babel and Liutov—after all, the eyes are the most spiritually expressive and physically vulnerable part of the face, and, in Babel as in Levinas, their vulnerability is expressive and their expressiveness is vulnerable. We enter the world through our eyes and, in a manner at times gruesome, vice versa.) It is striking that Babel incorporates the bulk of his aesthetic intrusions into the narratives of his two most savage *skaz* narrators.[49]

It would seem that Babel makes himself (or at least his aesthetics) accomplice to Balmashev and Pavlichenko. Of course, the contamination goes both ways, since the *skaz* pieces are also appropriations of the Cossacks' discourse and are, as such, related to the linguistic theft Liutov commits throughout the stories whenever he wants to strike a pose. After killing a goose in "My First Goose," Liutov declares, "Gospada boga dushu mat'—ska-zal ya, kopaias' v guse sablei—izzhar' mne ego, khozaika" ("Fucking Mother of Goddamn you!" I said digging into the goose with the saber, "go fry him up for me, lady") (SS 2:77). Inessa Medzhibovskaya describes Liutov as a "sly chameleon-like narrator" in this story, as he follows up his performance by reading Lenin's speech to the Cossacks who had just earlier thrown his trunk out of the house and farted in his direction:

> He steals the thunder of Lenin's triumph thanks to his first stealing a goose that he kills with somebody else's sword. . . . And ultimately, he manages to steal the craved-for place at the campfire through another act of theft—this time of the discourse of the "fighting proletariat"—and by speaking in a way not at all typical of a St. Petersburg Candidate of Law.[50]

The ethical and aesthetic significance of this discursive cross-pollination becomes even more disturbing once we take into account Babel's *1920 Diary*, which contains much of the raw material for *Red Cavalry*.

In the *Diary*, Babel's ethical inclinations are unambiguous. For instance, he has no love for the actual person·on whom Pavlichenko is based—Iosif Rodionovich Apanasenko:

> Apanasenko's irritability, his swearing—is this what's meant by strength of will? . . . Must penetrate the soul of the fighting man, I'm penetrating, it's all horrible, wild beasts with principles. . . . I hate life, murderers, it's unbearable, baseness and crime. . . . The military commissar and I ride along the line begging the men not to massacre prisoners. Apanasenko washes

his hands of it. . . . Apanasenko—don't waste cartridges, stick them. That's what Apanasenko always says—stick the nurse, stick the Poles. . . . Lvov's defenses—professors, women, adolescents. Apanasenko will massacre them, he hates the intelligentsia, and it goes deep, he wants a government of peasants and Cossacks, aristocratic in its own peculiar way. (*SS* 2:300–309)[51]

Given this judgment, Babel's decision to blur his aesthetic distinction from this most detestable narrator appears especially self-conscious.

If, as Hugh McLean writes, *skaz* is a "stylistically individualized inner narrative placed in the mouth of a fictional character and designed to produce the illusion of oral speech"[52] then it would appear that the distinction between author and narrator is central to the genre. This separation, as Bakhtin notes, is necessary to permit the *skaz* narrator with "his manner of seeing and portraying [to fulfill] his direct function as a narrator replacing the author" (*PDP* 190). McLean adds that the "phenomenon of emotional and judgmental distance between narrator and author (and therefore reader) frequently accompanies the required stylistic distance. A tension is thus created forcing the reader to discount the narrator's values and attitudes."[53]

Babel infuses his narrators' uneducated declamations with his own authorial lyricism, and thereby subverts this putative distance between author, narrator, and reader. This is a kind of travestying of the "Tynyanov effect," which describes the *skaz* narrator's oral performance as something that becomes, in a sense, an oral performance by the reader. The *skaz* here does indeed "make the word palpable" and does encourage the reader to "play" the story as opposed to just reading it.[54] But in so doing, Babel reinforces the obvious fact that these gruesome and morally dull-witted narratives are pleasurable and are thereby guilty pleasures. Mimesis, while certainly not an approval of amorality, can never be strictly neutral or innocent. The very notion of aesthetic neutrality is what Richard Rorty calls bad aestheticism:

> This idea that somehow language can be separated from authors, that literary technique is a godlike power operating independently of mortal contingencies, and in particular from the author's contingent notion of what goodness is, is the root of "aestheticism" in the bad sense of the term, the sense in which the aesthetic is a matter of form and language rather than of content and life.[55]

Here Rorty is defending Nabokov's fiction against the author's own theoretical proclamation of art as a realm free of moral concerns. Rorty makes a convincing case that "Nabokov's best novels are those which exhibit his own inability to believe his own general ideas."[56]

Babel, however, claimed to have no "general ideas" and was always reticent about giving an uncensored and straight-faced opinion about any large question, even in his private correspondence. He once said that as a literary critic he was "not just bad but terrible" (*SS* 3:396). But Babel's art, his every ornamental flourish and vocal trick, radiates with ethical subtlety and anxiety. And in this sense, the *skaz* in *Red Cavalry* is especially important, for it is only within this realm of literary performance that the narrator (and in a way, the reader) vicariously acquires the "ability to kill" his fellow man. Babel's *skaz* is related to the symbolic acts of violence Liutov commits (killing the goose, scratching Gulimov's cheek, striking the epileptic Ivan). And much like these acts—many of them committed in awkward self-defense—*skaz* reminds (without wholly indicting) the bloodless intellectual of his bloody humanity. This is perhaps especially apparent in the ending of "Pavlichenko," in which the Red general returns to kill his former master (who had compromised his wife and enslaved him with debt):

> Then I stomped on my master Nikitinsky. I trampled on him for an hour or maybe more than an hour, and in that time I got to know life in full. With shooting—I'll put it like this—you only rid yourself of a person: shooting is showing him mercy, and wickedly easy on yourself, you don't get at the soul by shooting, where it is in a person and how it shows itself. But there are times I don't spare myself, and trample an enemy for an hour or more than an hour, since I want to get to know life, such as it is with us. (*SS* 2:108)

Here, Babel's writerly urge to get at "what is Kiperman?" et cetera, is lent to the murderous Pavlichenko, son of Rodion—an allusion to Rodion Raskolnikov's more pretentious mystification of murder in *Crime and Punishment*.[57] As Elif Batuman puts it, pointedly conflating Babel and Pavlichenko, "You can live with someone, follow him around, take him to meet your parents, kick him for an hour, kick him for even more than an hour, and still not know who he is."[58]

To be sure, Babel's *skaz* also displays the humor and quaintness characteristic of Leskov's "Lefty." The standard *skaz* critique of intellectual elites can be found here in the Cossacks' travestying of the Communist establishment's egghead language. Gone, however, is the poignant innocence of Leskov's narrator and heroes. Cossack orality is yet another elitism, the dialect of Apanasenko's new "aristocracy." It is to some extent true, as Ragna Grøngaard notes, that one "occasionally senses that the *skaz* narrators, far from having mastered the language like the primary narrator, are indeed dominated by it."[59] But one also senses the opposite, that they ride roughshod over language. The Cossack narrators use literary language like a child dismembers a butterfly. They use lyricism, whereas Liutov often seems to be used *by* lyricism.

One of *Red Cavalry's* most haunting stories, "Zamost'e," is relevant in this respect. In it Liutov falls asleep having tethered his hungry horse to his foot. A woman, dressed up for a ball, visits him in a dream. As she raises her breast to him "like a nurse proffering food" (*SS* 2:122, 168), Liutov longs to cry out to her: "The earth is dragging me like a gibbering cur by the cord of its calamities, but nevertheless I have seen you, Margot" (*SS* 2:169). But the words remain stuck in his stiff jaw; and instead of offering nourishment Margot places copper coins over his eyes and pronounces last rites: "Jesus, receive the soul of thy departed servant." Margot is the incarnation of beauty as betrayal, death's handmaiden—and her role here is eerily reminiscent of the Yael of Judges, who gives Sisera milk or curds and invites him to sleep in her tent before running a spike through his skull. Margot's copper coins—meager, churchly, deadly—also make for an ironic parallel to the gold coins that Vera returns to the hero of "My First Fee" along with his "honorarium."

When Liutov awakens, his face bloody, a peasant sentry tells him that his horse had dragged him along the steppe for "almost half a verst." The earth stops dragging Liutov only when he stumbles upon the human company of this lonely sentinel, who has a "longing to have a talk with another person" and informs Liutov:

> "The Poles are slaughtering the yids [of Zamost'e]. . . . The yid is to blame for everything, on our side and yours. There'll be mighty few of them left after the war. How many yids are there in the whole world?"
>
> "Ten million," I answered . . .
>
> "There'll be only two hundred thousand left!" cried the peasant, and touched my hand, afraid I would go. But I got into the saddle and galloped off . . . (*SS* 2:170–71)

The affectionate, casually genocidal peasant is a (literally) repulsive figure of redemption through human dialogue. Beauty is a dream that betrays Liutov, but so does the waking nightmare of the Polish campaign. At the end of the story, his comrade Volkov asks him whether he is married. "My wife left me," Liutov replies. Since Liutov has never before mentioned a wife or a divorce, we might read this response allegorically: Margot, Faust's prize and redemption, has abandoned him. After a pause, Volkov mutters, "We've lost the campaign." "Yes," answers Liutov (*SS* 2:173). There is nothing, no dream and no poetic turn that can redeem the war.

Curiosity is a one-way street through which one loses one's innocence by bearing witness. Beauty and lyricism cannot extract Liutov from the reality he has chosen to witness out of eager curiosity; they can only pluck his strings. *Skaz* draws on the power of song, which can often involve a suspension of judgment, almost a seduction. As Paul Zumthor writes:

In the end, the meaning of the words no longer matters: voice alone, in its obvious mastery of itself, suffices to seduce (like that of Circe so vaunted by Homer for its tones and warmth or that of the Sirens). . . . The listener listens, in the silence of the self, to this voice that comes from elsewhere; lets the sound waves resonate, and, all judgment suspended, gathers together their modifications.[60]

But Babel's craft invests this otherwise physiological, participatory aestheticism with critique and hidden meaning. Where beauty and lyricism take one's breath away, Babel's labor of whittling and polishing a story through dozens of drafts brings your breath back. Walter Ong writes that the "song incorporates all of life. The text simply lies there, waiting for voice."[61] If Babel does lyrically intrude into these narratives, it is to draw attention to his and our readiness to sing along. In Babel's *skaz*, it is voice that lies waiting for a text, that is, for a careful reading.

Rorty describes this complicity as the moment in which the reader is "suddenly revealed to himself as, if not hypocritical, at least cruelly incurious, [and] recognizes his *semblable*, his brother," in the psychotic narrator.[62] To restate this point in Levinasian terms, Babel's *skaz* narrators, in their borrowed lyricism, seem to invert the "consent" of author and reader "into *participation*, . . . a dance to music."[63] Jill Robbins notes that Levinas derives this term and concept from the ethnologist Lucien Levy-Bruhl, who "calls the law or logic governing [the] connections [between primitive belief and practice] *participation*, a way of thinking which is indifferent to the law of contradiction, 'which finds no difficulty in imagining the identity of the one and the many, the individual and the species, of entities however unlike they may be.'" This "pre-logical stage of modern mentality"[64] is fairly close to that of Babel's Cossacks, who may express more passion and tenderness for a horse than any other creature but can flog it senseless the very next day. And when the pursuit of curiosity through the writing or hearing of *skaz* becomes participation, it can function as a cold incuriosity.

As Rorty notes, psychotics "are, after all, a lot more imaginative than the rest of us,"[65] and some literary works are structured to help us realize the ease with which we can participate in their aestheticism, in their radiant blindness to the suffering of others. Babel reminds readers that they shouldn't take direct sustenance even from the most performative of his stories. Babel's subversion of the Tynyanov effect brings to mind Trilling's admission of his respectful fear of even reading *Red Cavalry* in the first place.

It is possible to evaluate Babel's *skaz* in *Red Cavalry* on several levels. The basic value of oral narrative for Babel rests with the desire of his curiosity to aspire to the mimetic worship of a compelling otherness. The next level is his wish to educate the public about the kinds of voices, events, and personalities produced by the violent fusion of Cossacks and Communism in the Polish campaign—this is perhaps the aspect best understood by current Babel criticism. Third, the preeminence of textual legibility and the pervasiveness of aesthetic intrusion underscore the importance of the readily accessible pleasure of the texts. And finally, the unconsciously reprehensible narrators serve to draw attention to the perils of these pleasurable oral texts and of a genre that makes it particularly easy for author and reader to absent themselves from responsibility. In this way, the *skaz* stories in *Red Cavalry* become, in Adam Zachary Newton's parlance, "models of narrative as an ethics, paradigms which in turn imply fundamental ethical questions about what it means to generate and transmit narratives, and to implicate, transform, or force the persons who participate in them."[66]

These four levels themselves suggest a peculiar procedure for reading the *skaz* stories considered here. Babel's *skaz* should first be recited, then read to oneself, then recited once more, then read a second time. These are texts which physiologically delight the ear and which should also be picked at on the page exegetically. The second recitation would echo and expand the questions raised by the first exegesis and inform the second reading, which would reflect the reader's self-indictment. We should consider that orality for its own sake might be an insidious participation. However, orality that travels between sound and text, again and again, uncovers Babel's unique achievement of teaching without invocation. Babel reveals that the presence of others that precedes speech, which *skaz* suggests, always risks turning into a hardened cliché of folksy sociality. Instead, the dynamic interaction between voice and text will throw the dully cunning "spoken word" of what might otherwise become a novelty genre back into ethically intelligent discourse, into what Levinas would call "the language that at each instant dispels the charm of rhythm and prevents the initiative from becoming a role. Discourse is rupture and commencement, breaking of rhythm which enraptures and transports the interlocutors—prose" (*TI* 203).

It can be argued that Babel, who composed his stories on tiny strips of paper, was really a poet. It has even been suggested that he wrote prose as a somewhat mercenary adjustment, to fulfill the young Soviet establishment's desire for a "Red Tolstoy," and that *Red Cavalry* was Babel's version of *The Cossacks* (1863). Perhaps the assumption here is that only a repressed poet could compress a 150-page draft of "My First Goose" into a few sheets. But I would offer another view: Babel was a committed writer of prose, one who admired Tolstoy's obsession with fiction as a mode of seeking the truth, of following the aesthetic and ethical imperative to love experience—an obligation that compels narrative. Tolstoy and Babel shared a specific kind of curiosity, if utterly different temperaments. As Babel once put it:

> When you read Tolstoy, you feel the world is writing, the world in all its variety, . . . [but] although I am a devotee of Tolstoy, in order to achieve something I have to work in a way opposite to his. . . . Tolstoy was able to describe what happened to him minute by minute, . . . whereas I, evidently, have it in me to describe the most interesting five minutes I've experienced in twenty-four hours. (SS 3:396–98)

Characteristically modernist, Babel's world does not "write itself"; and in this sense Babel's condensed art seems more humble and perhaps more honest than Tolstoy's immense, ambitious narrative spread. One may also suggest that Babel's "most interesting five minutes"—released from the formal parameters of the realist novel—are a response to Dostoevsky's novels, which are strung together from scores of intense five-minute encounters. Then again, to return to Clay's helpful formula—Tolstoy as what happens the most, Dostoevsky the most that can happen—Babel's Dostoevskyan "five minutes" are taken from Tolstoy's "twenty-four hours." In other words, where Dostoevsky, according to Babel and others, offers us a revealing (but often unkind) intensification of the human condition, and where Tolstoy is the apotheosis of a transparent (and often overbearing) objective descriptiveness, Babel arrives at a poetic and narrative *distillation* of the world as it is. Babel's best fiction reduces the world to its irreducible ambivalence—but it is a passionate ambivalence that will forever call out for some kind of ethical and aesthetic commitment. To remain in some kind of decadent poetic indifference would be to misread Babel's lyrical reduction entirely. Poetic precision in fiction, besides having aesthetic force, often cuts with more ethical depth and subtlety, just as a faint light shining through a crack can seem more intense than a fluorescent lamp. Babel, however, needed to move past the stasis of the purely lyrical, past its prophetic eruption and otherworldly challenge.

Only prose can move beyond the daughter's implacable question at the end of "Crossing the Zbruch." There might be a simple reason why Babel did not write poems: prose takes you places. And Babel's *skaz* may be the most radical example of such movement. For indeed, if one compares Babel's *1920 Diary* to the *skaz* stories in *Red Cavalry,* one finds in the former a clear record of Babel's ethical integrity; and yet it is the *fiction* that is moved by a far more complex responsibility—an obligation to convey the world as it wants to be seen, without simply singing along in participation. In the *1920 Diary* Babel reminds himself to be responsible and lucid in his description of the things he least wanted to see: the aesthetic richness of the published stories attempts to fulfill this responsibility. This sense of obligation reflects an ethics that cannot be separated from aesthetics. In fact, this profound and subtle attention to what is other in the world is precisely what makes it so powerful *as an ethics.* And this ethics is porous, prone to defilement, while avoiding the irresponsibility of fusion and participation.

This art-as-ethics is perhaps what Babel means by the messianic literary sunshine in his manifesto. After all, although "Odessa" may be casually alfresco in tone, Babel's literary example, a rewriting of Maupassant's story "L'Aveu" or "Confession," presents a rather different, less sentimental vision of what the sun does to us:

> Now, Maupassant, maybe he doesn't know anything, but then again—maybe he knows everything. A carriage clatters down a road scorched by the heat, and in that carriage there's a fat, sly fellow named Polyte and a strapping, ungainly peasant girl. What they're doing in there, and why they're doing it—that's really their business. The sky is hot, the earth is hot. Sweat pours off Polyte and the girl, and the carriage clatters down the road scorched by the bright heat. And that's all. (SS 1:47)

The detail about the sweat is nowhere to be found in Maupassant's brief story, which is arguably more a satire about the hard-boiled frugality of Norman farmers than anything else. Celeste, the peasant girl, decides one day to accept Polyte's standing offer to do "a dance for two without music" because she was shocked to realize how much she had paid him over the past two years to drive her to the market. But this story is framed as Celeste's confession to her mother, who stops beating her only to ask:

> "Have you told him about the baby?"
> "No, of course not."
> "Why haven't you told him?"
> "Because very likely he'd have made me pay for all the free rides!"
> The old woman pondered awhile, then picked up her milk pails. "Come on, get up, and try to walk home," she said, and, after a pause, continued: "And don't tell him as long as he doesn't notice anything, and we'll make six or eight months' fares out of him."
> And Celeste, who had risen, still crying, disheveled and swollen round the eyes, started off again with dragging steps, murmuring: "Of course I won't say."[67]

In Babel's retelling of "Confession" in "Odessa," the pastoral-sexual mystery ("really their business") is amplified while the story's cultural context—which makes this mystery something at once brutal and ridiculous in Maupassant's telling—is effaced.[68] For Babel, the sun's Apollonian clarity is not merely bright and revealing but is above all relentlessly hot, opening our pores and sweat glands, melting our boundaries, throwing us back upon our animal selves as it burns away Dostoevsky's human fog, the fog that "stifles" us in "deeply felt" ideas.[69] In this sense, Babel's sun is oddly close not only to the "carnal" aspects of the Jewish tradition (to borrow Daniel Boyarin's term), but also to

*Karamazovshchina,* the earthy and sensuous force that is shared not only by Dmitri, Ivan, Smerdyakov, and Fyodor, but also by Alyosha—who transforms its biological vitality into the living ethics that inspired Levinas: "Each of us is guilty in all before all, and I more than all the others." Babel's work links this credo to a recognition of the fundamental impurity of the self, an impurity that always makes the other (ontologically and often psychologically, though not always practically) my affair, whether this other likes me or not.

One should be suspicious of a transgressive ethics, since transgression is often accompanied by self-absorption and insult and can lead to a cheaply aesthetic politics. And I certainly do not want to suggest, in some antinomian way, that defilement is not only vaguely cool but ethical too. Polyte and Celeste sweating through their dance without music, as the carriage slowly coasts along the road—compared to Sonya Marmeladova and Alyosha Karamazov, this image is an odd place to look for a literary ethics. Then again, the most profoundly ethical acts are often "dirty"—physically, emotionally, and sometimes morally. One might recall the discussion of Levinas and the metaphor of pregnancy, as well as Gedali's words about the wounded immortality of the mother: what is more "dirty"—scatalogically, biologically, and psychologically compromising—than childbirth? And indeed, what is more ethical (or beautiful) than the sacrifices (chosen or not) mothers make in bringing a new other into the world? Before he dies, the rabbi's son Ilya Bratslavsky tells Liutov "a mother in a revolution . . . is an episode" (*SS* 2:194). To borrow from another of Babel's metafictions, "Line and Color," such revolutionary language—which is also the language of Christ when he rejects his own family—is a messianism of the "line." In "Line and Color," the narrator associates the line not only with aesthetic precision but also with political cunning—with Trotsky's sharp and implacable oratory, as opposed to Kerensky's mystical and colorful myopia (*SS* 1:266). But although Babel's narrator tries (without success) to convince Kerensky to wear glasses and thus appreciate the beauty and importance of the line, his loving portrait of Kerensky (and, indeed, of the supremely "colorful" Apolek and Gedali) makes it clear that Babel's core sympathies remain with color. Color is fluid and impure, whereas the purity of line describes the impenetrable boundaries of asserted truths. In this sense, Babel, the shifty anti-philosopher who resisted literary movements, is a purist of the impure. As "Odessa" suggests, Babel lives by a literary messianism more than a political one—the former leaves room for color, the latter only for line. And the pattern that appears in Antonina Pirozhkova's account of life with Babel in the 1930s is that Soviet politics would indeed eventually cross out any colorful old Bolshevik that Babel thought to write about.[70] Until 1940, of course, when the line catches up with Babel himself.

George Eliot's old notion of literary ethics proposes an ethics based not in theory and abstraction but in the individual experiences of the artist and audience. As always, such an approach risks collapsing the distinction between self and others and thus risks the subjugation or effacement of these others. The impulse to imagine others seems inherently human. But is it also humane?[71] This concern is shared by Levinas, who insists on the irreducible otherness of other people. And I hope I have shown how this concern is resolved, beautifully and generously, in Babel's fiction, in which ethical integrity is inherently compromised, impure, contaminated by others, taking on their shame, while helping the self remain intact and others remain others.

## Chapter Four

# Osip Mandelstam's Judaism: Chaos and Cares

POETRY IS A SYNECDOCHE for all aesthetic activity because it seems like the most autonomous, least instrumental art, even as it retains a denotative link to the world at large. This paradoxically concrete signification-for-its-own-sake perhaps explains why almost anything remotely aesthetic may be described as poetic, if not always fictional or musical or architectural. It is appropriate, then, to conclude a book on ethics and aesthetics by examining a poet. Likewise, it is fitting to conclude a book on Levinas and Russian literature with Osip Mandelstam, a Jewish-Russian poet whose work strives toward an aesthetic imperative that is, for him, indistinguishable from ethical urgency and who reconfigures his "Judaism" accordingly.[1]

Unlike Babel, who spoke Yiddish and had been exposed to a traditional Hebrew education, Mandelstam grew up speaking Russian in a more assimilated Petersburg Jewish household. Odessa and its suburbs would have presented much less rigid models of plural identity for Babel than did czarist Petersburg for Mandelstam, where Jews could only reside by special permit and where the very street grid is an attempt to repress the anxiety that lurks beneath Russia's fraught identity as a European power. Accordingly, the Yiddish world of Mandelstam's Baltic grandparents was repellent and alien to him. Also unlike Babel, Mandelstam converted to Finnish Methodism when he was nineteen, largely—though not entirely—to avoid czarist restrictions on university entrance.[2]

Several scholars have examined the evolution of Mandelstam's literary attitude toward his Jewish heritage. Clare Cavanagh, for example, views this evolution (and perhaps Jewishness in general) as linked to the idea of the Jew and the poet as outsiders,[3] honorable jesters who thumb their noses at the tyranny of official culture. According to Cavanagh, when Mandelstam, after an early, pre-Soviet period of Hellenistic anti-Judaism, embraces this notion of what she calls the "irresponsible poet-Jew,"[4] he is pursuing the kind of subversive modernist ethics that one may find in Hannah Arendt's "Jews-in-spirit" (Heine, Chaplin, and other pariah figures).

Nancy Pollak, on the other hand, makes the case that Mandelstam's late poetics are infused with a "'Judaic' principle" that goes deeper than modernist subversiveness.[5] To be sure, Pollak agrees with Robert Alter, who writes that "Osip Mandelstam did not believe either in Judaism or Christianity: he believed in poetry. For a time, he was inclined to associate poetry with Christianity because of his notions of Christian order and of the apparent spiritual seriousness of Christianity."[6] However, Pollak notes that by 1933

> Mandelstam associated poetry—and authority—with a "Judaic" principle. . . . His conception of order was correspondingly transformed. The late poetry departs from the classical verse forms and lexicon that characterized the earlier periods; poetry came to be equated with the raw material rather than the finished product. . . . At the same time, the acute sense of opposition between the poet's Jewish origins and the orderly Russian milieu is tempered. In the earlier poems the opposition might appear a fatal one, but in the 1930's, Mandelstam realized . . . the inevitability of the return to Jewish roots.[7]

I might add that perhaps Mandelstam returned to the benignly chaotic order of his Jewish roots when the "orderly Russian milieu"—a dubious term that can only refer to the crisp European formalities of czarist Petersburg—gave way to a bloody revolutionary farce. In other words, his return to Judaism might have been less "inevitable" without the inexorable degeneration of Russian "orderliness."

Indeed, Efraim Sicher concludes that despite this philo-Judaic tendency in Mandelstam's late poetics, "there seems to be no incontrovertible evidence that Mandelstam might have reevaluated his [sometimes aloof] relationship with the Jewish people and the Zionist cause, as Kafka apparently did." And though it may be true that such kinds of basically political positions would have been unappealing (and perhaps unavailable) to an ideologically jaded Soviet poet, the broader point here is well taken. While "Judaism can be discerned somewhere on Mandelstam's idiosyncratic iconostasis," ultimately his "poetic credo enshrined play and freedom within a modernistic fleshing of the word that was christological in its identification of poet and Crucified Jew, [while] his goddess was classical simplicity."[8] In other words, it would be an abstract exaggeration to imply that Mandelstam ever became anything like a born-again Jew, poetically or otherwise.

Then again, Mikhail Epstein argues precisely the opposite—that in the context of the history of Russian poetry, Mandelstam's poetics was Judaic through and through. Epstein evocatively, if perhaps at times too expansively, identifies Mandelstam's consonance as Hebraic, his compressed poetic allusiveness as Kabbalistic, and his "scribal" approach to poetry as *Litvisch* (characteristic of Lithuanian Mitnagdim, rabbinic opponents of Hassidism).[9]

Such critical dissonance is not surprising, given the complex cultural geography one finds in Mandelstam's work. In his remarkable book-length study of Mandelstam's Judaism, Leonid Katsis writes:

94

The Jewish complexion of Babel's prose is strong.

In Mandelstam's case, the issue is more difficult to evaluate. Mandelstam thought in cultures. Judaism for him was one of many cultures (like Catholicism and Lutheranism), but it occupied a special place as personal, intimate experience, with roots reaching deep into his youth.[10]

Babel's prose is "strongly Jewish" because of the author's upbringing and education, his ethnographic proclivities, his explicit engagement with Jewish storytelling, and the key role of a certain Jewish sensibility even in an early manifesto like "Odessa." Mandelstam's work, in comparison, displays a tension between a poetic desire to thematize Judaism within a much broader cultural universe and the inchoate, often overwhelming and embarrassing, seemingly anti-poetic pull of Jewish ethnic origins. On the one hand, the universalizing quality of Mandelstam's verse (and perhaps of poetry in general) treats Judaism as one, in many ways marginal, culture among many; on the other hand, Judaism as Jewishness also represents his personal, unbidden, pre- or proto-poetic inheritance. Quite sensibly, Katsis sets aside the issue of Mandelstam's religious observance and focuses on the Judaic "subtexts and direct citations" in the poet's work.[11] Yet even this sort of intertextual attention to Mandelstam's "spiritual aesthetics" is complicated by the fact that Judaism (and for that matter, Christianity, Islam, or Buddhism) typically appears as a code, euphemism, or trope that has at best a tenuous connection to any of its concrete manifestations. This inevitably lends some tentativeness to this chapter. Here, however, I am ultimately less concerned with refining such Jewish (ethnic) or Judaic (textual or ritual) claims than with understanding their relevance for the relationship between the poetic and the ethical as it takes shape in Mandelstam—a relation for which Levinas's thought provides compelling commentary.

If modern poetry is indeed a supposedly less social genre, might the private sphere that it shapes actually serve a basic ethical function? Mandelstam, evolving from a certain youthful lyric preciousness into a more mature poetic ethos, develops into a poet who understands the indispensable nature of his relation to his "boring neighbors." At the same time, his attitude toward his Jewish origins gradually changes from self-alienation and self-loathing into an identification of "Judaism" with the spiritual roots of the poetic process. Mandelstam's early anxiety about "Judaic chaos" (to be overcome poetically through an identification with Russian and "world" culture) matures in his later verse into "Judaic cares," a term which suggests how the mundane order should be broken up into creative disorder to be recomposed as verse—a process mirrored by the ethical-aesthetic dynamics of Levinas's thought. Mandelstam's evolution may be fruitfully read alongside the shift in Levinas's work away from an early Platonic distrust of poetry to its reemergence in his later work as an ethically central category—the poetic not as the way being shows itself in language (à la Heidegger) but as the way "tenderness," a breaking forth of a kind of private rectitude, rehumanizes a world that has been objectified by public use.

Many have suggested that modernist art is a turning away from an incarnate and pagan aestheticism toward what Stephen Schwarzschild has called the "aboriginal Jewish aesthetic . . . of a phenomenal world in eternal pursuit of the ideal" and is therefore, in a sense, an assimilation of Judaism. According to this view—shared by Susan Handelman, Harold Bloom, Geoffrey Hartman, and a host of other Judeophile critics—both Judaism and modernism champion art that "struggles against idolatry and on behalf of ethicism: Art is action that envisions and suffers from the unattainability of Utopia."[12] If a modernist "Judaic" aesthetics indeed represents an ethically motivated reaction against certain iconic, figural, and charismatic aspects of both Christian and Hellenistic aesthetics, where might one situate the sensibilities expressed by Mandelstam's poetry and poetics?[13] Here I propose a consideration of Levinas's various notions of the poetic—as irresponsibility, as well as an exposure and attention to otherness—as a way to approach this question.[14]

The paradoxical quality of Levinas's relationship to the poetic finds its roots deep in the history of philosophy. In "Reality and Its Shadow," a lopsidedly anti-aesthetic essay published in 1948, Levinas aligns himself with Plato's notion of an "ancient war" between poetry and philosophy. Mark Edmundson offers a useful distillation of the Platonic position: "The poets must lie because they live among phantoms, at a third remove from reality."[15] As Jill Robbins notes, this tradition holds that "poetry is in tension with the philosophical project of wanting to get things right, to keep things straight, in tension with the self-control that characterizes philosophy's propositional style."[16] According to Levinas, there is a certain ethical irresponsibility that abides in the poet's lofty lack of self-control. The artist does not act upon reality, but instead plays, "participates" in it, chasing after its shadow. This is a negative version of a concept expressed by Socrates in Plato's *Parmenides, metexis,* by which things attain being by participating or sharing in ideal forms; so that, for example, something may be one by partaking of oneness, and many by partaking also of multitude (*Parmenides* 129). In Levinas's reading of art as participation, however, this partaking in an ideal form (such as the beautiful), instead of lending reality to phenomena, divests them of their specific autonomy. The artwork is a frozen distillation, in which artist and audience passively participate:

> To make or to appreciate a novel and a picture is to no longer have to conceive, is to renounce the effort of science, philosophy, and action. Do not

speak, do not reflect, admire in silence and in peace—such are the counsels of wisdom satisfied before the beautiful. Magic, recognized everywhere as the devil's part, enjoys an incomprehensible tolerance in poetry.[17]

Poetry is "magic" because it evokes being but evades time. And it is time— where continuous verbal interruption and qualification brings aesthetics back down to earth—that allows for the "perspective of the relation with the other without which being could not be told in its reality."[18] It is not that Levinas *cannot* comprehend why poetry tolerates magic; rather, in a fit of (poetic?) hyperbole, he suggests that one *should* not understand our tolerance for poetic magic.

Verbal magic is a fundamental aspect of the tradition of poetic charisma. Gregory Freidin examines Mandelstam precisely as a charismatic poet, noting contemporaries' reports about his "rather unusual appearance (a 'patriarch' . . . , a 'dervish' . . .), his frequent reliance on verbal formulas akin, and kin, to spells and exorcisms as well as his 'shamanistic' way of reciting poetry."[19] Freidin writes:

> The kind of magic that tradition associates with the poetic word—it heals, it casts a spell, it prophesies. And just as it is not necessary to believe in Santa Claus to covet a present at Christmas, it is not necessary to believe in the magic of the word in order to continue expecting from poets the coveted assurance that they indeed possess the extraordinary gift and would share it with us, if only on rare and special occasions.[20]

This is what Levinas does not desire to comprehend: why poetic magic can be effective even when nobody believes in it. He implies that poetic irresponsibility does not deserve understanding but correction.

But perhaps Levinas's bellicose tone in "Reality and Its Shadow" is less a reflection of his feelings about art than a visceral expression of philosophy's envy of poetry. If indeed the philosophical project is about wanting to "get things right," poetry, in Mandelstam's words, is "the consciousness of being right."[21] Philosophy can only get things right by dispelling illusions, by arranging and untangling ideas. Poetic magic, on the other hand, does not need to *get* things right—it simply *is* right, by the fiat of its aesthetic power. Its ambition is completely naked, that is, brazen and vulnerable.

Levinas sees critical interpretation as the only thing that ethically redeems the work of art. "Not content with being absorbed in aesthetic enjoyment, the public feels an irresistible need to speak" (*LR* 130). There is a moral element in this need to speak, as if it seeks to counteract the literary imposition of fate upon the future, art's reduction of freedom to necessity, as Levinas describes it:

[The artwork's] presence, impotent to force the future, is fate itself, that fate refractory to the will of pagan gods, stronger than the rational necessity of natural laws. Fate does not appear in universal necessity. It is a necessity in a free being, a reverting of freedom into necessity, their simultaneity, a freedom that discovers it is a prisoner. Fate has no place in life. The conflict between freedom and necessity in human action appears in reflection: when action is already sinking into the past, man discovers the motifs that necessitated it. . . . Not that the artist represents being crushed by fate—beings enter their fate because they are represented. (*LR* 138)

Without criticism, the artistic endeavor remains trapped in a fatalistic, obscure, and shadowy relation to reality.

The most lucid writer finds himself in the world bewitched by its images. He speaks in enigmas, by allusions, by suggestion, in equivocations, as though he moved in a world of shadows, as though he lacked the force to arouse realities, as though he could not go to them without wavering, as though, bloodless and awkward, he always committed himself further he had decided to do, as though he spills half the water he is bringing us. The most forewarned, the most lucid writer nonetheless plays the fool. The interpretation of criticism speaks in full self-possession, frankly, through concepts, which are like the muscles of the mind. (*LR* 142–43)

The poem here is not muscular. It is a lazy burst, a magical release. The implication here is that criticism is an honest day's work, whereas poetry is a kind of self-absorbed physiological emission, a holy or unholy folly.[22]

The above passage is found under the subsection "For Philosophical Criticism" (*LR* 141); and Levinas is not alone in this conflation of philosophy and criticism, given that both disciplines tend to value lucidity, logic, causality, and analysis. Plato, after all, associates art with the relativistic juggling of the sophist (*Sophist* 235). Mark Edmundson notes that this conflation is justified by both genealogy and current practice:

Literary criticism in the West begins with the wish that literature disappear. Plato's chief objection to Homer is that he exists. For to Plato poetry is a deception: it proffers imitations of imitations when life's purpose is to seek eternal truth; poetry stirs up refractory emotions, challenging reason's rule, making men womanish; it induces us to manipulate language for effect rather than strive for accuracy. . . . As of late literary criticism—egged on by a number of developments both conceptual and material—has taken up a philosophical attitude toward the poets. . . . The attitude of criticism to literature has become less celebratory, more inquisitive, even inquisitorial (more Platonic).[23]

Levinas's notion of a "muscular" criticism is akin to the contractions of philosophical skepticism. And though Levinas does not embrace the absolutist negativity of Socratic skepticism, he does see its restless movement, its perpetual unsaying of the said, to be a kind of constant "facing," inherently ethical.[24] Indeed, if Levinas is "anti-philosophical" in his rejection of idealist epistemology and his distrust of ontology and metaphysics, then skepticism is among the streams of the philosophic tradition that he admires—the other being the notion of infinity, the idea that exceeds its representation. Levinas also proclaims loyalty to what he calls the "Greek" language of philosophy, a language that he esteems as the transparent lingua franca of the academic world.

This is an oddly mixed philosophical legacy. If the "Greek" language of academic discourse is really transparent, and if philosophy leaves us with both skepticism and conceptual infinity, then what is there to see through Levinas's window of philosophical language? Even shorn of ontology, this language remains no better equipped to prove or affirm what is central to Levinas's thought: the ethical. Skepticism is the art of saying no; and while "infinity" may offer a broader conceptual category for radical ethics, unlike ethics it can be mathematically if not empirically expressed. On the other hand, the obligation that comes from the face of the other is a nonmathematical affirmation; the face partakes of no universal truth, but rather suggests its own singular authority. The ethics of the face is transitive: as Levinas puts it, "consciousness is always late for the rendezvous with the neighbor."[25] But this implies that consciousness—of which philosophy is arguably the apotheosis—does somehow eventually get to the meeting. If it did not, why would Levinas wonder if it is ethical to offer the other (his reader) a philosophy that preaches asymmetrical responsibility, holiness without heaven? "Does one have the right to preach to the other a piety without reward? . . . It is easier to tell myself to believe without promise than it is to ask it of the other. That is the idea of asymmetry. I can demand of myself that which I cannot demand of the other."[26] If Levinas were truly convinced that philosophical argument by itself could affirm the ethical, there would be little room for such doubts. After all, philosophy offers truth as its own consolation: it cannot be held responsible for what you see through the window.

Philosophical "transparency" cannot reveal Levinas's ethics—if only because goodness does not stand still long enough to become "The Good."[27] Moreover, it appears that, if anything, the notion of the ethical as a relation that is otherwise than being resembles the "shadowy" realm of poetry. As Gerald Bruns suggests, the anti-aesthetic hyperbole in "Reality and Its Shadow" certainly "appeals to Levinas's iconoclasm," but does not necessarily "square with his thought."[28] In this case, Levinas was reacting violently to Heidegger's "poetic turn" in the 1930s and '40s—a turn that easily looks like aesthetic escapism in view of Heidegger's parallel turn toward National

Socialism. A brief digression on Heidegger and poetry will help flesh out Levinas's own evolution on this subject.

Heidegger's poetic turn (and ultimately Levinas's) is hardly surprising. After all, phenomenologists wanted philosophy to return to the study of experience, to "the things themselves." Most people attending to the things themselves have already been seeking and finding them in art and literature. Indeed, Husserl and Wittgenstein's anti-theoreticism is at least as old as Aristophanes' attack on Socrates in *The Clouds,* in which the philosopher is ridiculed for perching in a basket above the earth. As Catherine Zuckert notes:

> Failing to recognize the limitations of his own existence, Socrates does not feel and so does not understand the desire of others to overcome them. . . . Any account of the whole which does not recognize the tensions among different parts is patently inadequate. . . . Because the poet begins with the human and examines it in relation to both what is higher and what is lower, he provides a more accurate picture of the whole. Whereas philosophy is reductive and hence destructive, Aristophanes' poetry not only provides a salutary teaching but also reveals the truth, if in a "cloudy" form, to those able to understand.[29]

Or, more succinctly, as Leo Strauss puts it, "philosophy is repulsive to the people because philosophy requires freedom from attachment to 'our world.'"[30] And it is literature that not only attends to "our world" but also to our attachment to it.

I would suggest that Heidegger's turn to poetry leaves this opposition of disciplines intact. He writes:

> Obedient to the voice of Being, thought seeks the Word through which the truth of Being may be expressed . . . Out of long-guarded speechlessness and the careful clarification of the field thus cleared, comes the utterance of the thinker. Of like origin is the naming of the poet. But since like is only like insofar as difference allows, and since poetry and thinking are most purely alike in their care of the word, the two things are at the same time at opposite poles in their essence. The thinker utters Being. The poet names what is holy.[31]

In this description, the thinker keeps quiet, clearing the ground until he can speak of (and for) the whole of Being itself. On the other hand, the poet, who uncovers and names the traces of Being in the underbrush of the world, can talk all he wants. One doesn't even need to consider the verbal economy of a writer like Isaac Babel (leaving aside the verbosity of a thinker like Sartre) to sense the absurd essentialism in Heidegger's apparently generous opposition.

100

In Levinas's "Reality and Its Shadow," however, it is art that invites the silence of admiration—albeit a silence that is passive and participatory, unlike the active speechlessness of Heidegger's thinker—and it is philosophical criticism that reflects our need to talk back to the work of art. One could argue that, in attacking Heidegger's alleged poeticism, Levinas switches terms and gives philosophy—or "philosophical criticism"—the "muscular" task of uncovering and naming the world as shadowed by art. It is the neo-pagan and inhuman ontology of Heidegger's aesthetics that is the target for Levinas,[32] for whom "*criticism* [and not poetry] is the basic capacity for human dwelling in so far as the term signifies a primordial relation with the other."[33] Of course, this also implies that philosophy as criticism becomes parasitic upon the art that prompts it.

Indeed, Levinas seems to avoid philosophy's inability to affirm a radical ethics by recourse to the very thing he condemns in "Reality and Its Shadow." That is, if the ethical cannot be affirmed in philosophically absolute terms, perhaps poetry is necessary to *invoke* it; or as Jill Robbins puts it, "Levinas needs the resources of the literary to say his philosophy."[34] He litters "Reality and Its Shadow" with poetic castigations of the poetic: that is, descriptions of the writer "spilling half of what he brings us," of concepts as "the muscles of the mind." Elsewhere in the same piece, Levinas uses the following analogy to underscore what he calls the "derisory . . . lifeless life" of an image: "Eternally the smile of the Mona Lisa about to broaden will not broaden" (*LR* 138). In *Totality and Infinity* he compares the naked face to "those industrial cities where everything is adapted to a goal of production, but which, full of smoke, full of wastes and sadness, exist also for themselves" (74). Levinas is not only a literary maven but is also a writer who fully relies on the poetic force and complexity of the French language as well as an expansive sense of biblical and secular literary diction.

Certainly, one can argue that there is a difference between poetry and poetic devices, and that an anti-aesthetic argument does not necessarily subvert itself by being well written. But if many of the most effective moments of this argument reach us through striking metaphors and allusions, then it would be wrong not to pursue the irony.[35] Indeed, as Edmundson reminds us, you cannot "qualify as a philosopher (or as a major theorist) unless you confer aura, charismatic glow, on particular words." What's more, often the best "philosophers are propounding myths, fictions that are open to broad interpretation, . . . flights of imagination . . . [that] move away from definitions, from truth,"[36] and into the incantatory realm inhabited by many poets.

I would suggest that poetry does not persuade. Poetry invokes and evokes, and then it is up to the reader to recognize or not recognize the "truth" of the poem or to shape a philosophical but ultimately provisional truth inspired by the poem. Similarly, it makes little sense to preach Levinasian ethics, since persuasion is an inherently coercive, verbal projection of my power. Instead, Levinas engages with the philosophical tradition and makes phenomenological observations on the one hand, and writes what he calls "confessional" Jewish essays and Talmudic readings on the other—all the while insisting on the *formal* separation between the two.[37] His work does not seek to compel in the way philosophy typically does: his reader either recognizes something authoritative in it or not—and this is also how we respond to a face. If philosophical language can be compared to legal prose in that it ideally relies on evidence, logic, and proofs to bind, to *compel* a decision, then perhaps Levinas's writing is closer to poetry than prose.

It is not surprising then that, twenty years after "Reality and Its Shadow," the word *poetry* reappears in Levinas's work as something central to his ethics. By the late 1960s, his postwar anger at the amorality of Heideggerian poeticism had cooled.[38] In "Language and Proximity" (1967) Levinas links poetry to "proximity," one of the key ideas of his late ethics—a link that will resurface in *Otherwise Than Being*.[39] Proximity introduces the sense of touch into Levinas's earlier notion of ethics as vision and speech. Indeed, touch comes to include sight and hearing, an idea Levinas borrows from a certain lyrical synesthesia: "One can see and hear as one touches: 'The forest, ponds, and fertile plains have touched my eyes more than looks. I leaned on the beauty of the world and held the odor of the seasons in my hands' (La Comtesse de Noailles)" (*OTB* 191n9). Proximity implies a closeness that is not palpation, not an assimilation of the other into the same:

> As a subject that approaches, I am not in the approach called to play the role of a perceiver that reflects and welcomes, animated with intentionality, the light of the open and the grace and mystery of the world. Proximity is not a state, not a repose, but a restlessness, null site, outside of the place of rest. . . . No site then, is ever sufficiently a proximity, like an embrace. Never close enough, proximity does not congeal into a structure, save when represented in the demand for justice as reversible, and reverts into a simple relation. Proximity, as the "closer and closer," becomes the subject. It attains its superlative as my incessant restlessness, becomes unique, then one, forgets reciprocity, as in a love that does not expect to be shared. Proximity is the subject that approaches and consequently constitutes a relationship in which I participate as a term, but where I am more, or less, than a term. This surplus or this lack throws me outside of the objectivity characteristic of relations. . . . One can no longer say what the ego or I is. From now on one has to speak in the first person. I am a term irreducible to the relation, and yet in a recurrence which empties me of all consistency. (*OTB* 82)

Proximity cannot be an embrace because it cannot be static—else it would mean death. And while at first it may look something like the "exile" of Socrates' philosophical position, Levinasian proximity is in fact a type of wandering—unable and unwilling to leave this world, just as it is unable and unwilling to fully inhabit it.

The emblematic gesture of Levinas's proximity is the caress, where one touches the surface of the other in her distance, contacting the unpossessible, the inexpressibly more than the sum of its parts:

> In a caress, what is there is sought as though it were not there, as though the skin were the trace of its own withdrawal, a languor still seeking, like an absence which, however, could not be more there. The caress is not the coinciding proper to contact, a denuding never naked enough. The neighbor does not satisfy the approach. The tenderness of skin is the very gap between approach and approached, a disparity, a non-intentionality, a non-teleology. Whence the disorder of caresses, the diachrony, a pleasure without present, pity, painfulness. Proximity, immediacy, is to enjoy and suffer by the other. But I can enjoy and suffer by the other only because I am-for-the-other, am signification, because the contact with skin is still a proximity of a face, a responsibility, an obsession with the other, being-one-for-the-other, which is the very birth of *signification* beyond *being.* (*OTB* 90)

Here Levinas seems to be retooling language that in "Reality and Its Shadow" characterizes the insidious nature of aesthetic fatalism—like an "Edgar Allan Poe character" who does not die but is always "dying . . . in the interval, forever an interval."[40] Except that now, in the caress, the dynamic of the "interval" is positive and ethical—indeed, it recalls the figuration of pregnancy and maternity in Levinas's later thought. One could say that this retooling has to do with a shift from the aesthetic object to the human subject. But human others are not the only faces that can haunt with their proximity, according to Levinas.

In a major departure for his thought—which shies away from the philosophical animism of someone like Buber—Levinas suggests that *things* may be proximal. In a remarkable endnote to *Otherwise Than Being,* Levinas writes:

> It is as possessed by a neighbor, as relics, and not as clothed with cultural attributes, that things first obsess. Beyond the "mineral" surface of things, contact is an obsession by the trace of a skin, the trace of an invisible face, which the things bear and which only reproduction fixes as an idol. The purely mineral contact is privative. Obsession breaks with the rectitude of consumption and cognition. But caresses are dormant in all contact, and contact in all sensible experience: the thematized disappears in the caress, in which the thematization becomes a proximity. There is indeed a part of metaphor in that, and the things are taken to be true and illusory before being near. But is not the poetry of the world prior to the truth of things, and inseparable from

what is proximity par excellence, that of a neighbor, of the proximity of the neighbor par excellence? (*OTB* 191n10)

In an earlier essay, "Language and Proximity," Levinas voiced this idea without reticence:

> The proximity of things is poetry; in themselves the things are revealed before being approached. In stroking an animal already the hide hardens under the skin. But over the hands that have touched things, places trampled by things, the fragments of those things, the contexts in which those fragments enter, the inflexions of the voice and the words that are articulated in them, the ever sensible signs of language, the letters traced, the vestiges, the relics—over all things, beginning with the human face and skin, tenderness spreads. Cognition turns into proximity, into the purely sensible. Matter, which is invested as a tool, and a tool in the world, is also, via the human, the matter which obsesses me with its proximity. The poetry of the world is inseparable from proximity par excellence, or the proximity of the neighbor par excellence.[41]

It is not entirely clear what Levinas means when he uses the word "poetry" to describe the caress, tenderness, or "proximity par excellence." At first glance, it seems he is referring less to poetry per se than to that quality of the world that verse tries to capture. What is this quality, according to Levinas? It is the desire to approach, to be near the other—whether a person or a "humanized" animal or thing—before that desire is satisfied, that is, before the "hide hardens." This is called the "poetry of the world" partly because it is a fleeting, impossible interval. But, etymology aside, is this poetic quality of the world at all conceivable or meaningful without the craft of poetry? Is this quality accessible, can it be offered to the other, without poetry per se?

Without poetry, without a language that is not only representational but also succinctly memorable and emotionally expressive, the poetic quality of the world would be something lonely, fleeting, primitive, and interpersonally irrelevant. What is more, in the best verse, the mutely poetic quality of the world has the potential to expand our language, enriching our thoughts and sensibility as well as our relations with others, offering fresh paths of approach to another person. And perhaps most significantly, it is difficult to understand how Levinas's ethics could work without the art of metaphor—especially the key metaphor of the human face, which poetically expresses my responsibility for the "face" not just in the singular other, but also in undifferentiated others, in animals, and in things. Likewise the metaphor of pregnancy, which would be dangerously sexist and essentialist if it were not poetically expanded to apply to nongendered relations between parents and children, teachers and students, writers and readers, and so on.[42] In other words, even if poetry is not always proximity, the reverse is always the case.

The movement of the ethical and the dynamics of the poetical share another fundamental affinity: both reach toward a public realm that issues from the absolute privacy of proximity, toward an original language that arises from my confrontation with a peerless and unpredictable singularity, other without horizon. Contact, according to Levinas, can certainly "turn into palpation," where a "'doxic thesis' wells up to transform the event of contact into an informing, a cognition collected on the springy or rough surface of things, and thus slips the sensible into a thematizing, identifying, universal discourse."[43] And I would add that a bad poem, too, eagerly palpates the world, its grasp smothering "the poetry of the world" in verbal pyrotechnics or stale conventions.

Good poems, however, seem to be motivated by (and often motivate) the poetic dynamism of proximity. Levinas begins his 1972 essay on Paul Celan with a striking quote from the German poet's letter to Hans Bender, in which he writes: "I cannot see any basic difference between a handshake and a poem."[44] Levinas marvels at this outrageous assertion:

> There is the poem, the height of language, reduced to the level of an interjection, a form of expression as undifferentiated as a wink, a sign to one's neighbor! A sign of what? Of life? Of goodwill? Of complicity? Or a sign of nothing, or of complicity for nothing: a saying without a said. Or is it a sign that is its own signified: the subject signals that sign-giving to the point of becoming a sign through and through. An elementary communication without revelation, . . . such an awkward inclusion in the famous *language that speaks,* the famous *die Sprache spricht:* a beggar's entrance into *the house of being.*[45]

In this essay Levinas clarifies what he had meant by his association of poetry with tenderness in his earlier "Language and Proximity." And in this respect, he does nothing to conceal his debt to Celan:

> For Celan the poem is situated . . . [at a level that is] pre-disclosing: at the moment of pure touching, pure contact, grasping, squeezing—which is, perhaps, a way of giving, right up to and including the hand that gives. A language of proximity for proximity's sake, older than that of "the truth of being"—which it probably carries and sustains—the first of the languages, response preceding the question, responsibility for the neighbor, by its *for the other,* the whole marvel of giving. (*PN* 41)

By the end of his essay, Levinas seems to fuse Celan's language with his own, thereby including *poetry* among the key words of his own ethical thought:

The fact of speaking to the other—the poem—precedes all thematization; it is in that act that qualities gather themselves into things. But the poem thus leaves the real its alterity, which pure imagination tears away from it; the poem "lets otherness's ownmost also speak: the time of the other." . . . The absolute poem does not say the meaning of being; it is not a variation on Hölderlin's *dichterisch wohnet der Mensch auf der Erde* . . . ; it goes toward utopia, "along the impossible path of the impossible path of the Impossible." More and less than being. "The absolute poem; no, indeed, it does not, cannot exist." . . . Does [Celan] not suggest a modality other than those situated between the limits of being and non-being? Does he not suggest poetry itself as an unheard-of modality of the *otherwise than being*? (PN 44, 46)

By way of Celan, the poetic "magic" Levinas once disdained becomes the very paragon of Saying, of otherwise-than-being.[46] Certainly, the poem is also a text, a Said; but the absolute poem, the utopian, impossible poem of which all great poems bear a ("magic") trace, is a purely exposed reaching out toward the other: pure Saying.[47]

By no means does Levinas explicitly renounce "Reality and Its Shadow." It is just that Celan permits him to rescue poetry from that essay's aesthetic rogues' gallery.[48] By 1974, when *Otherwise Than Being* was published, it appears that only "iconography" remains implicated in what Levinas still calls "an idolatry of the beautiful" (*OTB* 199n21). Alongside its valorization of poetry, *Otherwise Than Being* contains the following iconophobic passage:

> In its indiscrete exposition and in its stoppage in a statue, in its plasticity, a work of art substitutes itself for God. (Cf. our study "Reality and Its Shadow," 1948.) By an irresistible subreption, the diachronic, the non-contemporaneous, through the effect of a deceitful and marvelous schematism, is "imitated" by art, which is iconography. The movement beyond being is fixed in beauty. (*OTB* 199n21)

We may understand this lingering caveat as another warning about "fixing" the ever-transitive poetry of proximity into an icon that is above critique, into a frozen Said that pretends that it is the same as a Saying and thereby supplants it.

That Levinas's thinking about poetry and ethics was inspired by Celan (a Holocaust survivor whose parents were, like Levinas's, murdered by the Nazis) is significant for this chapter because Celan had adopted Osip Mandelstam as his most important predecessor, his poetic elder brother. In 1958 Celan was the first person to translate a substantial number of Mandelstam's poems. John Felstiner notes several of the biographical elements that comprised the kinship Celan perceived:

Many things occasioned this "shock of recognition" (Melville's phrase) in Celan. Mandelstam . . . had [also] worked as a translator and had once attempted suicide. Each grew up close to his mother and because of his father harbored ambivalence toward Judaism. Both underwent political and literary persecution not unrelated to their origins. And after a groundless plagiarism charge [something Celan endured as well], Mandelstam embraced the "proud title of Jew." This nexus may account for Celan's saying that Mandelstam "was murdered by Germans" rather than lost in Siberia, as was generally believed. (PC 129)

But there are also more profound affinities between the two poets.

Levinas's piece on Celan generously quotes or paraphrases three of the poet's essays, each of which alludes to Mandelstam. In particular, Celan draws on the early essay "O sobesednike," or "On the Interlocutor" (also somewhat imprecisely translated as "On the Addressee"), published in 1913 as an acmeist response to the Russian Symbolists. For instance, when Levinas writes, "The poem goes toward the other[;] it hopes to find him freed and vacant," he is paraphrasing (without citing) Celan's 1958 "Speech on the Occasion of Receiving the Literature Prize of the Free Hanseatic City of Bremen":

A poem, being an instance of language, hence essentially dialogue, may be a letter in a bottle thrown out to sea with the—surely not always strong— hope that it may somehow wash up somewhere, perhaps on a shoreline of the heart. In this way, too, poems are en route: they are headed toward. Toward what? Toward something open, inhabitable, an approachable you.[49]

The Bremen speech, Celan's "first full profession of poetic doubt and faith" (PC 117), echoes Mandelstam's 1913 essay:

At a critical moment, a seafarer tosses a sealed bottle into the ocean waves, containing his name and a message detailing his fate. Wandering along the dunes many years later, I happen upon it in the sand. I read the message, note the date, the last will and testament of one who has passed on. I have the right to do so. I have not opened someone else's mail. The message in the bottle was addressed to its finder. I found it. That means, I have become its secret addressee. . . . The ocean in all its vastness has come to its aid, has helped it fulfill its destiny. And that feeling of providence overwhelms the finder. . . . The message, just like the poem, was addressed to no one in particular. And yet both have addresses: the message is addressed to the person who happened across the bottle in the sand; the poem is addressed to "the reader in posterity" (see Baratynsky, "My gift is poor . . ."). (CPL 68–69)

There is perhaps no better image for the lucid paradox of what happens when a work of art—created, ostensibly, by someone and for someone who mean nothing to me—suddenly "speaks to me," when a poetic "Said" turns into a "Saying" upon reaching its "secret interlocutor." In Celan, Mandelstam's bottle finds its secret addressee. And passed on to Levinas, the message in this bottle attains ethical amplification and development.

There are other, even more striking examples of this sort of three-way intertextuality. In his discussion of language and ethics, Levinas quotes a long passage from Celan's "Conversation in the Mountains":

> Celan compares language with a "road" that is "so beautiful" in the mountains, "where, on the left the Turk's-cap lily blooms like nowhere else, and on the right the rampion, and where dianthus superbus, maiden-pink, rises not far away . . . a language not for you and not for me—for I ask for whom was it conceived then, the earth, it was not for you I say that it was conceived and not for me—a language of for ever, without *I* and without *You*, nothing but *He*, nothing but *It*, do you see, nothing but *She*, and that's all" [*CP* 18–20]. An impersonal language. The fact is, then, that for Celan the poem is situated precisely at that pre-syntactic and . . . pre-logical level, but a level also pre-disclosing. (*PN* 41)

Felstiner notes that, while traces of Martin Buber's 1913 "Gespräch in den Bergen" appear in Celan's "Gespräch im Gebirg," a "visceral presence in the [latter] must surely be Mandelstam. When Celan wrote it, his translations of Mandelstam were about to come out; and in Mandelstam's essay 'On the Interlocutor,' poetry is the search for an other and oneself—as Celan's translations make clear" (*PC* 141).

In Celan's "Conversation," Buber's focus on the unmediated and reciprocal *Ich-Du* relation is modulated by the idea of what Levinas calls an "impersonal language"—an idea that corresponds with Levinas's notion of the other as *il/elle* and of God as "illeity," an absence that is a trace of the other. And this modulation, elaborated by Celan in his Büchner Prize acceptance speech, "The Meridian" (another text extensively cited by Levinas in his essay), also owes much to Mandelstam. Felstiner writes:

> Celan once remarked that "a couple of formulations from [his] Mandelstam [radio] broadcast" made their way into "The Meridian." His broadcast of March 1960, before he was even slated for the Büchner Prize, fed into his acceptance speech because Mandelstam touched the core of his poetics. Celan's broadcast said of Mandelstam—and "The Meridian" makes it an axiom—that the poet speaks *"actualized* language, at once voiced and voiceless, set free under the sign of a radical individuation, which at the same time stays mindful of the limits set by language, the possibilities opened by

language." The broadcast insisted on poetry as *Gespräch,* "conversation" or "dialogue"—and "often it is despairing dialogue," he adds in "The Meridian." (*PC* 163)

These words were inspired by the following passage from Mandelstam's "On the Interlocutor":

> Without dialogue, lyric poetry cannot exist. Yet there is only one thing that pushes us into an addressee's embrace: the desire to be astonished by our own words, to be captivated by their originality and unexpectedness. Logic is merciless. If I know the person I am addressing, I know in advance how he will react to my words, to whatever I say, and consequently, I will not succeed in being astonished in his astonishment, in rejoicing in his joy, in loving in his love. The distance of separation erases the features of the loved one. Only from a distance do I feel the desire to tell him something important, something I do not utter directly seeing his face before me as a known quantity. (*CPL* 72)

Levinasian proximity—where the face of the other is never a "known quantity" even when seen directly—depends precisely on this kind of poetic distance: "an impersonal language, . . . pre-disclosing, . . . at the moment of pure touching, pure contact" (*PN* 41). Mandelstam's poetic distance, across which the poet writes to a secret and potentially phantom addressee, is a genre of the poetic irresponsibility so spurned in "Reality and Its Shadow"; and yet it includes the position of what I would call "engaged estrangement" that is so central to Levinasian ethics.

For Mandelstam, this finely attuned "irresponsibility" is hardly mystical or abstract. The unknown interlocutor is not the invention of indulgent fantasy or wish fulfillment. Rather, this providential addressee must exist just as the poet exists by virtue of having been someone (or something) else's providential addressee, as Mandelstam explains:

> And so, although individual poems, such as epistles or dedications, may be addressed to concrete persons, poetry as a whole is always directed toward a more or less distant, unknown addressee, in whose existence the poet does not doubt, not doubting in himself. Metaphysics has nothing to do with this. Only reality can bring life to a new reality. The poet is no homunculus, and there is absolutely no basis for ascribing to him characteristics of spontaneous generation. (*CPL* 73)

If there is magic involved in this poetic dynamic, it is not the "devil's part." Indeed, one might even ask if ethics is at all possible without such "magic."

The writer indeed spills half of what he brings us, as Levinas puts it in his anti-aesthetic essay; but it could well be that this cup is half full of things only the writer can offer in the first place. First of all, she brings us a text, a Said, that overflows with traces of the Saying, that begs for more Saying (the response that arises from a reader "not content with being absorbed in aesthetic enjoyment [and, accordingly, filled with] an irresistible need to speak" (*LR* 130). The reader must fill the rest of the cup, as Levinas himself intimates:

> Language would exceed the limits of what is thought, by suggesting, let-ting be understood without ever making understandable, an implication of a meaning distinct from that which comes to signs from the simultaneity of systems or the logical definition of concepts. *This possibility is laid bare in the poetic said, and the interpretation it calls for ad infinitum.* It is shown in the prophetic said, scorning its conditions in a sort of levitation. (*OTB* 169–70; my emphasis)

I would add that without poetry and prophecy, there would be little for crit-ics and sages to discuss. But perhaps even more importantly, the poem seeks to become a *place* where the poet and the reader might stand firm in an estranged proximity, in a groundless and *displaced* relation—a "null site," a restless "closer and closer" (*OTB* 82). The poet's "consciousness of being right" (*CPL* 69) is first and foremost a confidence about being able to invoke this realm that is no-place, the no-place of ethics. Levinas's references to poetry and proximity suggest that not only is the poem a handshake, but the handshake is really a poem. Without poetry, the ethical meaning of the handshake is latent, locked away behind a stale social convention, untroubled by poetic/ethical interruption.

Mandelstam's "On the Interlocutor" is an early formulation of a meta-poetics that will in many ways guide him until his death. But it is a difficult creed to follow: it is a general direction, not a road map. If the 1913 essay evokes the "saying" that gives rise to poetry, Mandelstam's career will address the way his "poetic said" might best relate this dynamic. And as one should expect, the course he charts is full of detours.

Interestingly, many of these detours parallel his struggle with his Jewish origins. Exploiting this correspondence is not an unusual critical approach, one perhaps motivated in part by the history that immediately followed Mandelstam's death in 1938.[50] Indeed, perhaps this is why it is not surpris-ing that Celan's translations often amplify this parallel, adding Judeocentric connotations that magnify those of the original, responsively softening and updating many of the somewhat standoffish, if not Judeophobic, allusions in Mandelstam's early verse.[51]

Unlike Babel, the young Mandelstam seems to have had little interest in or exposure to his Jewish roots. Also unlike Babel, who exaggerated his family's stereotypical Jewishness in the *Childhood Stories*, Mandelstam's early work was never explicitly autobiographical. The young Mandelstam deemed his origins too prosaic to escape the shroud of high allegory. Then again, autobiographical fortitude arrives later in life. Telling in this respect are Mikhail Karpovich's recollections of the teenage Mandelstam's feelings about his home life:

> About his family Mandelstam told me practically nothing. . . . Only on one occasion . . . he gave me to understand that his relationship with his parents was not altogether satisfactory. He even exclaimed, "It's terrible! terrible!" But since he was in general prone to abuse that expression, I immediately suspected him of overdoing it. And I still think that if Mandelstam's parents permitted him to live in Paris and occupy himself with whatever he wished, they must not have been so indifferent to his desires, and the family bonds did not lie so heavily upon him. In any case, he did not give one the feeling that he was constrained and bound. He was helpless in practical affairs, but spiritually he was independent and . . . sufficiently confident in himself.[52]

The young Mandelstam may have been spiritually sure of himself, but he was not yet completely confident about his nascent poetic persona, a persona apparently compromised by his rather "unlyrical" origins.

As Freidin notes, the charismatic poetic conventions (Symbolist and Futurist) of the second decade of the twentieth century called for a kind of confessional immediacy and sincerity that was ill-served by such autobiographical reticence. Freidin explains:

> In a different ideological climate, say, in Pushkin's time, with a better aware-ness of the conventional nature of art and, more importantly, without the emphatically charismatic view of poetry, one could fake sincerity and do this as often as the need arose, assuming it with as much ease or difficulty as any other mask. Not so in Mandelstam's time, when poets cultivated both in their work and in the minds of their readers the notion of poetry as the source of ultimate truth, which . . . made the requirement for sincerity central to con-temporary poetic practice. "I know that deception is unthinkable in a [poet's] vision." These words, affirming a common Symbolist belief in the truthful-ness of a poet's inner experience, were spoken by Mandelstam in 1911, the year of his poetic debut in *Apollon,* and they may indicate that he took this ideological desideratum to heart. . . . But it was not simple for Mandelstam to disclose in his poetry important elements of his "vision" with the "imme-diacy" demanded by the poetic convention he had apparently internalized. He was, after all, a Jew, and although he could find a sympathetic ear for a disclosure of his predicament, his milieu, on the whole, was either hostile or

indifferent to "confessions" of this sort, incapable, in any case, of recognizing in them any charismatic value.[53]

Accordingly, Mandelstam's "predicament" found expression in verses that betray a certain youthful Christological preciousness, as well as something that resembles Jewish self-loathing. In these poems, the lyrical self-identification with Jesus—a Jew who stood apart from his own kind and thus "redeemed the world"—seemed to offer the young poet a way of approaching the center of the Christian splendors and passions he so admired.[54]

"Kogda mozaik niknut travy . . ." ("When the mosaic grasses droop . . ."),[55] written in Lugano during the summer of 1910, is perhaps the earliest of such poems:

Когда мозаик никнут травы
И церковь гулкая пуста,
Я в темноте, как змей лукавый,
Влачусь подножию Креста.

Я пью монашескую нежность
В сосредоточенных сердцах,
Как кипариса безнодежность
В неумолимых высотах.

Люблю изогнутые брови
И краску на лице святых,
И пятна золота и крови
На теле статуй восковых.

Быть может, только призрак плоти
Обманывает нас в мечтах,
Просвечивая меж лохмотий,
И дышит в роковых страстях.

When the mosaic grasses droop
And the resounding church is still,
Like a cunning snake, I drag myself
Through the dark to the foot of the Cross.

I drink monastic tenderness
From concentrated hearts,
Like a cypress hopeless
In a pitiless sky.

I love the curving brows,
The color on the saints' faces,

The gold and blood that fleck
Their bodies made of wax.

Maybe it's only the illusion of flesh
Deceiving us in dreams,
Flickering through rags
And breathing fatal passions.

Here the poetic persona appears in the form of a serpent interloper, if not the devil himself (*lukavyi,* the Russian word for "cunning" or "the cunning one," is a folk term for the Evil One). But the subject desires to be more than a wicked vermin: this (Jewish) snake has been charmed by the lush and lofty sensuousness of the (here probably Catholic) Church. The last stanza seems to acknowledge this spell as such, wondering whether this resonant Christian beauty has innate spiritual significance or if it is more a matter of aesthetic magic. Cavanagh, however, argues that in these verses the Jewish poet

> remains aligned with the evil force that precipitated the Fall and drove humanity from Paradise into history at the Old Testament's outset, the force that led to the crucifixion but could itself not be saved by it. It is a chilling image. In this lyric Mandelstam himself embodies the evil power that bars him from the Eden of world culture. The Jewish interloper who [will later] inspire Notre Dame itself [in his "Notre Dame" of 1912] to reach new heights through his outsider's challenge, here remains trapped and alone beneath "implacable [or pitiless] skies." (*OM* 104)

Of course, such anxiety was justified given the climate of pre-Revolutionary Russia, in which the permit that permitted Mandelstam's family to live in the capital by virtue of his father's membership in a furriers' guild could be summarily revoked; and accordingly, the poem reflects the psychology of a tenuous and incomplete cultural assimilation.[56] But how "chilling" a poem is it, really? Indeed, more interestingly, one could argue that "When the mosaic grasses droop . . ." resembles Liutov's attitude of ironizing sensuality toward the Christian mystery in Babel's "Church at Novograd"—an attitude that gives way to appreciation and wonder in "Pan Apolek," and identification and protectiveness in "In St. Valentine's Church," where Liutov finds an image (probably painted by Apolek) of Christ as a tortured Polish Jew.[57] And in another way, the poem suggests Levinas's iconoclasm—which gives way to the idea of a Jewish symbiosis with Christian art. Sometimes it's good to be a snake—slithering unseen, you see what others do not.

Several of this poem's key words reappear in "Neumolimye slova . . .", or "Deaf words . . ." (August 1910),[58] a work charged with sharper Christological and Judeophobic themes and less apparent irony. (*Neumolimye* is the plural form of an adjective that can mean "implacable," "inexorable," and is etymologically suggestive of unanswered prayers and pointless begging, and which I also translate as "pitiless" or "deaf.") Here, the "thin cross and secret path" that Mandelstam had desired in an earlier four-line lyric ("Dushnyi sumrak kroet lozhe . . ." [*SDT* 1:73]) attains a more explicit context:

Deaf words . . .
Judea turned to stone,
And his head drooped
Heavier with every passing beat.

Soldiers stood around,
Kept watch over the waning body;
The halo head hung like a twig
On someone else's slender stem.

And He ruled and drooped
Like a lily in its native slough,
And the depths, where reed-stems drown,
Gloried in its law.

The word *neumolimye* returns, this time to set the tone. *Niknut'*, "to droop," reappears as well, also amplified. Christ's words are somehow unhearing, like the implacable heights in "When mosaic grasses droop . . . ," while the dark and smothering gravity of the Judaic depths, with its antiquated "law," causes the bearer of these remote heavenly words to droop earthward.

In "Iz omuta zlogo . . ." ("Out of the vicious slough . . ."), written several months later, it is the poetic "I" itself that is "drooping" into the "slough" of Jewish origins. The third stanza of this lyric ("I'm happy with this cruel insult,/And in this life, so dream-like,/I envy everyone in secret/And love everyone in secret") suggests a form of creative self-hatred. In other words, the young Mandelstam uses the "mismatch" between his origins and his adopted milieu as a kind of carrot and stick to prod himself into a heightened poetic state. This self-fulfilling prophecy might be summed up as follows: "If I feel surrounded by a family of smothering, outlandish philistines, then I must be a real poet." In the poem's ultimately excised final stanza, this childish prophecy envisions a "final victory" in which the poet will attain "vengeance for everything." Little wonder that Mandelstam excluded these lines from the 1928 edition of his verse, given that victory and vengeance over (lyrically fertile) insults and cruelties is not just immature but poetically deadening.[59]

In a passage omitted from his essay on "Scriabin and Christianity"

114

(winter 1916–17), Mandelstam renders the religious cosmology of the poems above more transparent. He writes:

> A Roman soldier guards the crucifixion and . . . must be removed. . . . The infertile, the graceless part of Europe has risen up against the fertile and the graced—Rome has risen up against Hellas. . . . Hellas must be saved from Rome. If Rome triumphs, it is not even Rome that triumphs, but Judaism— Judaism always stood behind its back and is only awaiting its hour, when it will celebrate its awful unnatural historical motion—the backward flow of time—Phaedra's black sun. (*SSCT* 1:276)

Here Mandelstam adopts the time-honored apocalyptic mode of Russian cultural commentary, as Clare Cavanagh makes clear.

> Belyi, Blok, Esenin, Akhmatova, Mayakovsky—all read the war and revo-lution in terms of cosmic, Christian transformation, and all worked . . . to place their poetic voice in relation to the upheaval by way of Judeo-Christian models of prophecy and redemption. For Mandelstam these models hold both special possibilities and special perils. He cannot claim as his birthright the Christian apocalyptic imagery and thought that enabled his contempo-raries to create the poetic cosmology that would, so they hoped, assure their place in world history. And he can use his Jewish legacy for such purposes only by abusing it. By enlarging his battles with his Jewish past to biblical proportions, he can justify his break with this legacy while placing himself at the heart of Christian culture. (*OM* 114)

Mandelstam's concern about cultural amnesia, his lament over what he calls the waning of "Christian" and "Hellenic" values—a lament that in this particular case invokes "Judaism" as an ominous, chaotic, and degenerative force—is something that stays with him in the years after the 1917 "apoca-lypse." His autobiographical prose and later verse, however, will help decode the euphemism of his spiritual poetics; the later work will ground and explain the "creative self-hatred" of the early verse, freeing his art from the rather limited context of his youthful Christological preciousness.

Furthermore, Cavanagh perhaps does not consider that the dramatic reductiveness of the apocalyptic model may ultimately have held less appeal for Mandelstam than it did for his contemporaries. Nadezhda Mandelstam's portrait of her husband certainly suggests that while his powers of prophecy were at times remarkable, his notion of the poet's role after "the upheaval" was less apocalyptic and redemptive than it was mundane and preservative. Care for language and culture was Mandelstam's response to Stalin's destruc-tion of both—a response that in a small way recalls the founding, in the wake of the destruction of the Second Temple in 70 C.E., of the Talmudic academy at Yavneh by Yochanan ben Zakai, who, incidentally, was also said to have declared that if you are "holding a sapling in your hand and someone tells you, 'Come quickly, the messiah is here!' first finish planting the tree and then go greet the messiah."[60]

During the 1920s and early '30s—largely coinciding with a period of unbroken poetic silence between 1925 and October 30, 1930—Mandelstam wrote four major prose works: *The Noise of Time, The Egyptian Stamp, Fourth Prose,* and *Journey to Armenia.* As Charles Isenberg notes, during these years "the Jewish theme is displaced to the prose, where it will undergo a substantial evolution."[61] In *The Noise of Time* (1923–25) Mandelstam sheds his autobiographical reticence, thereby confronting (without judging) the childhood aversions to Jewishness that had been too prosaic for verse. The memoir evokes the personal and psychological—not just the grandly cosmological—reasons why Mandelstam associated Judaism with chaos:

> All the elegant mirage of Petersburg was merely a dream, a brilliant cover-ing thrown over the abyss,[62] while round about there sprawled the chaos of Judaism—not a motherland, not a house, not a hearth, but precisely a chaos, the unknown womb world whence I had issued, which I feared, about which I made vague conjectures and fled, always fled. The Judaic chaos showed through all the chinks of the stone-clad Petersburg apartment: in the threat of ruin, in the cap hanging in the room of the guest from the provinces, in the hooked script of the unread books of Genesis, thrown into the dust one shelf lower than Goethe and Schiller, in the shreds of the black-and-yellow ritual. The strong, ruddy, Russian year rolled through the calendar with decorated eggs, Christmas trees, steel skates from Finland . . . But mixed up with all this there was a phantom—the new year in September—and the strange cheerless holidays, grating upon the ear with their harsh names: Rosh Hashanah and Yom Kippur. . . . As a little bit of musk fills an entire house, so the least influence of Judaism overflows all of one's life. (*SDT* 2:13)[63]

Judaism is chaotic and haunting here not only because Mandelstam's "books of Genesis" (in Russian literally "books of Being") are unread, but also because they are plural—suggestive of the semantic instability of *Bereshit,* the first book of the Hebrew Bible, in which the first sentence ("When God began" or "In the beginning of"), according to the best known of traditional Torah commentators, Rashi, says nothing but "Explain me!"[64] The hooked script, the collapsed foundation of the bookcase, raises more questions about "Being" and creation than it answers.

The childish Judeophobia that Mandelstam depicts here represents a fear of coming to grips with the creative process that transforms the "waste and wild" into civilized culture. The Russian model of this process—Vladi-

mir's conversion, Ivan's shaking off the Mongols and his imposition of imperial rule, the ascension of the Romanovs after the Time of Troubles, Peter the
Great's imposition of a European city on the Finnish swamps, the Bolshevik
experiment—tends to be abrupt and unstable. And since Russian order is
somehow inorganic, "a brilliant covering," there is always "the threat of
ruin" and a return to unknown chaos—something Mandelstam labels Judaic
probably because Judaism is the only alternate universe, the only "unknown
womb world," available to him. Hence, the Judaism described in the passage
above acts as "a universal solvent that undoes the singular synthesis of Russia
and Europe, past and present, history and new creation that is Petersburg,
the Russian capital of Mandelstam's world culture" (*OM* 106). Moreover,
Katsis contextualizes Mandelstam's "Judaic chaos" in Martin Buber's polemic
with Otto Weininger. Weininger, whose Jewish anti-Semitism was popular
in Russia in the early years of the twentieth century, describes Jewishness
as a chaos out of which a messiah could emerge only as an antithesis. Katsis
correlates this trope with Buber's discussion of the messianic potential of
a "broken, pathetic Jewish chaos," rich in time but not space.[65] Diachronic
time is also crucial to Levinas's idea of ethics as Saying, forever revising or
undoing the space of the Said. (In another prevailing stereotype, Russia is
belated and bloated: poor in time, too rich in space.)

The young Mandelstam could not detect many authentic voices in the
phantom Jewish realm to which he had been exposed as a child. He describes
how his parents,

> in a fit of national contrition . . . even tried hiring a real Jewish teacher
> for me. He came from Torgovaya Street and taught without taking off his
> cap, which made me feel awkward. His correct Russian sounded false. The
> Hebrew primer was illustrated with pictures which showed one and the same
> little boy, wearing a visored cap and a melancholy adult face, in all sorts of
> situations—with a cat, a book, a pail, a watering can. I saw nothing of myself
> in that boy and with all my being revolted against the book and the subject.
> There was one striking thing in that teacher, although it sounded unnatural:
> the feeling of national Jewish pride. He talked about the Jews as the French
> governess talked about Hugo and Napoleon. But I knew that he hid his pride
> when he went out into the street, and therefore did not believe him. (*SDT*
> 2:14; *NT* 78)

Just as Mandelstam claims he was never able to learn anything deep and
valuable about France from his governesses—"poor girls . . . completely
imbued with the cult of great [French] men" (*SDT* 2:12; *NT* 76)—so too was
he unable to imbibe the sheepish, canned nationalism of his Hebrew tutor.

The young Mandelstam does not actively seek and is not exposed to an
authentic and coherent Judaic voice. But there are premonitions: the cantor in

the Petersburg Synagogue, who "like Samson, collapsed the leonine building, [and] was answered by the velvet headdress, and the awesome equilibrium of vowels and consonants in the impeccably enunciated words imparted to the chants an invincible power" (*SDT* 2:19; *NT* 84). But the cantor's powerful notes, it seems, are soon dispelled by the *poshlost'* of the "crude speech of the rabbi: . . . 'His Imperial Highness.'" It is likely that the rabbi's Russian sermon sounds crude to Mandelstam because it is inauthentic—the fawning apologetics of an establishment Jew, representing a Judaism sanctioned by the czar. Later in life, however, Mandelstam does encounter other compelling Jewish voices: "In my childhood I absolutely never heard Yiddish [*zhargon*]; only later did I hear an abundance of that melodious, always surprised and disappointed, interrogative language" (*SDT* 2:19; *NT* 84). Indeed, linguistic self-possession, a self-possession that manifests itself in musical terms here, was the marker of aesthetic and cultural value for Mandelstam.

In its commentary on the language of his parents, *The Noise of Time* also reveals the oft-noted quasi-Oedipal tendency in Mandelstam's Judaic detours.[66]

> The speech of the father, and the speech of the mother—does not our language feed throughout all its long life on the confluence of these two . . . ? The speech of my mother was clear and sonorous without the least foreign admixture . . . —the literary Great Russian language. Her vocabulary was poor and constricted, the locutions were trite, but it was a language, it had roots and confidence. . . . Was she not the first of her whole family to achieve pure and clear Russian sounds? My father had absolutely no language; his speech was tongue-tie and languagelessness. . . . A completely abstract, counterfeit language, the ornate and twisted speech of an autodidact, where normal words are intertwined with the ancient philosophical terms of Herder, Leibniz, and Spinoza, the capricious syntax of a Talmudist, the artificial, not always finished sentence: it was anything in the world, but not a language, neither Russian nor German. In essence, my father transferred me to a totally alien century and distant, although completely un-Jewish, atmosphere. It was . . . the purest eighteenth or even seventeenth century of an enlightened Jewish ghetto somewhere in Hamburg. Religious interests had been eliminated completely. The philosophy of the Enlightenment was transformed into intricate Talmudist pantheism. (*SDT* 2:19–20; *NT* 84)

What is interesting in these recollections is that although the father here (and elsewhere, the paternal grandparents) are clearly associated with the antihistorical Judaic chaos described earlier, Mandelstam also insists that the alien atmosphere of his father was in fact "completely un-Jewish." Perhaps this is only an indication of the fact that his father was neither observant nor a Jewish cultural nationalist. But it is also possible that Mandelstam may be hinting that while chaos is "Judaic," for him Judaism is in fact beginning to represent a profound engagement with this chaos; and therefore, his father's haphazardly accreted, hybridized jumble is in a way un-Jewish. To put it another way, though Mandelstam's father is thoroughly Jewish in the historical sense, cast as a representative of a very specific moment in Jewish history (Hamburg during the Haskalah), his son's Judaism ultimately has little to do with history. Given the impossibility of maintaining the mirage of Christian cultural progress after World War I and the October Revolution, it becomes clear how an antihistorical "Judaic chaos"—anti-historical because history is a synchronic distillation of a diachronic world, in which, as Tolstoy had it, people do not know they are acting in history—might suddenly become more compelling.

While this notion of Judaism as diachronic chaos may be latent in *The Noise of Time*, there is a more apparent level on which Mandelstam can be said to identify with the Jewishness he describes. In talking about how biography begins from the composition of a childhood bookcase and from the speech of one's parents, Mandelstam, as Cavanagh notes,

> implicitly underscores the Jewishness of his efforts both to escape his past and to create a new self and new homeland through culture. Through his flight from "Judaic chaos" into Russian and European culture, he does not break with his immediate family past: he continues it. His very struggle to abandon this past extends the efforts of his parents . . . to shape new selves from what their son perceives as the rubble, or ruins, or chaos, of Jewish beginnings. . . . Unlike Boris Pasternak, who was born Jewish but raised in a thoroughly Russian cultural milieu, or Isaak Babel, who grew up "steeped in Jewish cultural and literary life," Mandelstam was brought up between cultures by parents who abandoned the past without mastering the new world that was to take its place. Mandelstam's Jewishness is chaotic because it signifies this no man's land, neither here nor there, inside or out. In *The Noise of Time*, he hints that his modernist creation of tradition is Jewish in crucial ways. (*OM* 110)

This "no man's land" resembles Kafka's description of his generation of Germanized Jews in a letter to Max Brod: "But with their posterior legs they were still glued to their father's Jewishness and with their waving anterior legs they found no new ground. The ensuing despair became their inspiration."[67] As every artist knows, chaos is protean, Dionysian, the wild element without which creation cannot be ordered. In his memoir, not only does Mandelstam identify Judaism with an inexorable and inscrutable chaos, he also begins the process by which he will fashion alternate Judaic models that, a few years later, will enable him to endure his period of poetic silence. But there may be something deeper at work here, revealed by way of a striking parallel in the development of Levinas's thought.

In Levinas, the terrifying, rustling *il y a* ("there is"), the passive non-sense or chaos that is associated with the shadowy realm of aesthetic activity in an early essay like "Reality and Its Shadow," becomes attached to the disorder of what is good beyond being—an ethics of proximity that is described as "poetry" in Levinas's mature work.[68] Furthermore, in his "Jewish" writings, Levinas presents a rabbinic tradition that treats the infinite demands of an invisible God as a threat and a challenge that must be embraced and negotiated though they are not freely chosen—a "subordination of a 'being able to die' to a 'knowing how to sacrifice oneself.'"[69] This threat and challenge may be phenomenologically linked to the "givenness" of the other and indeed of the world—a givenness expressed beautifully in two of Mandelstam's best-known early poems, "Dano mne telo . . ." ("A body is given . . .") of 1909 and "Obraz tvoi . . ." ("Your image . . .") of 1912:

Дано мне тело—что мне делать съ ним,
Таким единымъ и такимъ моимъ?

За радость тихую дышать и жить
Кого, скажите, мне благодарить?

Я и садовник, я же и цветок,
В темнице мира я не одинок.

На стекла вечности уже легло
Мое дыхание, мое тепло.

Запечатлеется на нем узор,
Неузнаваемый с недавних пор.

Пускай мгновения стекаетъ муть—
Узора милаго не зачеркнуть. (*SDT* 1:68–69)

A body is given: what to do with him?—
So singular, so mine.

For the quiet joy of living, breathing,
Tell me, whom should I be thanking?

I am a gardener as I am a flower,
And in this darkhouse I am not alone.

Upon eternal panes already lie
My breathing and my warmth, my sigh—

A pattern, pressed upon the glass,
Unrecognizable as seconds pass.

So let the momentary murk drip soft,
For this dear pattern cannot be wiped off.

Образ твой, мучительный и зыбкий,
Я не могъ въ тумане осязать.
"Господи!", сказал я по ошибке,
Сам того не думая сказать.

Божье имя, как большая птица,
Вылетело из моей груди . . .
Впереди густой туман клубится,
И пустая клетка позади . . . (*SDT* 1:78–79)

Your image, tormenting, shifty—
My hand missed it in the fog.
"Oh my Lord!" I said mistaken,
Meaning no such thing at all.

Like a great bird, the name of God
Fled winging from my breast.
Up ahead, dense fog is swirling,
A hollow cage behind.

In the first poem, Mandelstam discovers the "other" of his own body, its strange and miraculous preexistence—a preexistence that mirrors that of the "darkhouse of the world" (my rendering of "temnitza mira," which literally means "dungeon of the world" but also suggests *teplitza,* "hothouse," appropriately enough for this floral stanza). The second poem attempts to describe the way God cannot be distinguished from the involuntary and performative aspects of speech itself, as it draws toward an occluded and tormenting image of an unspecified thou (*obraz tvoi*). The body is given, the other is given, but neither can be taken, neither is quite mine. My body's breath leaves its fog on the glass—always a temporary mark (or "murk"), but also ineradicable as the "dear pattern" of the body's unstable relation to the self. And "your image" may be "shifty," but it is also the destination of "God's name" as it escapes my lungs. This consciousness of the given likewise suffuses Mandelstam's writing on poetics, such as "The Morning of Acmeism," with its understanding of language as something the poet finds already there and from which he works, as an architect builds with stone (*SDT* 2:141–44). But such givenness is also disorderly and inexorable—indeed, a pervasive "musk" that "overflows all of one's life."

When Mandelstam begins to come to grips with the Jewish aspects of his own givenness, however, he does not turn to the aesthetically repellent, incomprehensible, and traditionally Jewish household of his paternal grandparents in Riga, "the real locus of the 'Judaic chaos.'"[70] Rather than being vestigial, the Judaic elements he assembles will be adapted to his evolving brand of Russian poetics. Not surprisingly, given his neoclassical bent, Mandelstam turns to the Aegean-hued lens of antiquity in his quest for compelling Judaica. He turns south and east, to the Mediterranean and to the Levant. In his memoir he admires the father of a school friend, the Karaite Jew Boris Naumovich Siniani, whom he calls "the Abraham of positivism, [who] would not have hesitated to sacrifice his own son to it," and whose household was driven by "an aesthetic of the intellect" (*NT* 104–5). The Siniani family was especially attractive to Mandelstam, probably because they were as different from his Baltic relatives as any Jews could be: the Karaites were Jewish heretics found in warmer climes like Persia and, in Dr. Siniani's case, Crimea (the ancient Greek colony of Taurides, as Mandelstam points out in his verse).[71] They were a sect that had long ago rejected the Talmud in favor of biblical literalism—that is, had given up legalistic abstraction in favor of the shepherd's staff, if one chooses to imagine this trade-off in the allegorical terms that might have appealed to Mandelstam.

The Karaite Sinianis represent a kind of exotically Semitic, biblical nobility for the Russian Jewish poet, who sought cultural kinship not with the inhabitants of the Pale of Settlement or the ghettoes of Eastern Europe, but with Homer and Virgil and with Luis de León,[72] a Sephardi poet imprisoned by the Spanish Inquisition. But then even a thoroughly Ashkenazi Jew like S. A. Ansky, the Yiddish writer who was practically a member of the Siniani family, does not escape Mandelstam's neoclassical embrace: Ansky, the wandering storyteller, "gave the impression of a gentle Psyche afflicted with hemorrhoids" (*NT* 107). The great Yiddish actor Solomon Mikhoels is likewise rendered Hellenic, in an essay Mandelstam wrote in 1926:

> Mikhoels' face takes on the expression of world-weariness and mournful ecstasy in the course of his dance as if the mask of the Jewish people were drawing nearer to the mask of Classical antiquity, becoming virtually indistinguishable from it. The dancing Jew now resembles the leader of the ancient Greek chorus. All the power of Judaism, all the rhythm of abstract ideas in dance, all the pride of the dance whose single motive is . . . compassion for the earth—all this extends into the trembling of hands, into the vibration of the thinking fingers which are animated like articulated speech (*CPL* 261–62)

Here Mandelstam adds classical dramatic terms (masks, Dionysian intoxication) to the staples of Jewish consciousness (melancholy, irony, world-weariness).

Cavanagh's suggestion that such synthesis is the strategy by which Mandelstam-the-modernist-subversive marshals his forces is helpful here, but not entirely satisfying. Mandelstam continues:

> Mikhoels once said: "I implore my fellow artists to preserve my countenance for me." Indeed, the entire repertory of the Jewish State Theater revolves around the revelation of Mikhoels' masks. In each play he accomplishes the extremely difficult and glorious journey from Jewish meditation to dithyrambic ecstasy, to freedom and the unfettering of the dance of wisdom. (*CPL* 263)

Mikhoels' masks here are like rhetorical—and indeed, interpretive—devices. They mediate between inner states and outer realities, and they teach one how to respond to different faces. This might be what Mandelstam means by "Jewish meditation." But as a poet, Mandelstam is inevitably interested in the transformation of this synthetic Talmudic creativity into an organic, Dionysian poetic freedom, where wisdom is permitted to "dance," "unfettered" and yet ecstatically contained by the preexisting rhythms of the world. This interest has less to do with Hölderlin and Heidegger's idea that "poetically man dwells on the earth" than it does with the fact that poetry itself (even free verse) is a participation in the rhythmic structures of creation. In this essay, however, Mandelstam—through his admiration for Mikhoels' hybrid and elastic art—seems to be trying to understand the relationship between Jewish "compassion" and "meditation," on the one hand, and Greek lyrical "freedom," on the other.

Nadezhda Mandelstam claims that "for M., . . . the original unity of the Judeo-Christian world was far more real than its subsequent division. He saw the Mediterranean, to which he was so drawn, as a blend of Christian-Judaic with Hellenic culture." The poet's widow believes that he "yearns with such intensity for Judaism . . . not in response to the call of his blood, but because [it is] the source of all the European ideas and concepts from which poetry drew its strength."[73] Mandelstam himself might well have agreed with this assessment, and yet it doesn't quite address the specific philosophical dynamic that comprises Mandelstam's hybridized spiritual language. It may be plausible to read Judaism as a kind of source-culture for Mandelstam's favorite things. But it is more interesting to consider the extent to which the substance *behind* this ghostly source has any bearing on whatever it is that Mandelstam chooses to call "Judaism."

In "Mikhoels," Mandelstam ascribes Judaism's power to abstraction in the service of compassion. Rabbinic Judaism is abstract because it is diasporic and uprooted; and its compassion derives from an appreciation of the other's disruptedness and perpetual longing. In the late 1920s Mandelstam begins to ruefully accept and ultimately embrace his own uprootedness. In a 1928 response to the questionnaire "The Soviet Writer and October," he writes with thinly veiled sarcasm:

> The October Revolution could not but influence my work since it took away my "biography," my sense of individual significance. I am grateful to it, how-ever, for once and for all putting an end to my spiritual security and to a cultural life supported by unearned cultural income . . . I feel indebted to the Revolution, but I offer it gifts for which it still has no need. (*CPL* 375)

Gone is Mandelstam's unmediated ("unearned") communion not only with Hellenic world culture but also with the heroic self-absorption of the Russian lyrical tradition. In his prose Mandelstam mocks the Christological pseudo-martyrdom, the "self-burning" (*NT* 81) that had characterized so much of Russian literary culture since the 1880s and that was embodied by the poetic persona of Semyon Nadson (1862–87), whose father was from a family of Jewish converts to Russian Orthodoxy. Mandelstam gazes into the iconic face of the young Nadson and is "astonished by the genuine fieriness of those features and at the same time by their total inexpressiveness, their almost wooden simplicity" (*NT* 81).[74] The Revolution—that grim culmination of Russia's fin de siècle "smoldering"—has unmasked the moral and artistic vacuousness of "Nadsonist" preciousness. And Mandelstam has put away childish things, facile Christology and Judeophobia among them.

The poet now finds himself on the long road to reestablishing and reformulating his place in a new landscape, a more forbidding topography where his original destination looks quite different. October's "Judaic chaos" has congealed into a political and cultural order that is neither Judaic nor Greek. And Judeophobic apocalyptic allegory is neither original nor spiritu-ally useful once the "end of time" is already ten years running. The abstract disorder of Judaic ethics, so seemingly out of step with history, becomes sud-denly appealing given the questionable steps history has just taken.

This disruptive antihistorical sentiment challenges any easy poetic path from chaos to order. And it is also a sentiment that motivates much of Levinas's project, where it presents certain obvious difficulties for anyone concerned with justice, that is, with creating order out of ethics. As Steven Connor writes in his rich discussion of Joyce, Levinas, and Derrida,

> The notorious problem that Levinas's ethics poses for ethical thinking is its refusal to derive the ethical encounter from culture and history, or to see its operations within culture as anything other than a purifying disruption. Communication in and between cultures depends upon a "proximity" that works in a mode wholly other than that of "making common": "The neighbor is ordered to my responsibility; he is already uprooted and without a country as soon as he arises on the earth . . . torn up from culture, law, horizon, context,

by reason of an absence which is the very presence of infinity, finding itself in the null site of a trace . . ." (Levinas, "Language and Proximity," 121). . . . Derrida [warns] Levinas that the dream of a Judaic discourse capable of a purely vocative opening or approach to the other, as against the Greek *logos* that is always concerned rather to name and make intelligible the truth of the other, may itself commit the violence of asociality. For Derrida . . . the only possible way of ensuring a nonviolent opening to the other is by passing through history and its violence, rather than attempting to abstract oneself away from it.[75]

However, as Connor goes on to note, Levinas does not endorse an abstraction away from history so much as he urges a redefinition of it. Indeed, in 1947, when Levinas would have had reason to express bitterness about history and politics, he instead writes: "The situation of the face-to-face would be the very accomplishment of time; the encroachment of the present on the future is not the feat of the subject alone, but the intersubjective relationship. The condition of time lies in the relationship between humans, in history."[76] Then again, perhaps this definition is largely intuitive. Indeed, what is history, if not the face-to-face writ large—that is, the encounter, or the missed encounter?

In "Paul Celan" Levinas talks about the poem as the very paragon of disinterested goodwill, a "saying without a said, . . . a complicity *pour rien*." This lyrical turn inflects the basically prosaic, historical "face-time" of Levinas's ethics; just as Mandelstam's interaction with the mean prose of Soviet history inflected and pried open the poet's sealed literary communion with "world culture." And Levinas's implication that language—the dynamic between the *Saying* and the *Said*—is what accomplishes time, accomplishes history, parallels Mandelstam's notion of history as well. As Jane Gary Harris notes, "Mandelstam's 'historical love' was intimately connected with his 'love of the word,' since he equated Russian history with the Russian language."[77]

This "philological" approach to history is intimate and moody, primal and urbane—as characterized by the "literary savagery" (*zlost'*, also translated as "literary spite") of the *raznochinets littérateur*,[78] an attitude embodied by Mandelstam's teacher V. V. Gippius:

> [Gippius] differed from the other witnesses of literature precisely in his malign astonishment. He had a kind of feral relationship to literature, as if it were the only source of animal warmth. He warmed himself against literature, he rubbed against it with his fur . . . He was a Romulus who hated his wolf mother and, hating her, taught others to love her. (*NT* 114)

The literary werewolf-intellectual described here is connected to the very nerves of history, to humanity's notion of "the event" as defined by astonishment and then by language. The mytho-historical metaphor of Romulus and his wolf mother is quite apt: our ability to tell a story—a story that both sustains and betrays us—is indeed our "only source of animal warmth," because from the moment human beings leave the womb of nature and enter the world of history, this wolf becomes the indispensable surrogate mother of civilization and the historical consciousness that girds it. The relationship between wolf and ward, between history and its poet-charge, is tense and intimate, not just business but personal. As Mandelstam puts it, the bristling *raznochinets littérateur* "feels the centuries as he feels the weather, and he shouts at them" (*NT* 117).

Literary savagery is the manifestation of this relationship, its visible sparks. It is an expression of love for history, a philological love, that sees past the cruelty of its object of affection. "Literary spite! . . . You are the seasoning for the unleavened bread of understanding, you are the joyful consciousness of injustice, you are the conspiratorial salt which is transmitted with a malicious bow from decade to decade" (*NT* 112). Literary spite is a style, an attitude that presumes that the aesthetically responsive individual has the right and even the duty to respond to an apparently impersonal History in a thoroughly personal way. Harris suggests that it is a response of "wit and wisdom, not of naïveté. It combines the conscious and the unconscious, the cognitive and the instinctive response to life, emerging as it does from Mandelstam's fundamental esthetic impulses of 'astonishment' and 'sweet recognition' so evident in his lyrics" (*CPL* 18). These impulses are also ethical, since the other as other is astonishing and is then sweetly "recognized" when he is greeted and assisted as a neighbor; intersubjectivity can occur only with someone who is first faced as a stranger, absolutely other and therefore in need of translation and justice, someone whose demands deserve recognition.

The two impulses are forever in creative tension—an anarchic dynamic that both Levinas and Mandelstam ultimately find "Judaic" in certain ways. Mandelstam's likely reference to *matzo*—"the unleavened bread of understanding"—invokes an image of nourishment tempered by the awareness of injustice and exigency. The "conspiratorial salt" of literary spite— which could also be said to characterize the argumentative figures of the Talmud, who sought to make politics coincide with hermeneutics—lends a "joy" to an otherwise unleavened sense of injustice, generic and joyless without the disorder of astonishment and its reordering in sweet recognition. And we will recall that in "Judaism and Revolution," Levinas argues that the Talmud reflects a similar idea of justice—always rough, an imperfect contract that loses its ethical grounding when it becomes too impersonal, and yet the invocation of a future messianic time does not make the need for such justice disappear.[79] So too, literary spite enables the personality to be heard—even if only shouting like King Lear in the impersonal storms of history. One should add that "literary spite" also evokes the tone of Levinas's "Reality and Its Shadow," with its historically driven, nasty yet cozy brand of—ironically beautiful—anti-aesthetics. Indeed, Paul Ricoeur describes Levinas's hyperbolic writing as "the systematic practice of *excess* in philosophical argumentation . . . carried to the point of paroxysm" in *Otherwise Than Being*.[80]

Mandelstam's prose after *The Noise of Time* in the late 1920s and early '30s amplifies the ethics and aesthetics of literary spite. As Harris notes,

> [If] *Noise of Time* poses the issue of the poet's challenge to society and history, "Fourth Prose" takes up that challenge and hurls it in the form of a prophetic curse against the forces of death and destruction, and specifically against the Soviet literary establishment. . . . "Fourth Prose" resorts to the thunder and all-consuming moral passion of Old Testament prophecy as well as the Mosaic Law, "Thou shalt not kill," established in this work as a fundamental aesthetic concept. This piece confirms the aesthetic process in Mandelstam's poetics as a moral, intellectual, and cognitive act. The poet's renewed faith in himself and in the "creative spirit," following years of doubt and despair, seems to have resulted from an intensive personal revaluation of himself as a poet, as a man, and as a Jew.[81]

It is, however, in his subsequent prose work about his travels in Armenia—"that younger sister of the land of Judah," as he calls it (*NT* 182)—that Mandelstam arrives at a more explicit "philological" notion of ethics.

"Which tense do you want to live in?" Mandelstam asks in *Journey to Armenia*, replying, "I want to live in the imperative of the passive future participle—in the 'what ought to be'" (*NT* 221; *CPL* 374).[82] This was foremost a personal response, and ultimately one that led to an important poetic opening—as Harris notes:

> The recovery of Mandelstam's lyric voice is metaphorically revealed in *Journey to Armenia*, written in Moscow during the summer of 1931, a year after his memorable "two hundred days in the Sabbath land." This autobiographically engaged meditation joins the moral force of Old Testament prophecy, enunciated so firmly in "Fourth Prose," to the aesthetic force of contemplation, thereby providing a precious key to the lyrics of the 1930's.[83]

The "renewed sense of 'rightness'"[84]—lyric and ethical—recovered in Armenia coincided with a reversal of the Hebraic-Hellenic trajectory that had been suggested in Mandelstam's essay on Mikhoels, a doubling-back on what had been "the extremely difficult and glorious journey from Jewish meditation to dithyrambic ecstasy, to freedom and the unfettering of the dance of wisdom" (*CPL* 263).

In other words, Judaism is no longer merely a source-culture, a rich and unruly past, but a new way for Mandelstam to understand history and its unsettled trajectory as ethics. In "Oh, how we love to play the hypocrite . . ." of 1932, Mandelstam writes: "The cranky child/still tugs his grievance from his dish,/but I've got no one to pout at/and I'm alone on all my paths.//But I don't want to slumber, like a fish,/In the watery coma of the deep,/And I have a free choice of roads/Among my sufferings and cares" (*SSCT* 3:60–61). An earlier version concludes with the following stanza instead: "The beast molts, the fish plays/In the watery coma of the deep—/And if only one didn't have to look at the twists/of people's sufferings, people's cares" (*SSCT* 3:316). In this earlier version, there is the grudging realization that—unlike the child or the creature of nature—it is the poet's fate to be confronted with "people's sufferings, people's cares." The final version strikes a more definitive contrast: the poet affirms that he has "no desire to slumber like a fish" or a child, affirms the people's historically bound sufferings and cares as his own and, what's more, as constituting his very freedom ("a free choice of roads"). He shouts at the weather of centuries, as it were.

In the ninth of his "Octaves," completed early in 1934, Mandelstam takes up these cares (*zaboty*) again, this time adding a Jewish adjective:

Скажи мне, чертежник пустыни,
Арабских песков геометр,
Ужели безудержность линий
Сильнее, чем дующий ветр?
—Меня не касается трепет
Его иудейских забот—
Он опыт из лепета лепит
И лепет из опыта пьет
. . . (*SSCT* 3:79)

Tell me, draftsman of the desert,
Geometer of Arab sands,
Could the unruliness of lines
Be stronger than the blowing wind?
—Doesn't concern me, all the fuss
of his Judaic cares—
He forms forms from formlessness
And drinks formlessness from forms . . .

Literally, the last two lines read: "He shapes experience [or experiment] from babble/And drinks babble from experience [experiment]" ("On opyt iz lepeta lepit/I lepet iz opyta pyot").[85] To a certain extent my translation invokes

Genesis 1:1–3, with its similarly alliterative energy: "Bereshit bara elohim et hashamayim ve'et ha'arets. Veha'arets hayetah tohu vavohu vechoshech al-peney tehom veruach Elohim merachefet al-peney hamayim. Vayomer Elohim yehi-or vayehi-or." Mandelstam's lines, like the beginning of Bereshit, are redolent of chiasmus and parataxis, as if creation were not just the manifestation of God's will but is also rhythmic, reversible, and without apparent cause. Similarly, readers have noticed that Levinas—despite his condemnation of rhythm as irresponsible participation in "Reality and Its Shadow"—writes with rhythmic wavelike repetition to evoke his theme of a causeless ethics *pour rien,* of a Saying and a Said that revert one into the other.[86]

Moreover, *lepet* (babble) is the noun form of the verb *lepetat'* (to mumble, to move one's lips), which represented inspiration in Mandelstam's poetic practice—lexically associated with mouth, lips, books, the word. Petrified language came to represent petrified life for him.[87] Indeed, in May 1935 Mandelstam writes a stanza that reads like a more straightforward reply to the 1928 Soviet newspaper questionnaire quoted here earlier: "Having deprived me of seas, of running and flying away,/and allowing me only to walk upon the violent earth,/what have you achieved? A splendid result:/you could not stop my lips from moving."[88] As long as the poet can mumble (*lepetat'*), sculpting (*lepit'*) his work out of the soft clay of language, then culture is still alive.[89]

This lexical field, however, by no means resolves the identity of the interlocutors in this octave. In Jennifer Baines's view, the first four lines are the poet's question to the wind, while the last four are the wind's reply. She writes:

> The value of ["draftsman"], as of ["geometer"], lies in the connotations of precision and craftsmanship on which Mandelstam insisted that every artist should pride himself. The wind carefully outlines the shifting . . . sands of the desert into crescent-shaped dunes, in order to combat the formlessness of the open space, the ["desert"]. He questions the wind as to whether the instability of these geometrically exact shapes which it has molded out of sand, [the unruliness of lines], is not stronger than the force of the wind keeping them in place. The wind, in its self-confident reply, dismisses with contempt such a trivial and obvious enquiry . . . The Jewish poet is made to sound querulous and persnickety; the scale of their work differs. The wind sweeps freely without let or hindrance over limitless space, whereas Mandelstam's work appears minute and limited in comparison. But the wind has no quarrel with the poet's work, the synthesising of senseless noises into the final "*opyt,*" the enjoyment in drinking in these sounds once marshalled into order. Only in the phonetics does the sense of the poet's work emerge as charming child's play, compared with the wind's grandiose gestures.[90]

Pollak draws broader conclusions from a similar reading:

> The masculine singular pronoun *on,* which refers first of all to the wind ("it"), also suggests a person ("he"). The geometer, responding to the question about the wind, dismisses the poet's activity at the same time. The repetitive "Judaic cares" are the wind's, but they might be the poet's. The alternation of "babble" and "experiment" is the creative cycle. In the first two decades of his work, Mandelstam had tried to escape the primitive and inarticulate element he calls the "Judaic chaos" . . . ["which I fled, always fled"]. By the fall of 1933, as he realizes that the poet's activity is inextricably bound up with the fate of the Jew, "Judaic chaos" . . . has become "Judaic cares."[91]

Though the themes of this difficult poem now seem more accessible, the voicing is still irresolvably ambiguous. The draftsman of the desert seems to be the wind, or perhaps the force that controls the wind. The poet's question suggests that the untidiness of the dunes may be stronger than the wind that keeps them in place; of course, this untidiness is the result of wind erosion in the first place. But the geometer dismisses the poet's query because he simply does not care about such questions, doesn't care about what his winds wreak among the desert dunes. Only the poet is conscious of this creative cycle *as such;* and the crafted expression of this consciousness is the poet's vocation, his "Judaic cares." There is indeed a confusion between the activity of the wind and the poet: it is the poet who lends meaning to the world, whose metaphor, in this case, transforms the cold, unfeeling wind into a tender, childlike caretaker of the world. A mature and less feral version of "literary spite," the poet's fuss turns the grandly and dismissively neutral blowing of the wind into nature's taking-care.

When Mandelstam finally reads his "unread books of Genesis," so to speak, he becomes more than another renegade poet-Jew. He also acquires more than what has been called the Talmudic sensibility of reading the disparate events of a tradition in their simultaneity (which is really the ability to "choose one's time"). He has become attuned to what motivates the hermeneutic gymnastics of the rabbis: the poetry of the world, the anarchic ethos of "tenderness" or *nezhnost'*—a word that appears often in Mandelstam, in one case as the "sister" of *tyazhest'* or "heaviness"[92]—that "spreads over all things, beginning with the human face and skin," as Levinas puts it. Poetry is now a careful (and "Judaic") fuss, and no longer simply a Hellenic communion with the rhythmic structures of creation.

Bakhtin at one point associates rhythm with death: "Rhythm takes possession of a life that *has been lived:* the requiem tones at the end were already heard in the cradle song at the beginning." Mandelstam's long pacifist poem of 1937, "Verses on an Unknown Soldier," is an excellent example of what Bakhtin calls the "cherishing hopelessness of rhythm."[93] Mandelstam uses the slave drum anapest to evoke the horrors of rhythm, the anonymous terrors of aesthetic participation, of consciousness paralyzed in the play of its freedom (*LR* 32, 133). In these verses, Mandelstam testifies to the difficulty of being a sage, a local moral interpreter, in a totalitarian reality that leaves nothing unpalpated: under these circumstances he can only be a prophet, predicting the essence of the total war that he will not live to see. Eerily, Celan's line in "Todesfuge" of 1944–45—"we shovel a grave in the air/there you won't lie too cramped" (translated in *PC* 31)—was preempted by Mandelstam's "how the grave teaches the hunchback/and the airy pit entices" from "Unknown Soldier" of 1937 (*SDT* 1:242), a poem which Celan could not have seen until probably 1962.

A poetic obsession with otherness is ethical in its structure; it is related to the disorder of ethics. As Levinas notes, "In the form of responsibility, the psyche in the soul is the other in me, a malady of identity, both accused and self, . . . a possession and a psychosis; the soul is already a seed of folly" (*OTB* 69, 191n3). And however much we may disparage "soulfulness," it is also the seed of moral sensibility. The poet "plays" the other: but for whose sake? Certainly for his own, but in better poems this enacted otherness is also for the sake of the reader. As Celan wrote: "The poem speaks . . . True, it speaks only on its own, its very own behalf. But I think . . . that the poem has always hoped, for this very reason, to speak also . . . *on behalf of the other*, who knows, perhaps of an *altogether other*" (*CP* 48). Moreover, in Mandelstam's case, this fundamental poetic self-centeredness runs parallel to an effort to engage with the otherness—the material—of language, with the oft-neglected (and politically mangled) tools of sociality. It is indeed a commonplace that Mandelstam's verse was a form of aesthetic resistance to Stalinist ugliness.

It is, however, ethics, not language, that is "the hero of Mandelstam's experiment" or *opyt*, as he puts it: he only "cherished the ideal of language which he portrayed with the metaphor of 'Hellenism' because he hoped that language, understood in this way, could keep alive the tradition that humanity is called to be master in its own house."[94] Or, as Pollak notes, the "poet's confidence establishes the future addressee's existence."[95] This is how the poet takes on a sober—and even maternal—responsibility for everyone. No longer just a dream of joining the Hellenic dance, Mandelstam's more dissonant later verse was in fact *responsible*, precisely in the sense of responding to a distant interlocutor whom his work sought to protect as much as posit. Levinas suggests that in the modernist literary "intellectualism (which . . . goes back to Shakespeare, . . . Goethe, Dostoevsky), . . . the artist refuses to be only an artist, not because he wants to defend a thesis or cause, but because he needs to interpret his myths himself" (*LR* 143). This is precisely the sort of self-conscious, ethically honest modernism toward which Mandelstam (and Dostoevsky and Babel) strove.

And here we have arrived at a peculiar reversal, one that reveals the symbiotic entanglement—or covert affinity—beneath the elective antipathy that had been constructed between ethical disruption and aesthetic rhythm. Over time, Mandelstam's poetry—in which rhythm comes to evoke not just lyrical respiration but a forced march—becomes indistinguishable from an ethics. In Levinas poetry was initially identified as irresponsible participation, and rhythm understood as a charm to be dispelled by the prose of ethics. Levinas's later thought, however, invokes an ethics of tenderness ("the poetry of the world") that is nothing if not an expansive metaphor by which the world acquires a human face. Along the same lines, the dynamic between the Saying and the Said as well as Levinas's rhythmic philosophical style evoke the waves lapping against the Crimean shore in Mandelstam's "Sleeplessness. Homer . . .":

Like a wedge of cranes towards strangers' shores—
On the heads of kings there foams a holy frenzy—
Where are you sailing to? Were it not for Helen,
What is Troy alone to you, Achaean husbands?

And the sea and Homer—all things are moved by love.
Who then should I listen to? And now Homer is silent,
While the black sea, orotund, roars soft
And with weighty thunder laps gently at my bed.

In the caress of the poetry of the world, the Saying (an unfixable sea) and the Said (the Homeric text) are both moved by love and in fact form the basic meaning of love: *the need and desire for relation without identity,* to connect and not fuse with the other. And relation without identity is the very movement of Levinas's ethics, just as it is the goal of Mandelstam's verse. To say that Levinas's thought is poetic is not to suggest that poetry is some kind of sports massage for the main event of philosophical ethics. Certainly, the art of Dostoevsky, Babel, and Mandelstam shows that it is ultimately impossible to categorically separate ethics and aesthetics. So too, as Levinas reveals the impossibility of shaping an ethics from ontology, despite himself, his ethics-beyond-being emerges as another name for poetry.

# The Ethics of Aesthetics, the Aesthetics of Ethics

THE PREVAILING MODES of ethical criticism, in Robert Eaglestone's account, are "traditionalist" and "postmodernist." The first looks to realist, "readerly" texts for a content-based ethics *from literature*. The second favors more "writerly" works that interrupt reading by evoking the gap between life, text, and interpretation—suggesting literature's basic "unreadability" and therefore the need for an ethics *of criticism*.[1]

But we have long been tired of instruction, and we are now getting tired of constant interruption. The first presumes that literature still has any authority, and the second has become increasingly mechanical. Neither takes aesthetics seriously.

In an attempt to redress what he calls "aesthetic alienation"—modernity's categorical separation of art from truth and morality—Jay Bernstein locates what he calls "post-aesthetic" theories of art in the thought of such post-Kantians as Adorno, Heidegger, and Derrida. Such theories are "critiques of truth-only cognition insofar as their going beyond aesthetics implies a denial of the rigid distinctions separating the claims of taste from the claims of knowing or right action."[2] Unlike Bernstein's post-aesthetic philosophers, Levinas doesn't really mourn a pre-autonomous art, but ends up doing something that is both more and less than that. As a "Russian"—raised in a literary culture animated by an energetic belatedness that cannot take modernity's categorical distinctions at face value—Levinas sees art as something that cannot be severed from "the famous meaning of life" (ethics and truth). Or rather, as a "Russian," he *cannot* see aesthetics as categorically distinct. One could argue that even an aesthetic fundamentalist like Nabokov reveals this most salutary and most Russian inability in the moralistic absolutism of his insistence on the barrier between art and morality. As Rorty has suggested, Nabokov, repulsed by cruelty and ever curious, never fails to showcase in his fiction the cruelty and incuriosity of the committed aesthete.

If Wittgenstein's cryptic note that "ethics and aesthetics are one" is the unproven Fermat's Theorem of ethical criticism, where do we go from here? As I have indicated, this unity is a challenge and a threat. Worse than the instrumental approach suggested by the natural and social sciences, an undif-

133

ferentiated, faux-primitivist ethical-aesthetic monism would be an uncritical criticism. But the primitivism of the "Russian-Levinasian" approach developed here is richer than that, precisely because, as symbiosis, it suggests an unstable mingling of identities. I hope that this model is a more suggestive elaboration on Wittgenstein's assertion. In the ecology offered here, difference and opposition (elective antipathies) are potential sources of mutual survival and enrichment (covert affinities)—even as there is ever the risk of something more parasitic.

I also hope that the preceding chapters have offered dialogues that in retrospect seem intuitive. Levinas is the thinker of *la bonté,* of "goodness" as opposed to the systematic "Good" that moral philosophy has traditionally attempted to posit, and he finds *la bonté* in literature.[3] It is literature, not philosophy, that is best equipped to reveal goodness—not just in its content, but in the way a text approaches and even gives birth to a reader and vice versa.

At the very least, pairing Levinas with the three Russians in these pages recovers a key aspect of his autobiographical, cultural, and intellectual heritage that is generally underappreciated. His childhood and adolescence share broad similarities with those evoked by Isaac Babel and Osip Mandelstam. Here is an apposite Babel's pseudo-memoiristic "Story of My Dovecote" preceded by Levinas's "version":

> I entered a Russian gymnasium [in Kharkov, Ukraine] with the "five best Jews" who had made it through *the numerus clauses.* In 1916, my father, a bookseller in Kovno, thought that event merited a celebration. We were very attached to Pushkin—I knew Pushkin by heart. It is still today the literature that is my lifeblood.[4]

> I was shouting Pushkin's stanzas at the top of my lungs . . . "Tell your father that you are admitted to the first class" . . . My father organized a celebration. (*SS* 1:153–56)

And here is Levinas's adolescent—and Mandelstamian—"longing" for European culture: "In 1920, we returned to Lithuania . . . [where] I had my first contact with what I called Europe. . . . This was a point in my life when I found it shameful not to have seen Cologne cathedral!"[5] In "Notre Dame" (1912) Mandelstam looked to another cathedral of aspiration, whose example he vowed to follow by transforming "unkind heaviness" into "loveliness."

This twin longing, for Russia and Europe, appears in Levinas's thought as a figure that eventually links ethics to poetics, and as an orientation toward the Christian world—a turning that is both a plea for inclusion and a challenge to the Western "universal that is never universal enough." A dual discourse, here again: "I accept kenosis, absolutely," Levinas once declared, referring to the idea of a "self-emptying" Christlike ethical sacrifice in a discussion with Christian thinkers, "but what I say about the face of the neighbor, the Christian probably says about the face of Christ."[6] I would argue that Dostoevsky was perhaps Levinas's primary Christian interlocutor, precisely because his novels rely not on theology but on the secularization of Christian kenosis into human goodness (like Sonya Marmeladova's "insatiable compassion"). Hence, Myshkin's dramatic failure, Stepan's "conversion," and Alyosha's ethical muddling-through. And just as, in this dialogue, Levinas's description of justice reveals the ways in which Dostoevsky's fiction in fact *tempers* the stereotypical dualism of the Russian soul, so too, the novels provide a cultural context that situates and complicates Levinas's ethical hyperboles. Isaac Babel's aesthetics is revealed as a dirty ethics, even as it shows how Levinas's thought evokes a form of self-compromise that verges on pollution. Finally, the pairing with Mandelstam stresses how ethics and aesthetics may "pollute" each other, even as they "other" each other.

The tipping point between aesthetics and ethics can never be stabilized—each maintains a provisional identity, just as one may flow entirely into the other depending on how what has been written is being read. Perhaps the most to which an ethical criticism should aspire is to notice such fluidity, a symbiosis in the genitive case: the ethics of aesthetics, the aesthetics of ethics.

# Notes

## INTRODUCTION

The chapter epigraph is from Johann Wolfgang von Goethe, *Elective Affinities,* trans. David Constantine (New York: Oxford University Press, 1999), 32–33.

1. Robert Eaglestone suggests that "ethical criticism" has not yet met the challenge, suggested by Wittgenstein and articulated by Jay Bernstein, "to think through what truth, morality and beauty (or its primary instance: art) are when what is denied is their categorical separation from each other." See Ludwig Wittgenstein, *Tractatus Logico-Philosophicus,* trans. D. F. Pears and B. F. Guinness (London: Routledge, 1974), 6:421; J. M. Bernstein, *The Fate of Art* (London: Polity, 1992), 2; and Eaglestone, "One and the Same? Ethics, Aesthetics, and Truth," *Poetics Today* 25, no. 4 (Winter 2004): 595–608. Eaglestone attributes this failure to a reliance on "methodologies and presuppositions taken from the natural sciences, and this includes the natural sciences' way of understanding truth: the correspondence of a proposition with a state of affairs. Until we escape these and are prepared to defend a noninstrumental theory of truth, we may find that we cannot understand Wittgenstein's remark" (606).

2. Emmanuel Levinas, quoted in *Is It Righteous to Be?: Interviews with Emmanuel Levinas,* ed. Jill Robbins (Stanford, Calif.: Stanford University Press, 2001), 95. See also Judith Friedlander, *Vilna on the Seine: Jewish Intellectuals in France Since 1968* (New Haven, Conn.: Yale University Press, 1990), 85–86. As Judith Butler, Simon Critchley, and Thomas Caygill have recently pointed out, it is problematic that Levinas does not mention the obvious fact that Israel also has to come to terms with Islam. For more on the connection to Rosenzweig, see Robert Gibbs, *Correlations in Rosenzweig and Levinas* (Princeton, N.J.: Princeton University Press, 1992).

3. Levinas, quoted in Friedlander, *Vilna on the Seine,* 80.

4. Emmanuel Levinas, *Ethics and Infinity,* trans. Richard A. Cohen (Pittsburgh: Duquesne University Press, 1985), 22.

5. See, for example, Gabriella Safran, Harriet Murav, Maxim Shrayer, Brian Horowitz, Efraim Sicher, Gary Rosenshield, Judith Deutsch Kornblatt, Stanley

Rabinowitz, Michael Eskin, Leonid Katsis, Vladimir Kazan, David Patterson, Marat Grinberg, Susan McReynolds Oddo, Mikhail Krutikov, and Nina Perlina. Also interesting is James Rice's discussion of the connections between Freud and Dostoevsky, who both traced their family origins to the Lithuanian border provinces of the Russian Empire—as did Levinas. See Rice, *Freud's Russia: National Identity in the Evolution of Psychoanalysis* (New Brunswick, N.J.: Transaction, 1993).

6. The intellectual historian Samuel Moyn cogently links Levinas's philosophical development to interwar Protestant theology, rather than to any "organic" Jewish origins. Moyn's method is to underscore the contingency of philosophical concepts, and accordingly he situates the young Levinas in the milieu of a fairly typical upper-middle-class Jewish family seeking to assimilate into Russian economic and cultural life without shedding their religious observance. Moyn says little about the Russian literary connections that are of interest here. See Moyn, *Origins of the Other: Emmanuel Levinas Between Revelation and Ethics* (Ithaca, N.Y.: Cornell University Press, 2005).

7. For more on the recent controversies about Levinas's politics, see Howard Caygill, *Levinas and the Political* (New York: Routledge, 2002); Leora Batnitzky, *Leo Strauss and Emmanuel Levinas: Philosophy and the Politics of Revelation* (Cambridge: Cambridge University Press, 2006), who also compellingly exposes Levinas's theological and philosophical incoherence; Simon Critchley, "Five Problems in Levinas's View of Politics and the Sketch of a Solution to Them," *Political Theory* 32, no. 2 (April 2004): 172–85; and especially C. Fred Alford's excellent "Levinas and Political Theory," *Political Theory* 32, no. 2 (April 2004): 146–71. Alford persuasively accounts for Levinas's often contradictory and at times seemingly xenophobic political comments with the idea of "inverted liberalism," in which the individual must be protected for the sake of the *other* individual. Only the individual, not the state, can engage in the intimacy of responsibility. I suggest here that this ethical intimacy is rooted in a literary aesthetic sensibility—and a particularly Russian one at that.

8. Emmanuel Levinas, "Transcendence and Height," in *Basic Philosophical Writings,* ed. Adriaan Peperzak, Simon Critchley, and Robert Bernasconi (Bloomington: Indiana University Press, 1996), 23.

9. See Peter Atterton's remarkable essay, graciously shared in uncorrected proofs, "Art, Religion, and Ethics Post Mortem Dei: Levinas and Dostoevsky," *Levinas Studies* 2 (May 2007): 105–32: "In classical ethical theories, however different, obligations are always treated as universalizable. . . . Levinas's theory, which treats responsibility asymmetrically, thus offers for consideration an altogether different approach to ethics. But the notional of ethical symmetry is highly debatable in a philosophical context, which is why Levinas appeals to phenomenology and literature to ground it" (125).

10. For a fascinating study of "syncretistic" responses of Jewish converts to Russian Orthodoxy, see Judith Deutsch Kornblatt, *Doubly Chosen: Jewish*

*Identity, the Soviet Intelligentsia, and the Russian Orthodox Church* (Madison: University of Wisconsin Press, 2004). For more on such "Jewish Slavophiles" as Mikhail Gershenzon and Simon Frank, see Brian Horowitz, *The Myth of A. S. Pushkin in Russia's Silver Age: M. O. Gershenzon, Pushkinist* (Evanston, Ill.: Northwestern University Press, 1996); and Inessa Medzhibovskaya, "Dogmatism or Moral Logic? Simon Frank Confronts Tolstoy's Ethical Thought," *Tolstoy Studies Journal* 16 (2004): 18–32, and its continuation in *Tolstoy Studies Journal* 17 (2005): 43–58. In general, it is possible to situate Levinas's sensibility alongside those of Russian and Russian-Jewish "literary philosophers" or philosopher-critics such as Frank, Gershenzon, Soloviev, and Bakhtin.

11. See Victor Terras, *A Karamazov Companion* (Madison: University of Wisconsin Press, 2002), 77–78.

12. This is the opening sentence of Levinas's *Totality and Infinity*, trans. Alphonso Lingis (Pittsburgh: Duquesne University Press, 1961), 21. It is also, of course, part of Ivan Karamazov's challenge to Alyosha in "Rebellion."

13. Pavel Florensky, "Ikonostas," in *Izbrannye trudy po iskusstvu* (Moscow, 1996), first published 1922. See also Steven Cassedy, "Florensky and the Celebration of Matter," in *Russian Religious Thought*, ed. Judith Deutsch Kornblatt and Richard Gustafson (Madison: University of Wisconsin Press, 1996), 95–111; and Caryl Emerson, *An Introduction to Russian Literature* (forthcoming).

14. See, for example, Edith Wyschograd, "The Art in Ethics: Aesthetics, Objectivity, and Alterity in the Philosophy of Emmanuel Levinas," in *Ethics as First Philosophy: The Significance of Emmanuel Levinas for Philosophy, Literature, and Religion*, ed. Adriaan Peperzak (New York: Routledge, 1995); Adam Zachary Newton, *Narrative Ethics* (Cambridge, Mass.: Harvard University Press, 1997); Jill Robbins, *Altered Reading: Levinas and Literature* (Chicago: University of Chicago Press, 1999); and Robert Eaglestone, *Ethical Criticism: Reading After Levinas* (Edinburgh: Edinburgh University Press, 1997). For a partisan overview of some of these and other works, see Adam Newton's long review essay, "Versions of Ethics; or, The SARL of Criticism: Sonority, Arrogation, Letting-Be," *American Literary History* 13, no. 3 (Fall 2001): 603–37.

15. Emmanuel Levinas, "To Love the Torah More Than God," in *Difficult Freedom*, trans. Sean Hand (Baltimore: Johns Hopkins University Press, 1997), 145; Emmanuel Levinas, *Difficile liberté* (Paris: Livre de Poche, 2003), 205–6.

16. Emmanuel Levinas, quoted in Richard Cohen, *Face to Face with Levinas* (Albany, N.Y.: SUNY Press, 1986), 19.

17. The words are the reported deathbed speech of Zosima's brother Markel: ". . . vsiakii iz nas pred vsemi vo vsem vinovat, a ya bolee vsekh." Fyodor Mikhailovich Dostoevsky, *Polnoe sobranie sochinenii v 30-ti tomakh* (Leningrad: Nauka, 1972), 14:262. Fyodor Dostoevsky, *The Brothers Karamazov*, trans. Richard Pevear and Larissa Volokhonsky (New York: Vintage, 1991), 289. Whenever Levinas quotes this line from memory (and not from the Pléiade

edition), his French translation is literal; see Levinas, "Philosophie, justice et amour," in *Entre nous* (Paris: Grasset, 1991), 115: "Nous sommes tous coupables de tout et de tous, et moi plus que tous les autres."

18. For a book-length treatment of Dostoevsky and Levinas, see Jacques Rolland, *Dostoïevski: La question de l'autre* (Lagrasse: Verdier, 1983). See also Alain Toumayan, "'I More Than the Others': Dostoevsky and Levinas," in "Encounters with Levinas," ed. Thomas Trezise, special issue of *Yale French Studies* 104 (2004): 55–66; William Edelglass, "Asymmetry and Normativity: Levinas Reading Dostoyevsky on Desire, Responsibility, and Suffering," in *Analecta Husserliana LXXXV: The Enigma of Good and Evil: The Moral Sentiment in Literature,* ed. A. T. Tymienicka (Dordrecht, Neth.: Springer, 2005), 709–26; Leslie Johnson, "The Face of the Other in *Idiot*," *Slavic Review* 50, no. 4 (Winter 1991): 867–78; and Atterton, "Art, Religion, and Ethics." All of these compellingly link Dostoevsky's saintly characters and his emphasis on suffering to Levinas's ethics, and all suggest that Dostoevsky's novels provide concrete examples of what Levinas's ethics would look like; in my view, however, only a few consider these links critically with respect to either Levinas or Dostoevsky.

19. Emmanuel Levinas, quoted in Tamra Wright, Peter Hughes, and Alison Ainley, "The Paradox of Morality: An Interview with Emmanuel Levinas," in *The Provocation of Levinas: Rethinking the Other,* ed. Robert Bernasconi and David Wood (London: Routledge, 1988), 174.

20. See also Emmanuel Levinas, *Entre Nous: On Thinking-of-the-Other,* trans. M. B. Smith and Barbara Harshav (New York: Columbia University Press, 1998), 105.

21. See L. Rosenblum, "Umor Dostoevskogo," *Voprosy Literatury* 1–2 (1999): 152–53. In his youth Dostoevsky once wrote: "Thought is born in the soul" (letter to Mikhail Mikhailovich, October 31, 1838). Many of the writer's characters also give voice to this notion: "'Great thoughts come not so much from a great mind as from great feeling'— you said that yourself," Trusotsky reminds Velchaninov in "The Eternal Husband." In *Demons,* Stavrogin and Kirillov speak of "feeling an idea," and the hero of *A Raw Youth* talks about "idea-feelings." In fact, as Rosenblum notes, Dostoevsky derided purely "cerebral" thoughts—those that arose from science and reason, even when accompanied by great enthusiasm—as mere "office desk" ideas.

22. Victor Shklovsky, "I. Babel: A Critical Romance," in *Modern Critical Views: Isaac Babel,* ed. Harold Bloom (New York: Chelsea House, 1987), 12.

23. See Bruce Wilshire, *Get 'Em All! Kill 'Em!: Genocide, Terrorism, Righteous Communities* (Lanham, Md.: Lexington Books, 2004), x.

24. See Caryl Emerson, who writes (echoing Bakhtin) that "the poeticality of both epic and lyric is registered primarily by their great simplification in matters of time. . . . With its ability to collapse apparent oppositions into a perfect emotional 'suspension,' a texture that is both spontaneous and highly crafted, intimately singular and universal, the lyric does not need to know everyday time

and its responsibilities—its accretions and corrosions—at all." Emerson, "Prosaics and the Problem of Form," *Slavic and East European Journal* 41, no. 1 (Spring 1997): 19.

25. Clare Cavanagh, "The Forms of the Ordinary: Bakhtin, Prosaics and the Lyric," *Slavic and East European Journal* 41, no. 1 (Spring 1997): 49–50.

26. Notable exceptions are Gerald Bruns, "The Concepts of Art and Poetry in Emmanuel Levinas's Writings," in *The Cambridge Companion to Levinas,* ed. Simon Critchley and Robert Bernasconi (Cambridge: Cambridge University Press, 2002), 206–33; Steve McCaffrey, "The Scandal of Sincerity: Toward a Levinasian Poetics," in *Prior to Meaning: The Protosemantic and Poetics* (Evanston, Ill.: Northwestern University Press, 2001), 204–21; and William Edelglass, "Levinas's Language," in *Analecta Husserliana LXXXV,* 47–62.

## CHAPTER ONE

An earlier version of this chapter appeared as "The End of Consciousness and the Ends of Consciousness: A Reading of Dostoevsky's *The Idiot* and *Demons* after Levinas," *Russian Review* 59, no. 1 (January 2000): 21–37.

1. For more on the face in Dostoevsky, see Konstantin Barsht, "Defining the Face: Observations on Dostoevskii's Creative Processes," in *Russian Literature, Modernism, and the Visual Arts,* ed. C. Kelly and S. Lovell (Cambridge: Cambridge University Press, 2000), 23–57. See also the relevant section in Bruce French's superb book, *Dostoevsky's "Idiot": Dialogue and the Spiritually Good Life* (Evanston, Ill.: Northwestern University Press, 2001), 126–53.

2. Mikhail Bakhtin, *Problems of Dostoevsky's Poetics,* ed. and trans. Caryl Emerson (Minneapolis: University of Minnesota Press, 1989), 77n12. We will return to Bakhtin's distinction between normal and abnormal death in Dostoevsky.

3. We should keep in mind that in this unfinished final reworking of his Dostoevsky book Bakhtin suffered from the same Soviet-era self-censorship— with its attendant apathy—that plagued him all his life. He confided to Sergey Bocharov that the Dostoevsky book "was a product of self-limitation: a phenomenological description of the Dostoevsky novel as an aesthetic object and no more." Sergey Bocharov, "Conversations with Bakhtin," *PMLA* 109, no. 5 (October 1994): 1020.

4. A reference to "the third" occurs twice in Bakhtin. In "The Problem of the Text," he discusses a "higher *superaddressee* (third) . . . (God, absolute truth, the court of dispassionate human conscience, the people, the court of history, science, and so forth)" that is internally posited by the author of an utterance. Mikhail Bakhtin, *Speech Genres and Other Late Essays,* ed. Caryl Emerson and Michael Holquist, trans. Vern W. McGee (Austin: University of Texas Press, 1994), 126. The other instance is found in his "Notes Made in 1970–71," where Bakhtin mentions the "abstract *position of a third party* that is identified with

the 'objective position' as such, with the position of some 'scientific cognition.'" This position applies when I can replace myself as interlocutor with an abstracted aspect of myself—with my role as, say, "chemist" (*Speech Genres*, 143–44).

5. Levinas, quoted in Wright, Hughes, and Ainley, "Paradox of Morality," in *Provocation of Levinas*, 174.

6. Dostoevsky's emphasis. See his "Letter to Sofya Ivanovna" (January 13, 1868): "There is only one positively beautiful person—Christ . . . Of beautiful persons in Christian literature, the most fully realized is Don Quixote; but he is only beautiful because he is at the same time ridiculous . . . Compassion is shown for the beautiful that is ridiculed and does not know its own worth—and so sympathy appears in the readers . . . I have nothing like that, decidedly nothing, and that's why I'm terribly afraid [the novel] will be a positive failure" (Dostoevsky, *Polnoe sobranie sochinenii*, 28, part 2:251).

7. Dostoevsky, *Polnoe sobranie sochinenii*, 8:57; Fyodor Dostoevsky, *The Idiot*, trans. Richard Pevear and Larissa Volokhonsky (New York: Vintage, 2003), 66.

8. Johnson, "The Face of the Other." Inspired by Levinas's ethical philosophy of facing, Johnson appropriately emphasizes the centrality of the visual aspect in Prince Myshkin's goodness. But by equating ethical vision with the apprehension of images and icons and by ignoring what Levinas calls the "appearance of the third face," Johnson does not consider this philosophy in its fullest sense, and in so doing avoids a critical assessment of Myshkin's ethics. Then again, Levinas himself in an interview once praised the "feeble-minded" and "inspired" Myshkin for his "acts of stupid, senseless goodness." I show here how Myshkin's holy foolishness is problematic, precisely in the Levinasian sense. See Levinas, quoted in *Is It Righteous to Be?* ed. Robbins, 90.

9. Johnson, "The Face of the Other," 877.

10. Fyodor Mikhailovich Dostoevsky, *Zapisnye tetradi F. M. Dostoevskogo*, ed. E. N. Konshina (Moscow: Akademia, 1935), 292, 221. Cited in Robert Louis Jackson, *Dostoevsky's Quest for Form: A Study of His Philosophy of Art* (New Haven, Conn.: Yale University Press, 1966), 56.

11. Robin Feuer Miller, *Dostoevsky and "The Idiot"* (Cambridge, Mass.: Harvard University Press, 1981), 105.

12. Mikhail Bakhtin, *Art and Answerability: Early Philosophical Essays*, ed. Michael Holquist and Vadim Liapunov, trans. Vadim Liapunov (Austin: University of Texas Press, 1990), 24 (my emphasis).

13. Jackson, *Dostoevsky's Quest for Form*, 56–57.

14. Johnson, "The Face of the Other," 876.

15. Jackson, *Dostoevsky's Quest for Form*, 52.

16. Emmanuel Levinas, "Reality and Its Shadow," in *The Levinas Reader*, ed. Sean Hand, trans. Alphonso Lingis (Oxford: Blackwell, 1992), 132.

17. Another shocking example of Myshkin's physiological and spiritual evasion is his refusal to accept the testimony of his own eyes, when ambushed

by Rogozhin in the stairwell: "Rogozhin, I don't believe it!" he exclaims, and then has an epileptic fit. Aglaya recognizes this trait when she calls Myshkin a "Knight of Mournful Countenance," a Quixote.

18. Levinas, "Reality and Its Shadow," 132–34 (first set of italics is mine). Levinas indeed seems harsh here. One should consider, however, that he published this piece in 1948, after Heidegger's "poetically man dwells" (Martin Heidegger, *Poetry, Language, Thought* [New York: Harper and Row, 1971], 211–29), and after the Nazi experience of Paul Hindemith—who, even after the war, believed that people "who make music together cannot be enemies, at least not while the music lasts" (Heather Hadlock, "Program Notes," Juilliard String Quartet [Princeton University Concerts, May 11, 1995], 3). What happens when the music ends? Levinas stresses that life at large is not musical, and that therefore righteousness had better not be musical.

19. Emmanuel Levinas, "The Pact (Tractate Sotah 37a–37b)," in *Beyond the Verse*, trans. Gary D. Mole (Bloomington: Indiana University Press, 1994), 85. By this notion, Levinas suggests that since the infinite ethical obligation before the face of the other cannot ever be fulfilled, I am even responsible for the other's responsibility. I am obliged to teach the obligation of response; hence, the other's moral failings are in principle my responsibility.

20. For more on this notion of "the second day," see Caryl Emerson, "Word and Image in Dostoevsky's Worlds: Robert Louis Jackson on Readings That Bakhtin Could Not Do," in *Freedom and Responsibility in Russian Literature: Essays in Honor of Robert Louis Jackson,* ed. Elizabeth Cheresh Allen and Gary Saul Morson (Evanston, Ill.: Northwestern University Press, 1995), 246–306.

21. French, *Dostoevsky's Idiot*, 55.

22. Miller, *Dostoevsky and The Idiot*, 41–42.

23. Luke 8, in Dostoevsky, *Polnoe sobranie sochinenii*, 10:5; Fyodor Dostoevsky, *Demons,* trans. Richard Pevear and Larissa Volokhonsky (New York: Vintage Books, 1994), 3.

24. See Konstantin Mochulsky, *Dostoevsky: His Life and Work,* trans. Michael A. Minihan (Princeton, N.J.: Princeton University Press, 1967), who argues that with the deletion of the "Tikhon" chapter, Dostoevsky's hope that Stavrogin might yet be healed like the demoniac in the second epigraph "was destroyed and only the dark panel of the diptych remained: the picture of hell, of universal ruin, of the raging of the demonic snowstorm . . . [of] Pushkin's verses" (466). For more on the two competing epigraphs in *Demons,* see Val Vinokur, "'All of a Sudden': Dostoevsky's Demonologies of Terror," in *Just Assassins? The Culture of Russian Terrorism,* ed. Anthony Anemone (forthcoming).

25. Harriet Murav, *Holy Foolishness: Dostoevsky's Novels and the Poetics of Cultural Critique* (Stanford, Calif.: Stanford University Press, 1992), 121–22.

26. The inevitable question arises: does it make sense that *The Brothers Karamazov* followed *Demons*? Given that Alyosha Karamazov—a hero who truly listens, learns, and tries his best to make ethical decisions—is a complete

break from both Myshkin and Stavrogin, I would say yes. Alyosha is Myshkin purged of aesthesis, of the very aspect that wholly personifies Stavrogin. (One could even imagine that, with the death of Stavrogin—a kind of goat for Azazel—Myshkin reawakens as Alyosha.)

27. *Seichas* may also be less literally and more idiomatically translated as "just a moment" or "coming." For more on Kirillov's suicide, see Irina Paperno, *Suicide as a Cultural Institution in Dostoevsky's Russia* (Ithaca, N.Y.: Cornell University Press, 1997); and Maurice Blanchot, *The Space of Literature,* trans. Ann Smock (Lincoln: University of Nebraska Press, 1982), 96–102. The eeriness of Kirillov's suicide presages Istvan Szabo's film *Colonel Redl,* where the protagonist is railroaded by code and comrades into shooting himself, and does the deed while violently pacing about his room—a grossly inadequate gesture of anxiety.

28. Bakhtin doesn't quite finish formulating this, instead leaving the following fragment: "Interest in suicides as conscious deaths, as links in a conscious chain where a man finalizes himself from within" ("Toward a Reworking of the Dostoevsky Book," in *PDP,* 296.).

29. Walter Benjamin, "The Storyteller: Reflections on the Works of Nikolai Leskov," in *Illuminations* (New York: Schocken, 1969), 101.

30. See Caryl Emerson, who writes that the "most articulate opponents of Bakhtin today argue that Dostoevsky did indeed believe that 'to kill was to refute,' . . . that interaction within those novelistic worlds . . . takes place between bodies." Caryl Emerson, *The First Hundred Years of Mikhail Bakhtin* (Princeton, N.J.: Princeton University Press, 1997), 146–47.

31. Murav, *Holy Foolishness,* 32.

32. For an account of the circumstances of Dostoevsky's decision about the "Tikhon" chapter, see Joseph Frank, *Dostoevsky: The Miraculous Years, 1865–1871* (Princeton, N.J.: Princeton University Press, 1996), 434.

33. Murav, *Holy Foolishness,* 122.

34. Søren Kierkegaard, *The Concept of Anxiety,* ed. and trans. Reidar Thomte and Albert Anderson (Princeton, N.J.: Princeton University Press, 1980), 130–35.

35. Richard Pevear, foreword to *Demons,* xvii, xxi–xxii.

36. Aaron Steinberg notes that the "flaming enthusiasm with which Dostoevsky advocated Russia's right to possess Constantinople derived ultimately from the fact that the Turkish capital seemed to offer him the key to the 'Holy Land.' . . . The land in which Christ was born had to become thoroughly Russian . . . so that Russia might some day become the land for the return of the Messiah. . . . However, so long as the Jewish people . . . was still alive, Palestine had to be regarded as the 'land of Israel,' and Russia's right and her world-historic mission were once again in doubt." Compare this alongside Stepan Trofimovich's only somewhat ridiculous desire to be a "living reproach" among his neighbors. Aaron Steinberg, "Dostoevsky and the Jews," in *The Jew: Essays from Martin*

*Buber's Journal "Der Jude," 1916–1928,* ed. Arthur A. Cohen (University: University of Alabama Press, 1980), 169. For more on Dostoevsky and Judaism, see chapter 2 of this book.

37. Of course, for Dostoevsky himself, if not his narrator here, "artistic receptivity," by which beauty is accepted without conditions, is in fact linked to the unconditional acceptance of something that many of the author's young intellectual heroes cannot accept—God's world. See Susan McReynolds, "Dostoevsky in Europe: The Political as the Spiritual," *Partisan Review* 69, no. 1 (Winter 2002): 95.

38. Bakhtin, *Art and Answerability,* 107.


CHAPTER TWO

1. Nina Pelikan Straus, "Dostoevsky's Derrida," *Common Knowledge* 6, no. 4 (Fall 2002): 559. An earlier version of this chapter appeared as an article in response to Straus. See Val Vinokurov, "Levinas's Dostoevsky," *Common Knowledge* 9, no. 2 (Spring 2003): 322–44, copyright 2003 by Duke University Press; it is used here with permission of the publisher.

2. It is also possible to connect Levinas to Ivan by linking the former's condemnation of theodicy in "Useless Suffering" to the latter's rejection of any salvation that requires the tears of even one child. See Richard Bernstein, "Evil and the Temptation of Theodicy," in *Cambridge Companion to Levinas,* 257–58. As Bernstein points out, Levinas's ethical response to useless suffering is very different from Ivan's refusal "to accept God's world."

3. The state of the field with respect to Dostoevsky's beliefs is represented by Steven Cassedy's rich and engaging book *Dostoevsky's Religion* (Stanford, Calif.: Stanford University Press, 2005). For an interesting discussion linking the theology of *The Brothers Karamazov* to that of another modern Jewish religious thinker, see Gary Rosenshield, "Mystery and Commandment in *The Brothers Karamazov:* Leo Baeck and Fedor Dostoevsky," *Journal of the American Academy of Religion* 62, no. 2 (Summer 1994): 483–508.

4. The context of this famous midrash is too juicy to omit: the gentile had first approached and offered the same challenge to Hillel's great colleague and rival Shammai, an engineer by profession, who repulsed the proselyte with a builder's rule that was in his hand.

5. Robbins, *Altered Reading,* 149.

6. Emmanuel Levinas, "The Temptation of Temptation," in *Nine Talmudic Readings,* trans. Annette Aronowicz (Bloomington: Indiana University Press, 1994), 33.

7. Ibid.

8. Levinas, "Reality and Its Shadow," 138.

9. Levinas, *Difficult Freedom,* 65.

10. Levinas, "Temptation of Temptation," 33.

11. Robbins, *Altered Reading*, 150.

12. See Steinberg, "Dostoevsky and the Jews"; and Maxim D. Shrayer, "The Jewish Question and *The Brothers Karamazov*," in *A New Word on "The Brothers Karamazov*," ed. Robert Louis Jackson (Evanston, Ill: Northwestern University Press, 2003).

13. Robert Louis Jackson, *Dialogues with Dostoevsky* (Stanford, Calif.: Stanford University Press, 1993), 109.

14. Cohen, *The Jew*, 158.

15. Felix Dreizin, *The Russian Soul and the Jew: Essays in Literary Ethnocriticism* (Lanham, Md.: University Press of America, 1990), 75.

16. Ibid., 83.

17. See ibid., 107: "The writer's image of his father as 'Jewish' may explain the acutely intimate quality of Dostoyevskian anti-Semitism. As a son of a 'Jew,' he could not but himself feel somewhat Jewish ('I cough like a yid'). Such ephemeral Jewishness might have been perceived by Dostoevsky as one of his 'sins,' which demanded constant vigilance and 'cleansing'—in particular, with the aid of vehemently 'Russian' gambling losses, with acts of the most noble and wild generosity, with paranoid projection, and with wild anti-Semitic outbursts."

18. Mochulsky, *Dostoevsky*, 385.

19. Sigmund Freud, "Dostoevsky and Parricide," in *Writings on Art and Literature* (Stanford, Calif.: Stanford University Press, 1997), 249.

20. Edward Wasiolek, introduction to *The Notebooks for "The Brothers Karamazov*," by Fyodor M. Dostoevsky, ed. and trans. Edward Wasiolek (Chicago: University of Chicago Press, 1971), 8.

21. Nadezhda Kashina, *The Aesthetics of Dostoyevsky*, trans. Julius Katser (Moscow: Raduga, 1987), 168.

22. Emmanuel Levinas, quoted in Richard Kearney, *Dialogues with Contemporary Continental Thinkers* (Manchester, U.K.: Manchester University Press, 1984), 60.

23. Wladimir Weidle, *Russia: Absent and Present*, trans. A. Gordon Smith (London: Hollis and Carter, 1952), 146.

24. Marina Kostalevsky, *Dostoevsky and Soloviev: The Art of Integral Vision* (New Haven, Conn.: Yale University Press, 1997), 9.

25. Boris Shragin, *The Challenge of the Spirit*, trans. P. S. Falla (New York: Knopf, 1978), 135.

26. Dostoevsky, *Polnoe sobranie sochinenii*, 25:73; Fyodor Dostoevsky, *The Diary of a Writer*, trans. Boris Brasol (New York: Charles Scribner, 1949), 635. I have adjusted Brasol's translation as I have believed necessary.

27. For a brief history of the fusion of religious and economic anti-Semitism in Russia, see Kirill Postoutenko, "Imaginary Ethnicity: Jews and Russians in Russian Economical Mythology," *American Behavioral Scientist* 45 (2001): 282–95.

28. Vladimir Solovyov, *A Solovyov Anthology*, trans. Natalie Duddington

(New York: Charles Scribner, 1950), 113–15. For excellent discussions of Dostoevsky and Soloviev on the Jewish Question, see Judith Deutsch Kornblatt and Gary Rosenshield, "Vladimir Solovyov: Confronting Dostoevsky on the Jewish and Christian Questions," *Journal of the American Academy of Religion* 68, no. 1 (March 2000): 69–98; and Kornblatt, "Vladimir Solov'ev on Spiritual Nationhood," *Russian Review* 56 (April 1997): 157–77.

29. Karl Barth, *Church Dogmatics,* vol. 4 (Edinburgh: T. and T. Clark, 1961), part 1:671.

30. Ibid., vol. 2, part 2:209, 263–64.

31. Ibid., vol. 4, part 1:671.

32. Dreizin, *Russian Soul and the Jew,* 113.

33. David I. Goldstein, *Dostoevsky and the Jews* (Austin: University of Texas Press, 1981), 129. Gary Rosenshield, on the other hand, points to the utopian section, "But Long Live Brotherhood," that follows "The Jewish Question" in *The Diary of a Writer,* to suggest a "certain duality": "There is part of Dostoevsky that is certainly Judeophobic, but it may, at least occasionally, alternate with another based on love, forgiveness, and mutual understanding. . . . He has vented his spleen and now is ready to entertain the idea of reconciliation." Gary Rosenshield, "Dostoevskii's 'Funeral of the Universal Man' and 'An Isolated Case' and Chekhov's 'Rothschild's Fiddle': The Jewish Question," *Russian Review* 56 (October 1997): 492. I am not fully convinced by this apologia, since Dostoevsky's Judeophobia still inflects his alternative vision of harmony. See also Gary Saul Morson's classic review article, "Dostoevsky's Anti-Semitism and the Critics," *Slavic and East European Journal* 27, no. 3. (Autumn 1983): 302–17.

34. Kostalevsky, *Dostoevsky and Soloviev,* 9.

35. Girard's explanation is that since Dostoevsky "fully understood the negative usefulness of religion as a social prop against anarchy and chaos but was personally unable to believe, his was the mood . . . which makes reactionary politics a real temptation." René Girard, *Resurrection from the Underground: Feodor Dostoevsky,* trans. James G. Williams (New York: Crossroad, 1997), 162–63. James Rice argues persuasively, however, that Dostoevsky never gave up the radical politics of his youth, and that his reactionary outbursts were a smokescreen for a profoundly pessimistic view of the very possibility of "the Russian idea." See James Rice, "Dostoevsky's Endgame: The Projected Sequel to *The Brothers Karamazov,*" *Russian History/Histoire Russe* 33, no. 1 (Spring 2006): 45–62.

36. Vladimir Soloviev, cited in Kostalevsky, *Dostoevsky and Soloviev,* 144.

37. Wasiolek observes that the Grand Inquisitor in the notes for *The Brothers Karamazov* is much more blunt about his doubts concerning "true theocracy": "The aggression against Christ in the final version is muted, but in the notes . . . [the Grand Inquisitor states]: '. . . you have been disgorged from hell and are a heretic, and the very people who fell down before you will rake up the coals tomorrow. . . . They sing of you as Alone without sin, but I say to you

that you alone are guilty.' Finally, Alyosha makes the point in the final version that the Grand Inquisitor does not believe in God, but in the notes Dostoevsky emphasizes the fact that there is no immortality and that 'those who suffer his cross will not find anything that had been promised exactly as he himself had not found anything after the cross.' There seems to be little doubt that some of these statements were eliminated or changed because of their shocking anti-Orthodox and anti-Christian character" (Wasiolek, *Notebooks for "The Brothers Karamazov,"* 17).

38. See Leora Batnitzky, "The Image of Judaism: German-Jewish Intellectuals and the Ban on Images" (paper presented at the conference "Icon, Image, and Text in Modern Jewish Culture," Princeton, N.J., March 7, 1999).

39. Franz Rosenzweig, *The Star of Redemption*, trans. William W. Hallo (Boston: Beacon, 1972), 413.

40. Literally, "an unconditional handing-over of oneself to (the other's) power." Yuri M. Lotman, "'Agreement' and 'Self-Giving' as Archetypal Models of Culture," trans. N. F. C. Owen, in *The Semiotics of Russian Culture*, by Yuri M. Lotman and Boris A. Uspenskij, ed. Ann Shukman (Ann Arbor: Department of Slavic Languages and Literatures, University of Michigan Press, 1984), 125—a somewhat flawed translation. The Russian original may be found in Yuri M. Lotman, *Izbrannye stat'i v trekh tomakh* (Tallinn, Estonia: Aleksandra, 1992–93), 3:345–55.

41. It is also significant that Dostoevsky saves most of his best lines for the morally questionable characters. In his novels, evil is usually eloquent, verbal; and goodness is generally clumsy, overbearing, mawkish, or—at its most effective—mute, visual, and iconic (that is, image-bound).

42. Yeshayahu Leibowitz, *Judaism, Human Values, and the Jewish State*, ed. Eliezer Goldman (Cambridge, Mass.: Harvard University Press, 1992), 109.

43. Baba Metsia 59a–59b.

44. Fyodor M. Dostoevsky, *Biografija, pisma i zametki iz zapisnoi knizhki F. M. Dostoyevskovo*, ed. Orest Miller and Nikolai Strakhov (St. Petersburg, 1883), 372; cited in Jackson, *Dostoevsky's Quest for Form*, 44.

45. Girard, *Resurrection from the Underground*, 152.

46. Emmanuel Levinas, "Useless Suffering," in *Provocation of Levinas*, ed. Bernasconi and Wood, 166n5. Some of the analysis that follows first appeared in my essay "'On the Brink of Tears and Laughter': The Uses of Joy and Suffering in Levinas's Thought," *Journal of Religion and Society* 6 (2004), 1-8. Available at http://moses.creighton.edu/jrs/pdf/2004-12.pdf.

47. Rolland, *Dostoïevski*, 88.

48. Levinas, *Basic Philosophical Writings*, 89.

49. See Emmanuel Levinas, "Signification and Sense," in *Humanism of the Other*, trans. Nidra Poller (Urbana: University of Illinois Press, 2003), 30. In Dostoevsky, see *Polnoe sobranie sochinenii*, 6:243; Fyodor Dostoevsky, *Crime and Punishment*, trans. Richard Pevear and Larissa Volokhonsky (New York:

Vintage, 1993), 318 (Dostoevsky's italics). For more on Levinas and Sonya Marmeladova, see Atterton, "Art, Religion, and Ethics," 127–29; Edelglass, "Asymmetry and Normativity," 712–16, 724; and Rolland, *Dostoïevski*, 55–66.

50. See Matthew 16:21–23: "Jesus began to explain to his disciples that he must go to Jerusalem and suffer . . . and that he must be killed and on the third day be raised to life. Peter took him aside and began to rebuke him. 'Never, Lord!' he said. 'This shall never happen to you!' Jesus turned and said to Peter, 'Get behind me, Satan! You are a stumbling block [*skandalon*] to me; you do not have in mind the things of God, but the things of men.'" For more on the diabolical forces in Dostoevsky's novel, see Linda Ivanits, "Folk Beliefs About the 'Unclean Force' in Dostoevskij's *The Brothers Karamazov*," in *New Perspectives on Nineteenth-Century Russian Prose,* ed. George Gutsche and L. Leighton (Columbus, Ohio: Slavica, 1982), 135–46. For more on the ethical significance of Ivan's devil, see Val Vinokur, "Facing the Devil in Dostoevsky's *The Brothers Karamazov*," in "Word, Music, History: A Festschrift for Caryl Emerson," ed. Lazar Fleishman, Gabriella Safran, and Michael Wachtel, special issue of *Stanford Slavic Studies* 29–30, part 2 (2005): 464–76.

The objection may be raised that the existence of God is not the real issue for Ivan, who claims in his anti-theodicy ("Rebellion") that it is not God "but his world" that he rejects. However, one suspects that it is not just Ivan's devil but Ivan, the principled egoist himself, who would like nothing better than to light a candle in church like "some fat, 250-pound merchant's wife" (Dostoevsky, *Polnoe sobranie sochinenii*, 15:74; Dostoevsky, *Brothers Karamazov*, 639). One also suspects that his rebellious and seemingly all-consuming love for humanity (for the children especially) is largely a snare for Alyosha, his young interlocutor in "Rebellion," whom he does not want to "give up" to Elder Zosima, for "perhaps I want to be healed by you" (ibid.: 14:215; 236). Again, Ivan is expressing his own desire for salvation; and he would torment and strain Alyosha's faith just to keep him at hand in case Ivan happens to be ready to resolve his own struggle "in a positive way" (14:65; 70).

51. *EI*, 98–99.

52. Levinas, quoted in Kearney, *Contemporary Continental Thinkers*, 67.

53. Kostalevsky, *Dostoevsky and Soloviev*, 170.

54. Levinas, "Judaism and Revolution," in *Nine Talmudic Readings*, 94–119, first published in 1968. To be sure, Levinas isn't exactly passionate about such liberal capitalism. It is possible to argue that for Levinas, Marxism represents an attempt at an ethics without a workable (that is, either practical or ethical) system of justice. Speaking of the Jewish Bund, Levinas notes that Marxism "represented a devotion to the other man. It wanted to save all men, not abandon them. Although Stalinism has compromised all of this" (Levinas, quoted in *Is It Righteous to Be?* ed. Robbins, 88). As Susan Sontag has suggested, fascism is inspired by the aesthetic utopia of physical perfection, while communism is inspired by "utopian morality." See Sontag, "Fascinating Fascism," in *Under the*

*Sign of Saturn* (New York: Picador, 2002), 92. Needless to say, the procrustean tendencies of any utopian project would render it unethical.

55. Michael Holquist, *Dostoevsky and the Novel* (Princeton, N.J.: Princeton University Press, 1977), 187.

56. As Bruce K. Ward notes, Alyosha "is intended not only to embody the 'positively good,' but to embody it in a way which speaks effectively to the modern world. This 'new type of man' who will 'live in the world like a monk' resembles to some extent a 'saintly fool,' but his saintliness is characterized by health rather than sickness, by practical intelligence, rather than fanaticism, and above all by the impulse towards truth rather than towards mystification." Bruce K. Ward, "The Absent Finger of Providence in *The Brothers Karamazov:* Some Implications for Religious Models," in *And Meaning for a Life Entire: Festschrift for Charles A. Moser on the Occasion of His Sixtieth Birthday*, ed. Peter Rollberg (Bloomington, Ind.: Slavica, 1997), 149. See also Terras, *Karamazov Companion*, 78.

57. Levinas, *Basic Philosophical Writings*, 168. One may detect the ironic echo of two famous titles (and catchphrases) from the history of Russian radicalism: Herzen's novel *Who Is to Blame?* and Chernyshevsky's and Lenin's books *What Is to Be Done?* The crucial Levinasian twist, of course, is the stress on "my" and not a disembodied, general call for justice.

58. Emmanuel Levinas, *Time and the Other*, trans. Richard A. Cohen (Pittsburgh: Duquesne University Press, 1987), 90–91.

59. James Rice cites striking evidence in the novel and in the biographical record that suggests that the unwritten sequel "will tell a story of rebellion and revolutionary violence," and that the "novelist's rhetorical strategy [is] a kind of ethical sleight of hand half-concealing evil with good" (Rice, "Dostoevsky's Endgame: The Projected Sequel to *The Brothers Karamazov*," *Russian History/ Histoire Russe* 33, no. 1 [Spring 2006], 61). But I am uncertain how to consider the evidence for a counterfactual "possible"—or even "probable"—sequel. After all, Dostoevsky's novels attain greatness partly in the ways they depart from his initial projections. See also Robert Belknap, *The Structure of "The Brothers Karamazov"* (Evanston, Ill.: Northwestern University Press, 1989), 98–104. Belknap's case for the projected sequel's status as a literary device rests on the fact that Dostoevsky did no work on it after sending in the last installment of *The Brothers Karamazov;* that the fictional "author" makes almost the same remark about incompleteness at the end of *Crime and Punishment* as he makes at the beginning of *The Brothers Karamazov;* and that Dostoevsky may have been inspired by the Romantics' use of incompleteness as a "roughening device [. . . that] disturbs the impact of the existing novel and suggests a grand scheme."

60. Rolland, *Dostoïevski*, 83; Toumayan, "'I More Than the Others,'" 58.

61. Somewhat like Kafka's ape Rotpeter in "Report to the Academy." The gesture also brings to mind the crafty moaning of the Underground Man with his toothache.

62. Gary Saul Morson, *Narrative and Freedom* (New Haven, Conn.: Yale University Press, 1994), 142.

63. George R. Clay, *Tolstoy's Phoenix: From Method to Meaning in "War and Peace"* (Evanston, Ill.: Northwestern University Press, 1998), 32.

64. The precise role of affect is an underappreciated key to Levinas's ethics: "One has to first enjoy one's bread, not in order to have the merit of giving it, but in order to give it with one's heart, to give oneself in giving it." Emmanuel Levinas, *Otherwise Than Being, or Beyond Essence,* trans. Alphonso Lingis (Boston: Martinus Nijhoff, 1981), 72. See also Vinokur, "'On the Brink of Tears and Laughter.'"

65. For a discussion of the resurgence of "ethics and literature" partly as a response to the de Man scandal and to the apparent relativism of multicultural-ism and the "formalism" of deconstruction, see Michael Eskin, "Introduction: The Double 'Turn' to Ethics and Literature?" *Poetics Today* 25, no. 4 (Winter 2004): 557–72.

66. Levinas, *Difficult Freedom,* 218. For a lucid critique of Levinas's Zionism, see Batnitzky, *Strauss and Levinas,* 151–62. The dangers that attend any ambition to see Israel as an opportunity to enact a Judaic utopia are obvi-ous. Only political Zionism, in its full ideological spectrum, can pragmatically address the historical and moral reasons and realities of Israel's founding and of its troubled (and, to many, troubling) existence.

67. Vasily Grossman, *Life and Fate,* trans. Robert Chandler (New York: New York Review Books, 1985), 805–6.

68. *Is It Righteous to Be?* ed. Robbins, 89–90. For more on Levinas and Grossman, see Michael Morgan, *Discovering Levinas* (Cambridge: Cambridge University Press, 2007).

## CHAPTER THREE

Parts of this chapter have appeared in an earlier version in Val Vinokur, "Morality and Orality in Isaac Babel's *Red Cavalry,*" *Massachusetts Review* 45, no. 4 (Winter 2005): 674–95. I presented another section of this chapter as a conference paper, "Isaac Babel's Ethics of Defilement," at the American Comparative Literature Association's annual convention (Princeton, N.J., April 2006).

1. While James Falen repeatedly (and often too readily) labels aspects of Babel's fiction as "Dostoevskian," the best comparative treatment of the two authors may be found in Alexander Zholkovsky, "A Memo from the Underground (Babel and Dostoevsky)," *Elementa* 1 (1994): 305–20. See also James E. Falen, *Isaac Babel: Russian Master of the Short Story* (Knoxville: University of Ten-nessee Press, 1974), 133–34, 147, 189.

2. Isaac E. Babel, *Sobranie sochinenii v chetyrekh tomakh* (Moscow: Vremia, 2006), 1:46. Translations are mine unless otherwise noted.

3. See Emmanuel Levinas, "Reality and Its Shadow," in *Collected Philosophical Papers*, trans. Alphonso Lingis (Boston: Martinus Nijhoff, 1987), 10: "This plastic issue of the literary work was noted by Proust in a particularly admirable page of *The Prisoner.* In speaking of Dostoevsky, what holds his attention is neither Dostoevsky's religious ideas, his metaphysics, nor his psychology, but some profiles of girls, a few images: the house of the crime with its stairway and its *dvornik* in *Crime and Punishment,* Grushenka's figure in *The Brothers Karamazov.* It is as though we are to think that the plastic element of reality is, in the end, the goal of the psychological novel." Interestingly, Babel—in his charming, affected naïveté—repeats Proust's aesthetic reduction and then chides the ethics of this "plastic element" of Dostoevsky's fiction: a somewhat farcical version of Wittgenstein's "ethics and aesthetics are one and the same."

4. See Hannah Arendt, *The Jew as Pariah: Jewish Identity and Politics in the Modern Age* (New York: Grove, 1978).

5. I am grateful to Janneke van de Stadt for graciously showing me part of the manuscript for her excellent book, *Fellow Traveler, Wondering Jew: Isaac Babel and the Writer's Path* (forthcoming).

6. Lionel Trilling's well-known phrase from his introduction to *The Collected Stories,* by Isaac Babel, trans. Walter Morrison (New York: Meridian Fiction, 1955), 17.

7. Ibid.

8. Bruns, "Concepts of Art and Poetry," 229.

9. Babel weathered Budenny's attack thanks to the intervention of Maxim Gorky. The full record of the Budenny-Gorky exchange may be found in part 4 of *Isaac Babel's Selected Writings,* trans. Peter Constantine, ed. Gregory Freidin (New York: Norton, 2007).

10. Judith Deutsch Kornblatt, *The Cossack Hero in Russian Literature* (Madison: University of Wisconsin Press, 1992), 112.

11. Lee Siegel, "The Tower of Babel," *The Nation,* December 5, 2005, 56.

12. Trilling, introduction to *Collected Stories,* by Babel, 9–10.

13. For a succinct overview of the theoretical issues that revolve around metaphor and metonymy, see Wallace Martin, "Metaphor," in *The New Princeton Encyclopedia of Poetry and Poetics,* ed. Alex Preminger and T. V. F. Brogan (Princeton, N.J.: Princeton University Press, 1993), 784.

14. See Elif Batuman, "Babel in California," *n+1* no. 2 (Spring 2005): 28–29.

15. I am grateful to Melissa Frazier for calling my attention to this challenge. David Danow makes a similar point in "The Paradox of *Red Cavalry,*" in "Centenary of Isaak Babel," special issue of *Canadian Slavonic Papers* 36, no.1–2 (March–June 1994): 43–54.

16. Nadezhda Mandelstam, *Hope Against Hope,* trans. Max Hayward (New York: Atheneum, 1970), 321.

17. See Gregory Freidin, "Isaac Babel," in *European Writers: The Twentieth Century,* ed. George Stade (New York: Charles Scribner's Sons, 1990), 1896.

Babel's better known "autobiographical stories" such as "Story of My Dovecot" and "Awakening" were, by his own admission, hardly autobiographical, but according to his second wife, he used this framework because "that way, the stories could be shorter. You don't have to describe the narrator" (Babel, *Sobranie sochinenii,* 4:454). See Antonina Pirozhkova's wonderful memoir, "Years at His Side (1932–1939) and Beyond," trans. Anne Frydman, in "Centenary of Isaak Babel," 205.

18. Isaac Babel, *You Must Know Everything,* ed. Nathalie Babel, trans. M. Hayward (New York: Dell, 1970), 11–12.

19. See Trilling, who writes of Babel's "defenseless commitment of himself" to the "moral issue that lies beneath the brilliant surface of his stories." Trilling, introduction to *Collected Stories,* by Babel, 17.

20. Alexander Zholkovsky, "Towards a Typology of 'Debut' Narratives: Babel, Nabokov and Others" (paper given at the conference on "The Enigma of Isaac Babel," Stanford University, Stanford, Calif., February 29–March 2, 2004). Available at www.usc.edu/dept/las/sll/eng/ess/babnab1.htm.

21. Zholkovsky, "Memo from the Underground," 313.

22. Ibid, 317.

23. According to Pirozhkova, Babel attributed this plot to the journalist P. I. Staritsyn, who had "gone to a prostitute, gotten undressed, and, glimpsing himself in the mirror, he saw that he resembled 'an overwrought pink swine.' Disgusted, he quickly dressed, told the woman he was a boy with the Armenians, and left. Sometime later he was on a tram when he saw this woman at a stop along the way . . . She called out to him: 'Greetings, little sister'" (Babel, *Sobranie sochinenii,* 4:454). Assuming Babel did not fabricate this source, it is interesting that in "First Fee" the narrator—unlike Staritsyn—seems disgusted by the prostitute and her rooms, not by himself. This means that the hero's invented childhood was more for her sake than his.

24. Zholkovsky, "Memo from the Underground," 318.

25. Ibid, 317.

26. Interestingly, the overly cautious bar owner is "blinded by flabbiness" (Babel, *Sobranie sochinenii,* 1:217)—words that also describe Vera's body before the hero's tale. Vera, whatever her other virtues and talents, is not a language artist, and thus cannot transform her friend's blind flabbiness into clear-eyed vitality as the young narrator transforms Vera.

27. See Levinas, *Otherwise Than Being,* 67–76. See also Claire Elise Katz, *Levinas, Judaism, and the Feminine: The Silent Footsteps of Rebecca* (Bloomington: Indiana University Press, 2003); and Robert Gibbs, "Book Review: The Silent Footsteps of Rebecca," *Continental Philosophy Review* 37, no. 3 (July 2004): 371–75.

28. Falen, *Isaac Babel,* 185–87.

29. *Deborah* is the Hebrew word for "bee," which, in Apolek's tale, is the metaphor that stings Jesus with sorrow after he lies with the aptly named

bride—even though, according to a Cossack legend recounted in "The Road to Brody," the bee was the only insect that did not sting Christ as he died on the cross. In Judges, Deborah's name likewise seems appropriate, given the (somewhat hilarious) way she goads the prevaricating Barak: "Hath not the LORD God of Israel commanded, saying, Go and draw toward Mount Tabor, and take with thee ten thousand men . . . ? . . . And Barak said unto her, If thou wilt go with me, then I will go: but if thou wilt not go with me, then I will not go. And she said, I will surely go with thee: notwithstanding the journey that thou takest shall not be for thine honor; for the LORD shall sell Sisera into the hand of a woman [that is, Yael]. . . . Up, [Barak,] for this is the day in which the LORD hath delivered Sisera into thine hand: is not the LORD gone out before thee?" (Judges 4:6–14).

30. See Avivah Zornberg's wonderful discussion of Judah and Tamar in *Genesis: The Beginning of Desire* (New York: Doubleday, 1996), 243–83.

31. An allusion to Rebbe Nachman of Bratslav, well known for his proto-Kafkaesque parables, and whose successor was never named—somewhat anomalous for a Hassidic sect, which typically revolves around a living, charismatic rebbe. Babel himself was raised in a modern Orthodox milieu that would have been hostile to Hassidism. For more on Babel and Hassidism, see M. P. Odesskii and D. M. Fel'dman, who argue, perhaps a bit tendentiously, that Babel came to associate the eschatological passion of Hassidism with the revolutionary violence of the Red Cossacks. Odesskii and Fel'dman, "Reinterpreting *Red Cavalry* in the Light of Chassidism (Justifying the Revolution)," in "Centenary of Isaak Babel," 148–54.

32. See Gabriella Safran, *Rewriting the Jew: Assimilation Narratives in the Russian Empire* (Stanford, Calif.: Stanford University Press, 2000).

33. Stephen Schwarzschild, "Aesthetics," in *Contemporary Jewish Religious Thought*, ed. A. Cohen and P. Mendes-Flohr (New York: Scribner, 1987), 1–6.

34. For a fascinating reading of the "strange" Jewish dialogue in such stories as "The Rebbe," see Sasha Senderovich, "The Hershele Maze: Isaac Babel and His Ghost Reader," in *Arguing the Modern Jewish Canon: Essays on Modern Jewish Literature in Honor of Ruth Wisse*, ed. Justin D. Cammy and others (Cambridge, Mass.: Harvard University Press, 2007).

35. This concern is implicit even when someone like Gogol, in his Ukrainian stories, seems to employ *skaz* largely in an effort to entertain the literate at the expense of the illiterate.

36. For Hugh McLean this sort of narration is a variant of "'pseudo-*skaz*,' in which the narrator . . . is himself not a genuine character, but an impersonal mechanism for restricting the point of view." McLean, "On the Style of a Leskovian *Skaz*," in *Harvard Slavic Studies* (Cambridge, Mass.: Harvard University Press, 1954), 2:300.

37. Nikolai S. Leskov, *Povesti i rasskazy* (Moscow: Russkii Yazyk, 1985), 38.

See also Nikolai Leskov, *Selected Tales*, trans. David Magarshack (New York: Noonday, 1961), 27. I have adjusted Magarshack's generally fine translation.

38. Leskov, *Povesti i rasskazy*, 24; Leskov, *Selected Tales*, 11.

39. Caryl Emerson, "Back to the Future: Shostakovich's Revision of Leskov's 'Lady Macbeth of Mtsensk District,'" *Cambridge Opera Journal* 1, no. 1 (March 1989): 68.

40. N. Stepanov, "Novella Babelja," in *Mastera sovremmenoj literatury* (1928), 14, cited in Ragna Grøngaard, *An Investigation of Composition and Theme in Isaak Babel's Literary Cycle KONARMIJA* (Aarhus, Den.: Arkona, 1979), 37. Victor Terras has noted that Babel's lyrical prose bears striking similarities to Osip Mandelstam's modernist verse. Terras, "Line and Color: The Structure of Babel's Short Stories," in *Red Cavalry: A Critical Companion,* ed. Charles Rougle (Evanston, Ill.: Northwestern University Press, 1996), 132.

41. Efraim Sicher, *Style and Structure in the Prose of Isaak Babel* (Columbus, Ohio: Slavica, 1986), 77–78.

42. The malapropos "unconsciousness" that Balmashev attributes to the "women who are harmful to [the cause]" (Babel, *Sobranie sochinenii*, 2:123) is really characteristic of him.

43. Boris Eichenbaum, "Illutsiya skaza (1918)," in *Skvoz' literaturu* (The Hague, Neth.: Mouton, 1962), 152–56.

44. Sicher underscores the fact that "Babel's stylization [conveys] colloquial language effectively and in an intelligible form to the standard Russian reader" and that it is neither a "reproduction of incomprehensibility . . . [nor an] ornamentalist play on linguistic deviancy" common in the *skaz* of the 1920s (Sicher, *Style and Structure*, 78–79).

45. Carol Luplow, *Isaac Babel's "Red Cavalry"* (Ann Arbor, Mich.: Ardis, 1982), 88.

46. Marc Schreurs, *Procedures of Montage in Isaak Babel's "Red Cavalry"* (Atlanta: Rodopi, 1989), 41.

47. See Terras, "Line and Color," 123–24: "The uneducated or semiliterate narrator finds it difficult to get to the point of his tale as he wades through a morass of irrelevant trivialities; when he finally does get there, it is awkwardly off balance, and as if by accident. The murders in 'Salt' and in 'A Letter' seem just to happen, anticlimactically almost . . . The entire narrative in these stories is characterized by what one might call 'wrong accents'—stylistically, structurally, and emotionally."

48. These structures, though certainly reflective of Babel's predilection for such voicings throughout his authorial narratives, are perhaps only quantitatively different from "prototypical" *skaz*—in which the illiterate narrator's sole points of literary reference are in fact the Bible and legend.

49. This is especially striking compared to Babel's aesthetic intrusions in the *skaz* of the relatively mild-mannered Konkin—the only narrator here who

bears some affinity to the author: Commissar Konkin is a "musical entertainer and drawing-room ventriloquist," an artist of sorts.

50. Inessa Medzhibovskaya, "'Creating a Life for Language': The Emancipatory Rejoinder of *Skaz*" (forthcoming), 15.

51. Isaac Babel, *1920 Diary*, trans. H. T. Willetts, ed. Carol Avins (New Haven, Conn.: Yale University Press, 1995), 69–76. I have adjusted the translation.

52. McLean, "Leskovian *Skaz*," 299 (italics in original).

53. Hugh McLean, quoted in *Handbook of Russian Literature*, ed. Victor Terras (New Haven, Conn.: Yale University Press, 1985), 420.

54. Ibid.

55. Richard Rorty, "The Barber of Kasbeam: Nabokov on Cruelty," in *Contingency, Irony, and Solidarity* (Cambridge: Cambridge University Press, 1995), 166–67.

56. Ibid., 168.

57. Matvei Rodionych Pavlichenko was based on Iosif Rodionych Apanasenko, who is described unsympathetically throughout the *1920 Diary;* understandably, Babel could not resist retaining the Dostoevskyan patronymic.

58. Batuman, "Babel in California," 32

59. Grøngaard, *Investigation of Composition and Theme*, 53.

60. Paul Zumthor, *Oral Poetry: An Introduction* (Minneapolis: University of Minnesota Press, 1990), 9.

61. Walter Ong, introduction to *Oral Poetry*, by Paul Zumthor, xi.

62. Rorty, "Barber of Kasbeam," 163.

63. Levinas, "Reality and Its Shadow," in *Levinas Reader*, 132–33.

64. Jill Robbins, "Aesthetic Totality and Ethical Infinity: Levinas on Art," *L'Esprit Créateur* 35, no. 3 (Fall 1995): 75.

65. Rorty, "Barber of Kasbeam," 164.

66. Newton, *Narrative Ethics*, 7.

67. Guy de Maupassant, "L'Aveu," in *Contes du jour et de la nuit* (Boston: Adamant, 2006), 31.

68. "L'Aveu" is also recounted and even further embellished in Babel's "Guy de Maupassant." Here, too, Babel rewrites Maupassant's story into something far more pastoral and romantic, inventing details about how the "sun's direct rays and wine and apple-cider burnished the coachman's mug" (Babel, *Sobranie sochinenii*, 1:231). See Alexander Zholkovsky, "Isaak Babel, Author of Guy de Maupassant," in "Centenary of Isaak Babel," 85–105.

69. Babel's fixation with perspiration is remarkable: Christ sweats in "Pan Apolek," as do the narrator and the samovar in "My First Fee." Pirozhkova recalls that Babel told her that in the days when people used to drink tea properly, they would take it strong and boiling hot, cup after cup, until it "beaded on the stomach" (Pirozhkova, in *Sobranie sochinenii* 4:433). For Babel sweat seems to be a metaphor for the way we absorb the world (morally and bodily) until we physically exude it.

70. For example, when the NKVD arrested the legendary party leader of Kabardino-Balkariya, Betal Kalmykov, "Babel's cycle of tales about Kabardino-Balkariya remained unwritten" (Pirozhkova, in *Sobranie sochinenii* 4:395, 183). It seems something similar happened after Beria did away with the Abkhazian leader Nestor Lakoba and his kin.

71. This formulation is based on a description for three seminars at the American Comparative Literature Association's annual convention, on "Imagining Our Others," co-organized by Ann Jurecic, Anne Caswell Klein, Amanda Irwin Wilkins, Cole Bentley, and Val Vinokur (Princeton, N.J., April 2006).

## CHAPTER FOUR

1. Like Dostoevsky and Levinas, Mandelstam's family—from Courland, Warsaw, and the Baltics—also had roots in the Polish-Lithuanian border regions.

2. For more on Mandelstam's conversion, see Michael Stanislawski, *Autobiographical Jews: Essays in Jewish Self-Fashioning* (Seattle: University of Washington Press, 2004), 86–88.

3. Marina Tsvetaeva's 1924 "Poem of the End" provides the oft-cited gloss on the *poète maudit* (*à la russe*): "In this most Christian of worlds, the poets are the yids."

4. Clare Cavanagh, *Osip Mandelstam and the Modernist Creation of Tradition* (Princeton, N.J.: Princeton University Press, 1995), 207.

5. Nancy Pollak, *Mandelstam the Reader* (Baltimore: Johns Hopkins University Press, 1995), 3.

6. Robert Alter quoted in Pollak, *Mandelstam the Reader,* 3.

7. Pollak, *Mandelstam the Reader,* 3.

8. Efraim Sicher, *Jews in Russian Literature After the October Revolution: Writers and Artists Between Hope and Apostasy* (Cambridge: Cambridge University Press, 1995), 136.

9. Mikhail Epstein, "Judaic Spiritual Traditions in the Poetry of Pasternak and Mandel'shtam," trans. Ruth Rischin, *Symposium: A Quarterly Journal in Modern Literatures* 52, no. 4 (Winter 1999): 205–31. In Epstein's scheme, Pasternak, with his southern Jewish origins and ecstatic verse, becomes the Hassid to Mandelstam's Litvak. It must be said, however, that Hassidic tzaddiks were often gifted scholars, just as Lithuanian yeshiva deans could be charismatic figures.

10. Leonid Katsis, *Osip Mandel'shtam: Muksus iudeistva* [The Musk of Judaism] (Jerusalem: Gesharim; Moscow: Mosty Kul'tury, 2002), 585. My translation.

11. Katsis, *Osip Mandel'shtam,* 13.

12. Schwarzschild, "Aesthetics," 5–6. See also Schwarzschild's "The Legal Foundation of Jewish Aesthetics," in *The Pursuit of the Ideal: Jewish Writings*

*of Steven Schwarzschild,* ed. M. Kellner (Albany, N.Y.: SUNY Press, 1990), 109–16. For a discussion of Russian Jewish modernism in art and literature, see Sicher, "Modernist Responses to War and Revolution: The Jewish Jesus," chapter 2 in *Jews in Russian Literature,* 40–70.

13. One should note that Mandelstam's poetry and poetics are often at odds with one another, something fairly common among poet-critics.

14. Michael Eskin has suggested a connection between Mandelstam and Levinas via Paul Celan, who translated many of Mandelstam's poems into German and who greatly influenced Levinas. I explore this three-way link later in the chapter. See Eskin's *Ethics and Dialogue in the Works of Levinas, Bakhtin, Mandel'shtam, and Celan* (Oxford: Oxford University Press, 2000); and his "Translating the Other: Celan's Encounter with Mandelstam," *Germano-Slavica* 11 (1999): 27–38.

15. Mark Edmundson, *Literature Against Philosophy, Plato to Derrida: A Defence of Poetry* (Cambridge: Cambridge University Press, 1995), 4.

16. Jill Robbins, *Altered Reading,* 52–53.

17. Levinas, "Reality and Its Shadow," in *Levinas Reader,* 141.

18. Ibid., 143.

19. Gregory Freidin, *A Coat of Many Colors: Osip Mandelstam and His Mythologies of Self-Presentation* (Berkeley: University of California Press, 1987), 14

20. Ibid., 33.

21. Osip Mandelstam, "On the Addressee," in *Critical Prose and Letters,* trans. J. G. Harris and C. Link (Ann Arbor, Mich.: Ardis, 1990), 69. See Osip Mandelstam, *Sochinenia v dvukh tomakh,* ed. Averintsev, Nerler, and Mikhailov, 2 vols. (Moscow: Khudozhestvennaya Literatura, 1990), 2:147. See also Osip Mandelstam, *Sobranie sochinenii v chetyrekh tomakh,* ed. Nerler, Nikitaev, and Sergeeva (Moscow: Art-Biznis-Tsentr, 1993). Russian citations of Mandelstam in this chapter are taken from the more readily available edition, *Sochinenia v dvukh tomakh.*

22. This is, of course, a very ancient stance: Socrates' and Plato's condemnation of poetry as feminizing, irrational, and paradoxically both impotent and potently dangerous. For another contemporary response to this position, see Elaine Scarry's *On Beauty and Being Just* (Princeton, N.J.: Princeton University Press, 1999). Edmundson, however, also praises critical muscle: "Strong analytical critique can revise our valuations of art in bracing, salutory ways, provided that someone is willing to respond to the disenfranchising theory when response is tenable" (*Literature Against Philosophy,* 15).

23. Edmundson, *Literature Against Philosophy,* 1, 15.

24. See Jean Greisch, "The Face and Reading," trans. Simon Critchley, in *Re-Reading Levinas,* ed. Robert Bernasconi and Simon Critchley (Bloomington: Indiana University Press, 1991), 78. Greisch notes that in Levinas, "as in Hegel, skepticism is not a philosophical trend relevant to the history of ideas;

it is an internal moment of philosophical comprehension itself. But the Levinasian rehabilitation of skepticism follows very different paths from those of the Hegelian dialectic. Skepticism cannot be eliminated, because 'language is already skepticism' [Levinas, *Otherwise Than Being*, 170]. Wanting to get rid of it once and for all—which indeed a certain type of philosophy has always sought to do—would mean wanting to get rid of transcendence itself." See also Simon Critchley, *The Ethics of Deconstruction: Derrida and Levinas* (Cambridge: Blackwell, 1992), 156–68.

25. Emmanuel Levinas, "Language and Proximity," in *Collected Philosophical Papers,* 119.

26. Levinas, quoted in Wright, Hughes, and Ainley, "Paradox of Morality," in *Provocation of Levinas,* 176.

27. See Inessa Medzhibovskaya, "Frank Confronts Tolstoy's Ethical Thought (the Later Years)," *Tolstoy Studies Journal* 27 (2005): 52 and 55: "Vicious circles of the type A = A occur when man accords exhaustive meaning to only one instance (his or others') of knowing All. . . . There is no logical substitute for moral knowledge." Such moral knowledge can only come from the specificity and self-corrections of life and art.

28. Bruns, "Concepts of Art and Poetry," 229.

29. Catherine Zuckert, *Postmodern Platos* (Chicago: University of Chicago Press, 1996), 136–37; cited in Batnitzky, *Strauss and Levinas,* 170.

30. Leo Strauss, *Natural Right and History* (Chicago: University of Chicago Press, 1952), 113; cited in Batnitzky, *Strauss and Levinas,* 171.

31. Martin Heidegger, *Existence and Being,* ed. Werner Brock (London: Vision, 1956), 391.

32. See Bruns, "Concepts of Art and Poetry," 222: "Levinas's objections to Heidegger's phenomenology of disclosure are well known: the world that is opened in Heidegger's analysis has no people in it. *Dasein* listens for the peal of stillness across a nuclear landscape." For a reading more generous to Heidegger, see Krzysztof Ziarek, *Inflected Language: Toward a Hermeneutics of Nearness: Heidegger, Levinas, Stevens, Celan* (Albany, N.Y.: SUNY Press, 1992).

33. Sean Hand, in *Levinas Reader,* 129.

34. Robbins, *Altered Reading,* xxiii.

35. See Robbins, *Altered Reading,* xxiv: "The face faces, Levinas warns, 'without any metaphor' (*EDE,* 186) [Levinas, *En découvrant l'existence avec Husserl et Heidegger* (Paris: Vrin, 1974)]. Because metaphor would be derivative upon the more originary summons to responsibility that Levinas calls *face,* caution is required before comparing Levinas's descriptions to figural and tropological operations such as prosopopoeia, synecdoche, or metonymy. But what is Levinas's reader to make of the obvious metaphoricity of 'The face is a hand, an open hand,' or, 'The whole body—a hand or a curve of the shoulder—can express as a face' (*TI,* 212), which even suggest a transfer between synecdochic figures for the human?"

36. Edmundson, *Literature Against Philosophy*, 13–14.

37. "There is a very radical distinction between them; they are not even published by the same publishers. . . . But there is certainly a relationship between them." Levinas, quoted in Wright, Hughes, and Ainley, "Paradox of Morality," in *Provocation of Levinas*, 173–74.

38. Perhaps the later Levinas's more balanced, less polemical attitude toward art is related to the fact that he dedicates *Otherwise Than Being* to the memory of (1) "those who were closest among the six million murdered by the National Socialists, and of the millions . . . of all confessions and all nations, victims of the same hatred of the other man, the same anti-semitism"; and (2) to the memory of each member of his immediate family that perished in the Shoah. In other words, by airing the heart of his grievance against Heidegger in this double dedication (the first in French, the other in Hebrew), perhaps Levinas no longer feels compelled to vent against Heideggerian aesthetics. Elsewhere in the same book, however, he includes this telling footnote: "These lines, and those that follow, owe much to Heidegger. Deformed and ill-understood? Perhaps. At least this deformation will not have been a way to deny the debt. Nor this debt a reason to forget . . ." (Levinas, *Otherwise Than Being*, 189n28).

39. *Otherwise Than Being*, Levinas's second magnum opus, published in 1974, rehabilitates not only poetry but music (perhaps because his son Michael Levinas had become a classical musician and composer), as evident in the following passage that, in different ways, recuperates both: body and soul "are in accord prior to thematization, in an accord, a chord, which is possible only as an arpeggio" (Levinas, *Otherwise Than Being*, 68). Here Levinas is succinctly and eloquently suggesting that while the body and soul may be one prior to the sundering they endure through consciousness, this unity cannot be expressed in its simultaneity. Like an arpeggio, their accord does not exist as simple harmony.

40. Levinas, *Collected Philosophical Papers*, 11.

41. Levinas, "Language and Proximity," 118–19.

42. Gibbs makes a very similar point in "Book Review: The Silent Footsteps of Rebecca."

43. Levinas, *Collected Philosophical Papers*, 118.

44. Paul Celan, *Collected Prose*, trans. Rosmarie Waldrop (Manchester, U.K.: Carcanet, 1986), 26.

45. Emmanuel Levinas, *Proper Names*, trans. M. Smith (Stanford, Calif.: Stanford University Press, 1996), 40. See also Emmanuel Levinas, *Noms propres* (Montpelier, Fr.: Fata Morgana, 1976), 59. I have adjusted Smith's translation where necessary.

46. It is interesting that Levinas uses Celan's essays and not his poems here. Perhaps this choice betrays a certain desire to tip the balance away from the "said" of actual poetic texts toward the pure "saying" invoked by Celan's metaliterary prose. (I am grateful to Thomas Trezise for bringing this tendency to my attention.)

47. See Bruns, "Concepts of Art and Poetry," 229: "For Levinas . . . the priority of sound over semantics is meant to indicate the event of sociality: sound means the *presence* of others making themselves felt in advance of what is said. . . . The sound of words is an ethical event, which Levinas does not hesitate to characterize as *critique,* not only because others interrupt me in making themselves felt, setting limits to my autonomy, but because *even when I myself speak* . . . I am no longer an 'I,' am no longer self-identical, but am now beside myself: 'To speak is to interrupt my existence as a subject, a master' [Levinas, *Outside the Subject* (Stanford, Calif.: Stanford University Press, 1994), 149]."

48. So strongly does Levinas embrace Celan's definition of poetry that he hints that the poet's acquaintance with Heidegger might almost offer a realm of rapprochement with his teacher-betrayer: "Paul Celan (whom Heidegger was somehow able, nonetheless, to extoll during one of the former's stays in Germany). . . . Each of these visits 'changed Heidegger deeply' according to an unquestionable testimony I received in these very words" (Levinas, *Proper Names,* 40–41, 174n1). But if there is any chance that Levinas was looking to Celan to clear a path back to Heidegger, the poet went only halfway, according to John Felstiner. Despite their mutual admiration, Celan never succeeded in getting Heidegger to account for his Nazi past; and when the latter asked him to contribute a poem to his 1959 Festschrift, Celan refused. See John Felstiner, *Paul Celan: Poet, Survivor, Jew* (New Haven, Conn.: Yale University Press, 1995), 149, 247.

49. Celan, *Collected Prose,* 34–45.

50. As admirably demonstrated by such readers as Clare Cavanagh, Nancy Pollak, Omry Ronen, Gregory Freidin, Jane Gary Harris, and Charles Isenberg.

51. See Felstiner, *Paul Celan,* 129–33. Felstiner cites Pöggeler's report that when Heidegger came upon Celan's Judaically amplified translation of Mandelstam's 1916 elegy for his mother, he "brusquely whisked it off the table." If one wants to be generous, one could guess that Heidegger felt such interpretive anachronism to be unfairly self-righteous.

52. Mikhail Karpovich, "Moe znakomstvo s Mandel'shtamom," *Novyi Zhurnal* 49 (1957): 258–61, as cited in Clarence Brown, *Mandelstam* (Cambridge: Cambridge University Press, 1973), 34.

53. Freidin, *Coat of Many Colors,* 47.

54. Cavanagh makes a similar point (see *Osip Mandelstam,* 116), citing Mandelstam's essay "Scriabin and Pushkin," in which he writes that "Christian art is an eternal return to the single creative act that began our Christian era, . . . the profound revolution that turned Hellas into Europe" (Mandelstam, *Critical Prose and Letters,* 91–92).

55. Literally, "When the grasses of the mosaics droop . . ." A note about the verse translations that follow: I have sought to balance a concern for conveying

the literal meaning of Mandelstam's poems with a desire to offer English versions that sound right to the ear.

56. See Cavanagh, *Mandelstam*, 105: "Unofficially, his Jewish past followed him even into the non-Jewish 'home and family' he attempted to construct for himself in Russian and European literature. . . . The young poet was known in Symbolist circles as 'Zinaida's [Gippius's] little Yid' (Gippius had been one of his early supporters); and Aleksandr Blok, no admirer either of Acmeists or of Jews, later noted in his diary that 'Mandelstam has grown a great deal. Gradually one gets used to the kike and sees the artist.'"

57. In the house of the Novograd priest, Liutov finds a painting of the severed head of John the Baptist with a "lively" snake looping out of his mouth—which, as Sicher points out, at the same time is a portrait of Saint John the Apostle-Evangelist, whose life, according to legend, was saved by a snake who extracted the venom from a poisoned chalice (Sicher, *Jews in Russian Literature,* 60). As in Mandelstam, Babel's cunning serpentine interloper is a savior as well.

58. An otherwise identical poem appears as "Neutolimye slova . . ." ("Unquenchable words . . .") of 1915, in an earlier edition of Mandelstam's complete works edited by Struve and Filipoff, *Sobranie sochinenii v trekh tomakh* (Washington, D.C.: Inter-Language Library Associates, 1964), 1:128. I have relied instead on Nerler's 1990 and 1993 editions, which correct the title, stanzaic division, and date of this poem. See Cavanagh, *Osip Mandelstam,* 331n28.

59. See "V ogromnom omute prozrachno i temno" ("The great slough is clear and dark"), also from 1910, where Mandelstam writes: "So heavy that [my heart] goes to the bottom,/Pining for that old sweet silt,/And then like a straw escaping the depths,/it floats up effortlessly" (Mandelstam, *Sochinenia v dvukh tomakh,* 1:72). Here Mandelstam relies on a kind of fated inevitability to rescue him from the "sweet silt" of origins at the bottom of the slough.

60. Midrash Avot D'Rabbi Nathan 31b.

61. Charles Isenberg, *Substantial Proofs of Being: Osip Mandelstam's Literary Prose* (Columbus, Ohio: Slavica, 1986), 30.

62. This image is borrowed from Fyodor Tiutchev (1803–73)—along with many other motifs that appear in Mandelstam's art. See Tiutchev's "Den' i noch'" ("Night and Day"), where day appears as the "shimmering veil" that is ripped off the "abyss" as night falls. See Fyodor Tiutchev, "Den' i noch'," in *The Heritage of Russian Verse,* ed. D. Obolensky (Bloomington: Indiana University Press, 1976), 135.

63. Osip Mandelstam, *The Noise of Time and Other Prose Pieces,* trans. Clarence Brown (London: Quartet Books, 1988), 76–77.

64. See Zornberg, *Genesis,* 3.

65. Katsis, *Osip Mandel'shtam,* 244–46.

66. For a clear and sympathetic account of the relevance of Freud's "family romances" throughout Jewish literature, see Marshall Berman, "'A Little Child

Shall Lead Them': The Jewish Family Romance," in *The Jew in the Text: Modernity and the Construction of Identity,* ed. Linda Nochlin and Tamar Garb (London: Thames and Hudson, 1995), 253–75.

67. Franz Kafka, "Letter to Max Brod, June, 1921," trans. Richard Winston and Clara Winston, in *The Basic Kafka* (New York: Simon and Schuster, 1979), 292. Furthermore, Kafka's infamous undelivered letter to his father could have easily been written by Mandelstam to his own: what little Judaism there was "to be handed on to the child . . . dribbled away while you were passing it on" (217).

68. See Bruns, "Concepts of Art and Poetry."

69. Levinas, "Temptation of Temptation," 50.

70. Isenberg, *Substantial Proofs of Being,* 55.

71. The evocation of Taurides, as a way of tying Crimea and hence Russia to ancient Greece, also occurs more than a dozen times in Pushkin's work. See J. Thomas Shaw, *Konkordans k stikham A. S. Pushkina* (Moscow: Yazyk Russkoi Kultury, 2000), 2:1072.

72. See Pollak, *Mandelstam the Reader,* 125.

73. Nadezhda Mandelstam, *Hope Abandoned,* trans. Max Hayward (New York: Atheneum, 1974), 554.

74. In 1935 Mandelstam writes that "lyrical self-love, even in its best forms, is deadening; it always impoverishes the poet" (Mandelstam, *Sobranie sochinenii v chetyrekh tomakh,* 4:165; see also Isenberg, *Substantial Proofs of Being,* 36).

75. Steven Connor, "'I . . . AM. A': Addressing the Jewish Question in Joyce's *Ulysses,*" in *The Jew in the Text,* 231–32.

76. Levinas, *Time and the Other,* 79.

77. J. G. Harris, "The Impulse and the Text," introduction to *Critical Prose and Letters,* by Mandelstam, 16–17.

78. See David Danow's definition in *Handbook of Russian Literature,* ed. Terras, 363: *raznochintsy* is "a social term referring to 'people of diverse rank' or 'people of no particular estate.' These were a new breed within Russian society of mixed background below the gentry. . . . Having emerged from provincial, clerical, and petty-bourgeois squalor, they rose with difficulty from poverty and social obscurity, frequently by tutoring, doing translation work, or through journalism." By the 1860s, *raznochintsy* had come to dominate and define what had become known as the intelligentsia.

79. Levinas, "Judaism and Revolution," 118.

80. Paul Ricoeur, *Oneself as Another,* trans. Kathleen Blamey (Chicago: University of Chicago Press, 1992), 337.

81. J. G. Harris, *Osip Mandelstam* (Boston: Twayne, 1988), 80.

82. See the Russian original in Mandelstam, *Sochinenia v dvukh tomakh,* 2:128: "Ty v kakom vremeni khochesh zhit'?—Ya khochu zhit' v povelitel'nom prichastii budushchego, v zaloge stradatel'nom—v 'dolzhenstvuyushchem byt.'"

83. Harris, *Osip Mandelstam,* 81.

84. Ibid., 99.

85. Richard and Elizabeth McKane's version hews close to this—see "Octets," in Osip Mandelstam, *The Moscow Notebooks*, trans. Richard McKane and Elizabeth McKane (Newcastle upon Tyne, U.K.: Bloodaxe Books, 1991), 76. Nancy Pollak translates *lepit* ("forms," "mashes together," "sculpts out of clay") as "fashions" and *opyt* ("experience") as "the experiment." My own rather free translation of the last two lines tries to convey some of the tongue-twisting cadence and aesthetic agenda of the Russian original. See also Ilya Bernstein, ed., *Osip Mandelstam: New Translations* (New York: Ugly Duckling, 2006), 23, for a rather nice rendering by Eugene Ostashevsky: "It molds matter out of mutter/And drinks mutter out of matter."

86. I am grateful to Jacob Meskin for first bringing this to my attention during a conversation about *Otherwise Than Being.*

87. See Clarence Brown, foreword to *A Concordance to the Poems of Osip Mandelstam,* ed. Demetrius J. Koubourlis (Ithaca, N.Y.: Cornell University Press, 1974), xi.

88. Osip Mandelstam, *The Voronezh Notebooks*, trans. Richard McKane and Elizabeth McKane (Newcastle upon Tyne, U.K.: Bloodaxe Books, 1996), 43. See also Mandelstam, *Sochinenia v dvukh tomakh,* 1:216.

89. The lexical association of babble (*lepet*) with shaping something from clay (*lepit' iz gliny*) in Mandelstam's verse also suggests the image of continuous creation in Isaiah 29, 41, 45, and 64 and Jeremiah 18—in which God is a potter and humanity a clay pot constantly being reshaped, a theme grounded in the second account of man's creation by hand out of dust and breath in Genesis 2:7. Mandelstam's *"lepet-lepit"* dynamic fuses the logocentric and manual versions of divine creation, following the Greek definition of *poesis* as a "making."

90. Jennifer Baines, *Mandelstam: The Later Poetry* (Cambridge: Cambridge University Press, 1976), 96. For historical intertexts, see Katsis, *Osip Mandel'shtam,* 429–33.

91. Pollak, *Mandelstam the Reader,* 54.

92. See Osip Mandelstam, "Sestry tyazhest' i nezhnost . . ." of 1920 ("Heaviness and Tenderness, sisters with the same traits . . ."), in *Sochinenia v dvukh tomakh,* 1:126.

93. See Bakhtin, *Art and Answerability.*

94. Isenberg, *Substantial Proofs of Being,* 168.

95. Pollak, *Mandelstam the Reader,* 130, 161.

## CONCLUSION

1. Eaglestone, "One and the Same?" 605–6.

2. J. M. Bernstein, *The Fate of Art,* 3.

3. In Grossman's epic *Life and Fate,* specifically: see Levinas, quoted in *Is*

*It Righteous to Be?* ed. Robbins, 81. Mark Larrimore suggests the term "goods" instead of "The Good" as a fruitful way to approach the problem of goodness. See Larrimore, "The Problem of Good" (forthcoming).

4. Levinas, quoted in *Is It Righteous to Be?* ed. Robbins, 85.

5. Ibid.

6. Ibid., 280. Kenosis is derived from Philippians 2:5–7: "Your attitude should be the same as that of Christ Jesus: Who, being in very nature God, did not consider equality with God something to be grasped, but made himself nothing, taking the very nature of a servant, being made in human likeness." In the discussion above, Jean Borel refers to Levinas's "God and Philosophy" as a description of Christian kenosis: "As responsible, I do not leave off emptying myself of myself. There is an infinite increase in this exhausting of oneself, in which the subject is not simply an awareness of this expenditure but its locus and even, so to speak, goodness" (Levinas, *Basic Philosophical Writings*, 144).

# Bibliography

Alford, C. Fred. "Levinas and Political Theory." *Political Theory* 32, no. 2 (April 2004): 146–71.

Arendt, Hannah. *The Jew as Pariah: Jewish Identity and Politics in the Modern Age*. New York: Grove, 1978.

Atterton, Peter. "Art, Religion, and Ethics Post Mortem Dei: Levinas and Dostoevsky." *Levinas Studies* 2 (May 2007): 104–32.

Babel, Isaac. *The Collected Stories*. Translated by Walter Morrison. New York: Meridian Fiction, 1955.

———. *Isaac Babel's Selected Writings*. Translated by Peter Constantine. Edited by Gregory Freidin. New York: Norton, 2007.

———. *1920 Diary*. Translated by H. T. Willetts. Edited by Carol Avins. New Haven, Conn.: Yale University Press, 1995.

———. *Sobranie sochinenii v chetyrekh tomakh*. Moscow: Vremia, 2006.

———. *You Must Know Everything*. Edited by Nathalie Babel. Translated by M. Hayward. New York: Dell, 1970.

Baines, Jennifer. *Mandelstam: The Later Poetry*. Cambridge: Cambridge University Press, 1976.

Bakhtin, Mikhail. *Art and Answerability: Early Philosophical Essays*. Translated by Vadim Liapunov. Edited by Michael Holquist and Vadim Liapunov. Austin: University of Texas Press, 1990.

———. *Problems of Dostoevsky's Poetics*. Edited and translated by Caryl Emerson. Minneapolis: University of Minnesota Press, 1989.

———. *Speech Genres and Other Late Essays*. Translated by Vern W. McGee. Edited by Caryl Emerson and Michael Holquist. Austin: University of Texas Press, 1994.

Barsht, Konstantin. "Defining the Face: Observations on Dostoevskii's Creative Processes." In *Russian Literature, Modernism and the Visual Arts*, edited by C. Kelly and S. Lovell. Cambridge: Cambridge University Press, 2000.

Barth, Karl. *Church Dogmatics*. Edinburgh: T. and T. Clark, 1961.

Batnitzky, Leora. "The Image of Judaism: German-Jewish Intellectuals and the Ban on Images." Paper presented at the conference "Icon, Image, and Text in Modern Jewish Culture," Princeton, N.J., March 7, 1999.

————. *Leo Strauss and Emmanuel Levinas: Philosophy and the Politics of Revelation*. Cambridge: Cambridge University Press, 2006.

Batuman, Elif. "Babel in California." *n+1* no. 2 (Spring 2005): 22–68.

Belknap, Robert. *The Structure of "The Brothers Karamazov."* Evanston, Ill.: Northwestern University Press, 1989.

Benjamin, Walter. "The Storyteller: Reflections on the Works of Nikolai Leskov." In *Illuminations*. New York: Schocken, 1969.

Berman, Marshall. "'A Little Child Shall Lead Them': The Jewish Family Romance." In *The Jew in the Text: Modernity and the Construction of Identity*, edited by Linda Nochlin and Tamar Garb. London: Thames and Hudson, 1995.

Bernstein, Ilya, ed. *Osip Mandelstam: New Translations*. New York: Ugly Duckling, 2006.

Bernstein, J. M. *The Fate of Art*. London: Polity, 1992.

Bernstein, Richard. "Evail and the Temptation of Theodicy." In *The Cambridge Companion to Levinas,* edited by Simon Critchley and Robert Bernasconi. Cambridge: Cambridge University Press, 2002.

Blanchot, Maurice. *The Space of Literature*. Translated by Ann Smock. Lincoln: University of Nebraska Press, 1982.

Bocharov, Sergey. "Conversations with Bakhtin." *PMLA* 109, no. 5 (October 1994): 1020.

Brown, Clarence. Foreword to *A Concordance to the Poems of Osip Mandelstam,* edited by Demetrius J. Koubourlis. Ithaca, N.Y.: Cornell University Press, 1974.

————. *Mandelstam*. Cambridge: Cambridge University Press, 1973.

Bruns, Gerald. "The Concepts of Art and Poetry in Emmanuel Levinas's Writings." In *The Cambridge Companion to Levinas*, edited by Simon Critchley and Robert Bernasconi. Cambridge: Cambridge University Press, 2002.

Cassedy, Steven. *Dostoevsky's Religion*. Stanford, Calif.: Stanford University Press, 2005.

————. "Florensky and the Celebration of Matter." In *Russian Religious Thought,* edited by Judith Deutsch Kornblatt and Richard Gustafson. Madison: University of Wisconsin Press, 1996.

Cavanagh, Clare. "The Forms of the Ordinary: Bakhtin, Prosaics and the Lyric." *Slavic and East European Journal* 41, no. 1 (Spring 1997): 49–50.

————. *Osip Mandelstam and the Modernist Creation of Tradition*. Princeton, N.J.: Princeton University Press, 1995.

Caygill, Howard. *Levinas and the Political*. New York: Routledge, 2002.

Celan, Paul. *Collected Prose*. Translated by Rosmarie Waldrop. Manchester, U.K.: Carcanet, 1986.

Clay, George R. *Tolstoy's Phoenix: From Method to Meaning in "War and Peace."* Evanston, Ill.: Northwestern University Press, 1998.

Cohen, Arthur A., ed. *The Jew: Essays from Martin Buber's Journal "Der Jude," 1916–1928*. University: University of Alabama Press, 1980.

Cohen, Richard. *Face to Face with Levinas*. Albany, N.Y.: SUNY Press, 1986.

Connor, Steven. "'I . . . AM. A': Addressing the Jewish Question in Joyce's *Ulysses*." In *The Jew in the Text: Modernity and the Construction of Identity*. Edited by Linda Nochlin and Tamar Garb. London: Thames and Hudson, 1995.

Critchley, Simon. *The Ethics of Deconstruction: Derrida and Levinas*. Cambridge: Blackwell, 1992.

———. "Five Problems in Levinas's View of Politics and the Sketch of a Solution to Them." *Political Theory* 32, no. 2 (April 2004): 172–85.

Danow, David. "The Paradox of *Red Cavalry*." In "Centenary of Isaak Babel." Special issue of *Canadian Slavonic Papers* 36, no. 1–2 (March–June 1994): 43–54.

Dostoevsky, Fyodor M. *Biografija, pisma i zametki iz zapisnoi knizhki F. M. Dostoyevskovo*. Edited by Orest Miller and Nikolai Strakhov. St. Petersburg, 1883.

———. *The Brothers Karamazov*. Translated by Richard Pevear and Larissa Volokhonsky. New York: Vintage, 1991.

———. *Crime and Punishment*. Translated by Richard Pevear and Larissa Volokhonsky. New York: Vintage, 1993.

———. *Demons*. Translated by Richard Pevear and Larissa Volokhonsky. New York: Vintage Books, 1994.

———. *The Diary of a Writer*. Translated by Boris Brasol. New York: Charles Scribner, 1949.

———. *The Idiot*. Translated by Richard Pevear and Larissa Volokhonsky. New York: Vintage, 2003.

———. *Polnoe sobranie sochinenii v 30-ti tomakh*. Leningrad: Nauka, 1972.

———. *Zapisnye tetradi F. M. Dostoevskogo*. Edited by E. N. Konshina. Moscow: Akademia, 1935.

Dreizin, Felix. *The Russian Soul and the Jew: Essays in Literary Ethnocriticism*. Lanham, Md.: University Press of America, 1990.

Eaglestone, Robert. *Ethical Criticism: Reading After Levinas*. Edinburgh: Edinburgh University Press, 1997.

———. "One and the Same? Ethics, Aesthetics, and Truth." *Poetics Today* 25, no. 4 (Winter 2004): 595–608.

Edelglass, William. "Asymmetry and Normativity: Levinas Reading Dostoyevsky on Desire, Responsibility, and Suffering." In *Analecta Husserliana LXXXV: The Enigma of Good and Evil: The Moral Sentiment in Literature*, edited by A. T. Tymienicka. Dordrecht, Neth.: Springer, 2005.

———. "Levinas's Language." In *Analecta Husserliana LXXXV: The Enigma of Good and Evil: The Moral Sentiment in Literature*, edited by A. T. Tymienicka. Dordrecht, Neth.: Springer, 2005.

Edmundson, Mark. *Literature Against Philosophy, Plato to Derrida: A Defence of Poetry.* Cambridge: Cambridge University Press, 1995.

Eichenbaum, Boris. "Illutsiya skaza (1918)." In *Skvoz' literaturu.* The Hague, Neth.: Mouton, 1962.

Emerson, Caryl. "Back to the Future: Shostakovich's Revision of Leskov's 'Lady Macbeth of Mtsensk District.'" *Cambridge Opera Journal* 1, no. 1 (March 1989): 59–78.

———. *The First Hundred Years of Mikhail Bakhtin.* Princeton, N.J.: Princeton University Press, 1997.

———. *An Introduction to Russian Literature,* forthcoming.

———. "Prosaics and the Problem of Form." *Slavic and East European Journal* 41, no. 1 (Spring 1997): 16–39.

———. "Word and Image in Dostoevsky's Worlds: Robert Louis Jackson on Readings That Bakhtin Could Not Do." In *Freedom and Responsibility in Russian Literature: Essays in Honor of Robert Louis Jackson,* edited by Elizabeth Cheresh Allen and Gary Saul Morson. Evanston, Ill.: Northwestern University Press, 1995.

Epstein, Mikhail. "Judaic Spiritual Traditions in the Poetry of Pasternak and Mandel'shtam." Translated by Ruth Rischin. *Symposium: A Quarterly Journal in Modern Literatures* 52, no. 4 (Winter 1999): 205–31.

Eskin, Michael. *Ethics and Dialogue in the Works of Levinas, Bakhtin, Mandel'shtam, and Celan.* Oxford: Oxford University Press, 2000.

———. "Introduction: The Double 'Turn' to Ethics and Literature?" *Poetics Today* 25, no. 4 (Winter 2004): 557–72.

———. "Translating the Other: Celan's Encounter with Mandelstam." *Germano-Slavica* 11 (1999): 27–38.

Falen, James E. *Isaac Babel: Russian Master of the Short Story.* Knoxville: University of Tennessee Press, 1974.

Felstiner, John. *Paul Celan: Poet, Survivor, Jew.* New Haven, Conn.: Yale University Press, 1995.

Florensky, Pavel. "Ikonostas." In *Izbrannye trudy po iskusstvu.* Moscow, 1996. Originally published in 1922.

Frank, Joseph. *Dostoevsky: The Miraculous Years, 1865–1871.* Princeton, N.J.: Princeton University Press, 1996.

Freidin, Gregory. *A Coat of Many Colors: Osip Mandelstam and His Mythologies of Self-Presentation.* Berkeley: University of California Press, 1987.

———. "Isaac Babel." In *European Writers: The Twentieth Century,* edited by George Stade. New York: Charles Scribner's Sons, 1990.

French, Bruce. *Dostoevsky's "Idiot": Dialogue and the Spiritually Good Life.* Evanston, Ill.: Northwestern University Press, 2001.

Freud, Sigmund. "Dostoevsky and Parricide." In *Writings on Art and Literature.* Stanford, Calif.: Stanford University Press, 1997.

Friedlander, Judith. *Vilna on the Seine: Jewish Intellectuals in France Since 1968*. New Haven, Conn.: Yale University Press, 1990.

Gasparov, M. L. *O. Mandel'shtam: Grazhdanskaya lirika 1937 goda*. Moscow: RGGU, 1996.

Gibbs, Robert. "Book Review: The Silent Footsteps of Rebecca." *Continental Philosophy Review* 37, no. 3 (July 2004): 371–75.

———. *Correlations in Rosenzweig and Levinas*. Princeton, N.J.: Princeton University Press, 1992.

Girard, René. *Resurrection from the Underground: Feodor Dostoevsky*. Translated by James G. Williams. New York: Crossroad, 1997.

Goethe, Johann Wolfgang von. *Elective Affinities*. Translated by David Constantine. New York: Oxford University Press, 1999.

Goldstein, David I. *Dostoevsky and the Jews*. Austin: University of Texas Press, 1981.

Greisch, Jean. "The Face and Reading." Translated by Simon Critchley. In *Re-Reading Levinas*, edited by Robert Bernasconi and Simon Critchley. Bloomington: Indiana University Press, 1991.

Grøngaard, Ragna. *An Investigation of Composition and Theme in Isaak Babel's Literary Cycle KONARMIJA*. Aarhus, Den.: Arkona, 1979.

Grossman, Vasily. *Life and Fate*. Translated by Robert Chandler. New York: New York Review Books, 1985.

Hadlock, Heather. "Program Notes." Juilliard String Quartet. Princeton University Concerts, May 11, 1995.

Harris, J. G. Introduction to *Critical Prose and Letters*, by Osip Mandelstam. Translated by J. G. Harris and C. Link. Ann Arbor, Mich.: Ardis, 1990.

———. *Osip Mandelstam*. Boston: Twayne, 1988.

Heidegger, Martin. *Existence and Being*. Edited by Werner Brock. London: Vision, 1956.

———. *Poetry, Language, Thought*. New York: Harper and Row, 1971.

Horowitz, Brian. *The Myth of A. S. Pushkin in Russia's Silver Age: M. O. Gershenzon, Pushkinist*. Evanston, Ill.: Northwestern University Press, 1996.

Isenberg, Charles. *Substantial Proofs of Being: Osip Mandelstam's Literary Prose*. Columbus, Ohio: Slavica, 1986.

Ivanits, Linda. "Folk Beliefs About the 'Unclean Force' in Dostoevskij's *The Brothers Karamazov*." In *New Perspectives on Nineteenth-Century Russian Prose*, edited by George Gutsche and L. Leighton. Columbus, Ohio: Slavica, 1982.

Jackson, Robert Louis. *Dialogues with Dostoevsky*. Stanford, Calif.: Stanford University Press, 1993.

———. *Dostoevsky's Quest for Form: A Study of His Philosophy of Art*. New Haven, Conn.: Yale University Press, 1966.

Johnson, Leslie. "The Face of the Other in *Idiot*." *Slavic Review* 50, no.4 (Winter 1991).

Jurecic, Ann, Anne Caswell Klein, Amanda Irwin Wilkins, Cole Bentley, and Val Vinokur. "Imagining Our Others." Description for three seminars given at the American Comparative Literature Association's annual convention, Princeton, N.J., April 2006.

Kafka, Franz. "Letter to Max Brod, June, 1921." Translated by Richard and Clara Winston. In *The Basic Kafka*. New York: Simon and Schuster, 1979.

Karpovich, Mikhail. "Moe znakomstvo s Mandel'shtamom." *Novyi zhurnal* 49 (1957): 258–61.

Kashina, Nadezhda. *The Aesthetics of Dostoyevsky*. Translated by Julius Katser. Moscow: Raduga, 1987.

Katsis, Leonid. *Osip Mandel'shtam: Muksus iudeistva* [The Musk of Judaism]. Jerusalem: Gesharim; Moscow: Mosty Kul'tury, 2002.

Katz, Elise. *Levinas, Judaism, and the Feminine: The Silent Footsteps of Rebecca*. Bloomington: Indiana University Press, 2003.

Kearney, Richard. *Dialogues with Contemporary Continental Thinkers*. Manchester, U.K.: Manchester University Press, 1984.

Kierkegaard, Søren. *The Concept of Anxiety*. Edited and translated by Reidar Thomte and Albert Anderson. Princeton, N.J.: Princeton University Press, 1980.

Kornblatt, Judith Deutsch. *The Cossack Hero in Russian Literature*. Madison: University of Wisconsin Press, 1992.

———. *Doubly Chosen: Jewish Identity, the Soviet Intelligentsia, and the Russian Orthodox Church*. Madison: University of Wisconsin Press, 2004.

———. "Vladimir Solov'ev on Spiritual Nationhood." *Russian Review* 56 (April 1997): 157–77.

Kornblatt, Judith Deutsch, and Gary Rosenshield. "Vladimir Solovyov: Confronting Dostoevsky on the Jewish and Christian Questions." *Journal of the American Academy of Religion* 68, no. 1 (March 2000): 69–98.

Kostalevsky, Marina. *Dostoevsky and Soloviev: The Art of Integral Vision*. New Haven, Conn.: Yale University Press, 1997.

Leibowitz, Yeshayahu. *Judaism, Human Values, and the Jewish State*. Edited by Eliezer Goldman. Cambridge, Mass.: Harvard University Press, 1992.

Leskov, Nikolai S. *Povesti i rasskazy*. Moscow: Russkii Yazyk, 1985.

———. *Selected Tales*. Translated by David Magarshack. New York: Noonday, 1961.

Levinas, Emmanuel. *Difficile liberté*. Paris: Livre de Poche, 2003.

———. *En découvrant l'existence avec Husserl et Heidegger*. Paris: Vrin, 1974.

———. *Entre Nous: On Thinking-of-the-Other*. Translated by M. B. Smith and Barbara Harshav. New York: Columbia University Press, 1998.

———. *Ethics and Infinity*. Translated by Richard A. Cohen. Pittsburgh: Duquesne University Press, 1985.

———. "Judaism and Revolution." In *Nine Talmudic Readings*, translated by Annette Aronowicz. Bloomington: Indiana University Press, 1994.

———. "Language and Proximity." In *Collected Philosophical Papers*. Translated by Alphonso Lingis. Boston: Martinus Nijhoff, 1987.

———. *Noms propres*. Montpelier, Fr.: Fata Morgana, 1976.

———. *Otherwise Than Being, or Beyond Essence*. Translated by Alphonso Lingis. Boston: Martinus Nijhoff, 1981.

———. *Outside the Subject*. Stanford, Calif.: Stanford University Press, 1994.

———. "The Pact (Tractate Sotah 37a-37b)." In *Beyond the Verse*, translated by Gary D. Mole. Bloomington: Indiana University Press, 1994.

———. "Philosophie, justice et amour." In *Entre Nous*. Paris: Grasset, 1991.

———. *Proper Names*. Translated by M. Smith. Stanford, Calif.: Stanford University Press, 1996.

———. "Reality and Its Shadow." In *Collected Philosophical Papers*, translated by Alphonso Lingis. Boston: Martinus Nijhoff, 1987.

———. "Reality and Its Shadow." In *The Levinas Reader*, edited by Sean Hand, translated by Alphonso Lingis. Oxford: Blackwell, 1992.

———. "Signification and Sense." In *Humanism of the Other*, translated by Nidra Poller. Urbana: University of Illinois Press, 2003.

———. "The Temptation of Temptation." In *Nine Talmudic Readings*, translated by Annette Aronowicz. Bloomington: Indiana University Press, 1994.

———. *Time and the Other*. Translated by Richard A. Cohen. Pittsburgh: Duquesne University Press, 1987.

———. "To Love the Torah More Than God." In *Difficult Freedom*, translated by Sean Hand. Baltimore: Johns Hopkins University Press, 1997.

———. *Totality and Infinity*. Translated by Alphonso Lingis. Pittsburgh: Duquesne University Press, 1961.

———. "Transcendence and Height." In *Basic Philosophical Writings*, edited by Adriaan Peperzak, Simon Critchley, and Robert Bernasconi. Bloomington: Indiana University Press, 1996.

———. "Useless Suffering." In *The Provocation of Levinas: Rethinking the Other*, edited by Robert Bernasconi and David Wood. London: Routledge, 1988.

Lotman, Yuri M. "'Agreement' and 'Self-Giving' as Archetypal Models of Culture." Translated by N. F. C. Owen. In *The Semiotics of Russian Culture*, by Yuri M. Lotman and Boris A. Uspenskij, edited by Ann Shukman. Ann Arbor: Department of Slavic Languages and Literatures, University of Michigan, 1984.

———. *Izbrannye stat'i v trekh tomakh*. Tallinn, Estonia: Aleksandra, 1992–93.

Luplow, Carol. *Isaac Babel's "Red Cavalry."* Ann Arbor, Mich.: Ardis, 1982.

Mandelstam, Nadezhda. *Hope Abandoned*. Translated by Max Hayward. New York: Atheneum, 1974.

———. *Hope Against Hope*. Translated by Max Hayward. New York: Atheneum, 1970.

Mandelstam, Osip. *Critical Prose and Letters*. Translated by J. G. Harris and C. Link. Ann Arbor, Mich.: Ardis, 1990.

———. *The Moscow Notebooks*. Translated by Richard McKane and Elizabeth McKane. Newcastle upon Tyne, U.K.: Bloodaxe Books, 1991.

———. *The Noise of Time and Other Prose Pieces*. Translated by Clarence Brown. London: Quartet Books, 1988.

———. *Sobranie sochinenii v chetyrekh tomakh*. Edited by Nerler, Nikitaev, and Sergeeva. Moscow: Art-Biznis-Tsentr, 1993.

———. *Sobranie sochinenii v trekh tomakh*. Edited by Struve and Filipoff. Washington, D.C.: Inter-Language Library Associates, 1964.

———. *Sochinenia v dvukh tomakh*. Edited by Averintsev, Nerler, and Mikhailov. Moscow: Khudozhestvennaya Literatura, 1990.

———. *The Voronezh Notebooks*. Translated by Richard McKane and Elizabeth McKane. Newcastle upon Tyne: Bloodaxe Books, 1996.

Maupassant, Guy de. "L'Aveu." In *Contes du jour et de la nuit*. Boston: Adamant, 2006.

McCaffrey, Steve. "The Scandal of Sincerity: Toward a Levinasian Poetics." In *Prior to Meaning: The Protosemantic and Poetics*. Evanston, Ill.: Northwestern University Press, 2001.

McLean, Hugh. "On the Style of a Leskovian *Skaz*." In *Harvard Slavic Studies*, vol. 2. Cambridge, Mass.: Harvard University Press, 1954.

McReynolds, Susan. "Dostoevsky in Europe: The Political as the Spiritual." *Partisan Review* 69, no. 1 (Winter 2002): 93–101.

Medzhibovskaya, Inessa. "'Creating a Life for Language': The Emancipatory Rejoinder of *Skaz*," forthcoming.

———. "Dogmatism or Moral Logic? Simon Frank Confronts Tolstoy's Ethical Thought." *Tolstoy Studies Journal* 16 (2004): 18–32.

———. "Frank Confronts Tolstoy's Ethical Thought (the Later Years)." *Tolstoy Studies Journal* 17 (2005): 43–58.

Miller, Robin Feuer. *Dostoevsky and "The Idiot."* Cambridge, Mass.: Harvard University Press, 1981.

Mochulsky, Konstantin. *Dostoevsky: His Life and Work*. Translated by Michael A. Minihan. Princeton, N.J.: Princeton University Press, 1967.

Morgan, Michael. *Discovering Levinas*. Cambridge: Cambridge University Press, 2007.

Morson, Gary Saul. "Dostoevsky's Anti-Semitism and the Critics." *Slavic and East European Journal* 27, no. 3 (Autumn 1983): 302–17.

———. *Narrative and Freedom*. New Haven, Conn.: Yale University Press, 1994.

Moyn, Samuel. *Origins of the Other: Emmanuel Levinas Between Revelation and Ethics*. Ithaca, N.Y.: Cornell University Press, 2005.

Murav, Harriet. *Holy Foolishness: Dostoevsky's Novels and the Poetics of Cultural Critique*. Stanford, Calif.: Stanford University Press, 1992.

Newton, Adam Zachary. *Narrative Ethics*. Cambridge, Mass.: Harvard University Press, 1997.

———. "Versions of Ethics; or, The SARL of Criticism: Sonority, Arrogation, Letting-Be." *American Literary History* 13, no. 3 (Summer 2001): 603–37.

Odesskii, M. P. and D. M. Fel'dman. "Reinterpreting *Red Cavalry* in the Light of Chassidism (Justifying the Revolution)." In "Centenary of Isaak Babel." Special issue of *Canadian Slavonic Papers* 36, no. 1–2 (March–June 1994): 148–54.

Ong, Walter. Introduction to *Oral Poetry: An Introduction*, by Paul Zumthor. Minneapolis: University of Minnesota Press, 1990.

Paperno, Irina. *Suicide as a Cultural Institution in Dostoevsky's Russia*. Ithaca, N.Y.: Cornell University Press, 1997.

Pirozhkova, Antonina. "Years at His Side (1932–1939) and Beyond." Translated by Anne Frydman. In "Centenary of Isaak Babel." Special issue of *Canadian Slavonic Papers* 36, no. 1–2 (March–June 1994): 168–240.

Pollak, Nancy. *Mandelstam the Reader*. Baltimore: Johns Hopkins University Press, 1995.

Postoutenko, Kirill. "Imaginary Ethnicity: Jews and Russians in Russian Economical Mythology." *American Behavioral Scientist* 45 (2001): 282–95.

Preminger, Alex, and T. V. F. Brogan, eds. *The New Princeton Encyclopedia of Poetry and Poetics*. Princeton, N.J.: Princeton University Press, 1993.

Rice, James. "Dostoevsky's Endgame: The Projected Sequel to *The Brothers Karamazov*." *Russian History/Histoire Russe* 33, no. 1 (Spring 2006): 45–62.

———. *Freud's Russia: National Identity in the Evolution of Psychoanalysis*. New Brunswick, N.J.: Transaction, 1993.

Ricoeur, Paul. *Oneself as Another*. Translated by Kathleen Blamey. Chicago: University of Chicago Press, 1992.

Robbins, Jill. "Aesthetic Totality and Ethical Infinity: Levinas on Art." *L'esprit créateur* 35, no. 3 (Fall 1995): 66–79.

———. *Altered Reading: Levinas and Literature*. Chicago: University of Chicago Press, 1999.

———, ed. *Is It Righteous to Be?: Interviews with Emmanuel Levinas*. Stanford, Calif.: Stanford University Press, 2001.

Rolland, Jacques. *Dostoïevski: La question de l'autre*. Lagrasse, France: Verdier, 1983.

Rorty, Richard. "The Barber of Kasbeam: Nabokov on Cruelty." In *Contingency, Irony, and Solidarity*. Cambridge: Cambridge University Press, 1995.

Rosenblum, L. "Umor Dostoevskogo." *Voprosy Literatury* 1–2 (1999): 152–53.

Rosenshield, Gary. "Dostoevskii's 'Funeral of the Universal Man' and 'An Isolated Case' and Chekhov's 'Rothschild's Fiddle': The Jewish Question." *Russian Review* 56 (October 1997): 487–504.

———. "Mystery and Commandment in *The Brothers Karamazov:* Leo Baeck and Fedor Dostoevsky." *Journal of the American Academy of Religion* 62, no. 2 (Summer 1994): 483–508.

Rosenzweig, Franz. *The Star of Redemption.* Translated by William W. Hallo. Boston: Beacon, 1972.

Safran, Gabriella. *Rewriting the Jew: Assimilation Narratives in the Russian Empire.* Stanford, Calif.: Stanford University Press, 2000.

Scarry, Elaine. *On Beauty and Being Just.* Princeton, N.J.: Princeton University Press, 1999.

Schreurs, Marc. *Procedures of Montage in Isaak Babel's "Red Cavalry."* Atlanta: Rodopi, 1989.

Schwarzschild, Steven. "Aesthetics." In *Contemporary Jewish Religious Thought,* edited by A. Cohen and P. Mendes-Flohr. New York: Scribner, 1987.

———. "The Legal Foundation of Jewish Aesthetics." In *The Pursuit of the Ideal: Jewish Writings of Steven Schwarzschild,* edited by M. Kellner. Albany, N.Y.: SUNY Press, 1990.

Senderovich, Sasha. "The Hershele Maze: Isaac Babel and His Ghost Reader." In *Arguing the Modern Jewish Canon: Essays on Modern Jewish Literature in Honor of Ruth Wisse,* edited by Justin D. Cammy, Dara Horn, Alyssa Quint, and Rachel Rubenstein. Cambridge, Mass.: Harvard University Press, 2007.

Shaw, J. Thomas. *Konkordans k stikham A. S. Pushkina.* Moscow: Yazyk Russkoi Kultury, 2000.

Shklovsky, Victor. "I. Babel: A Critical Romance." In *Modern Critical Views: Isaac Babel,* edited by Harold Bloom. New York: Chelsea House, 1987.

Shragin, Boris. *The Challenge of the Spirit.* Translated by P. S. Falla. New York: Knopf, 1978.

Shrayer, Maxim D. "The Jewish Question and *The Brothers Karamazov.*" In *A New Word on "The Brothers Karamazov,"* edited by Robert Louis Jackson. Evanston, Ill.: Northwestern University Press, 2004.

Sicher, Efraim. *Jews in Russian Literature After the October Revolution: Writers and Artists Between Hope and Apostasy.* Cambridge: Cambridge University Press, 1995.

———. *Style and Structure in the Prose of Isaak Babel.* Columbus, Ohio: Slavica, 1986.

Siegel, Lee. "The Tower of Babel." *The Nation,* December 5, 2005.

Solovyov, Vladimir. *A Solovyov Anthology.* Translated by Natalie Duddington. New York: Charles Scribner, 1950.

Sontag, Susan. "Fascinating Fascism." In *Under the Sign of Saturn.* New York: Picador, 2002.

Stadt, Janneke van de. *Fellow Traveler, Wondering Jew: Isaac Babel and the Writer's Path,* forthcoming.

Stanislawski, Michael. *Autobiographical Jews: Essays in Jewish Self-Fashioning.* Seattle: University of Washington Press, 2004.

Steinberg, Aaron S. "Dostoevsky and the Jews." In *The Jew: Essays from Martin Buber's Journal "Der Jude," 1916–1928,* edited by Arthur A. Cohen. University: University of Alabama Press, 1980.

Stepanov, Nikolai. "Novella Babelja." In *Mastera sovremmenoj literatury* (1928).

Straus, Nina Pelikan. "Dostoevsky's Derrida." *Common Knowledge* 6, no. 4 (Fall 2002): 555–67.

Strauss, Leo. *Natural Right and History.* Chicago: University of Chicago Press, 1952.

Terras, Victor, ed. *The Handbook of Russian Literature.* New Haven, Conn.: Yale University Press, 1985.

———. *A Karamazov Companion.* Madison: University of Wisconsin Press, 2002.

———. "Line and Color: The Structure of Babel's Short Stories." In *Red Cavalry: A Critical Companion,* edited by Charles Rougle. Evanston, Ill.: Northwestern University Press, 1996.

Tiutchev, Fyodor. "Den' i noch'." In *The Heritage of Russian Verse,* edited by D. Obolensky. Bloomington: Indiana University Press, 1976.

Toumayan, Alain. "'I More Than the Others': Dostoevsky and Levinas." In "Encounters with Levinas," edited by Thomas Trezise. Special issue of *Yale French Studies* 104 (2004): 55–66.

Trilling, Lionel. Introduction to *The Collected Stories,* by Isaac Babel. Translated by Walter Morrison. New York: Meridian Fiction, 1955.

Vinokur, Val. "'All of a Sudden': Dostoevsky's Demonologies of Terror." In *Just Assassins? The Culture of Russian Terrorism,* edited by Anthony Anemone (forthcoming).

———. "Facing the Devil in Dostoevsky's *The Brothers Karamazov.*" In *Word, Music, History: A Festschrift for Caryl Emerson,* edited by Lazar Fleishman, Gabriella Safran, and Michael Wachtel. Special issue of *Stanford Slavic Studies* 29–30 (2005): part 2, 464–76.

———. "Morality and Orality in Isaac Babel's *Red Cavalry.*" *Massachusetts Review* 45, no. 4 (Winter 2005): 674–95.

———. See also Vinokurov, Val.

Vinokurov, Val. "The End of Consciousness and the Ends of Consciousness: A Reading of Dostoevsky's *The Idiot* and *Demons* after Levinas." *Russian Review* 59, no. 1 (January 2000): 21–37.

———. "Levinas's Dostoevsky." *Common Knowledge* 9, vol. 2 (Spring 2003): 322–44.

———. "'On the Brink of Tears and Laughter': The Uses of Joy and Suffering in Levinas's Thought." *Journal of Religion and Society* 6 (2004), 1-8. Available at http://moses.creighton.edu/jrs/pdf/2004-12.pdf.

————. See also Vinokur, Val.

Ward, Bruce K. "The Absent Finger of Providence in *The Brothers Karamazov: Some Implications for Religious Models.*" In *And Meaning for a Life Entire: Festschrift for Charles A. Moser on the Occasion of His Sixtieth Birthday,* edited by Peter Rollberg. Bloomington, Ind.: Slavica, 1997.

Wasiolek, Edward. Introduction to *The Notebooks for "The Brothers Karamazov,"* by Fyodor M. Dostoevsky, edited by Edward Wasiolek. Chicago: University of Chicago Press, 1971.

Weidle, Wladimir. *Russia: Absent and Present.* Translated by A. Gordon Smith. London: Hollis and Carter, 1952.

Wilshire, Bruce. *Get 'Em All! Kill 'Em!: Genocide, Terrorism, Righteous Communities.* Lanham, Md.: Lexington Books, 2004.

Wittgenstein, Ludwig. *Tractatus Logico-Philosophicus.* Translated by D. F. Pears and B. F. Guinness. London: Routledge, 1974. Vol. 6.

Wright, Tamra, Peter Hughes, and Alison Ainley. "The Paradox of Morality: An Interview with Emmanuel Levinas." In *The Provocation of Levinas: Rethinking the Other,* edited by Robert Bernasconi and David Wood. London: Routledge, 1988.

Wyschograd, Edith. "The Art in Ethics: Aesthetics, Objectivity, and Alterity in the Philosophy of Emmanuel Levinas." In *Ethics as First Philosophy: The Significance of Emmanuel Levinas for Philosophy, Literature, and Religion,* edited by Adriaan Peperzak. New York: Routledge, 1995.

Zholkovsky, Alexander. "Isaak Babel, Author of Guy de Maupassant." In "Centenary of Isaak Babel." Special issue of *Canadian Slavonic Papers* 36, no. 1–2 (March–June 1994): 89–106.

————. "A Memo from the Underground (Babel and Dostoevsky)." *Elementa* 1 (1994): 305–20.

————. "Towards a Typology of 'Debut' Narratives: Babel, Nabokov and Others." Paper given at the conference on "The Enigma of Isaac Babel," Stanford University, Stanford, Calif., February 29–March 2, 2004. Available at www.usc.edu/dept/las/sll/eng/ess/babnab1.htm.

Ziarek, Krzysztof. *Inflected Language: Toward a Hermeneutics of Nearness: Heidegger, Levinas, Stevens, Celan.* Albany, N.Y.: SUNY Press, 1992.

Zornberg, Avivah. *Genesis: The Beginning of Desire.* New York: Doubleday, 1996.

Zuckert, Catherine. *Postmodern Platos.* Chicago: University of Chicago Press, 1996.

Zumthor, Paul. *Oral Poetry: An Introduction.* Minneapolis: University of Minnesota Press, 1990.

# Index

# Index

# Index

Markel (*BK*), 11, 34, 51, 53
  credo of, 56, 57
  deathbed confession, 36
  on guilt, 50
  radical responsibility and, 38
Marmeladova, Sonya (*CP*), 50, 74, 91, 135
Marxism, 149n54
Marya Lebyadkina (*Demons*), 31
materialism, spiritual, 44, 46, 58, 61
Maupassant, Guy de, 60, 90, 156n68
Mayakovsky, Vladimir, 115
McCaffrey, Steve, 141n26
McKane, Richard and Elizabeth, 164n85
McLean, Hugh, 84, 154n36
McReynolds, Susan, 138n5, 145n37
Medzhibovskaya, Inessa, 83, 139n10, 159n27
Mendele Mokher Sforim, 4
"Meridian, The" (Celan), 108–9
messianism, 5, 61, 91
metaphysics, 16, 99, 109, 152n3
*metexis* (partaking of ideal forms), 96
metonymy, 64, 159n35
Mikhoels, Solomon, 122, 123, 127
"Mikhoels" (Mandelstam), 123
Mill, John Stuart, 13
Miller, Robin Feuer, 19, 25
mimesis, 12, 62, 75, 81, 84, 88
Mitnagdim, 94
Mochulsky, Konstantin, 40, 143n24
modernism, 4, 77, 89, 96, 131
Mongols, 117
"Morning of Acmeism, The" (Mandelstam), 121
Morgan, Michael, 151n68
Morson, Gary Saul, 56, 147n33
Moses (biblical), 46–47
Moyn, Samuel, 138n6
Murav, Harriet, 25, 31
Myshkin, Prince (*Idiot*), 10, 23, 57, 135, 142–43n17
  departure of consciousness from, 24–25
  faces and, 16, 18, 19, 142n8
  inability to deal with justice, 20, 21–22
  positive beauty and, 32

Nabokov, Vladimir, 133
Nachman of Bratslav, Rebbe, 154n31
*nadryv* (laceration, strain), 48
Nadson, Semyon, 124

Nastasya Filippovna (*Idiot*), 19, 20, 21, 22–23, 25, 49
Nazism (National Socialism), 7, 64, 106
  Heidegger and, 99–100, 143n18, 161n48
  Holocaust and, 160n38
New Testament, 39, 69
Newton, Adam Zachary, 88, 139n14
Nietzsche, Friedrich, 49
nihilism, 17, 31
*1920 Diary* (Babel), 63–64, 65, 72, 76, 83–84, 156
*Noise of Time, The* (Mandelstam), 116, 118, 127
*Notes from the Underground* (Dostoevsky), 68, 69
"Notre Dame" (Mandelstam), 113, 134

"Octaves" (Mandelstam), 128–30
October Revolution, 124
Odessa, Jewish ghetto of, 61–62
"Odessa" (Babel), 60, 61, 90, 95
*Odessa Tales* (Babel), 76
"Oh, how we love to play the hypocrite" (Mandelstam), 128
Old Testament, 33, 113, 127
  *See also* Bible, Hebrew
Ong, Walter, 87
"On the Interlocutor" ["O sobesednike"] (Mandelstam), 107, 108, 109, 110
ontology, 12, 50, 55, 132
  of Heidegger's aesthetics, 101
  Levinas's distrust of, 99
  relation to the other, 53
oral culture, 77
ornamentalism, 62, 63–64, 79
Orthodox Christianity, Russian, 5, 6, 7, 39
  Hagia Sophia (Constantinople), 61
  Jewish converts to, 124
  Roman Catholicism versus, 41–42
  *sobornost'*, 42, 44, 58
  *See also* Christianity; Constantinople
Other/otherness, 5, 92
  face of, 7, 19, 27
  poetry and, 13, 108
  proximity of caress and, 103
  responsibility for, 34, 51–52, 55, 131
  separateness from, 52
  suffering of, 87
*Otherwise Than Being* (Levinas), 71, 102–4, 106, 160nn38–39

# Index

"Out of the vicious slough . . . " ["Iz omuta
  zlogo . . . "] (Mandelstam), 114
Ozick, Cynthia, 4, 64

paganism, 45, 46
Pale of Settlement, 122
Paperno, Irina, 144n27
*Parmenides* (Plato), 96
participation, 87, 89, 129
Pasternak, Boris, 119, 157n9
pathos, 49, 56
"Paul Celan" (Levinas), 125
Pavlichenko (*Red Cavalry*), 72, 82–83,
  156n57
peasants, 33, 37, 41, 42, 51
pederasty, 69
penance, 35
Persia, 122
Petersburg, 6, 93, 94, 116
  founding of, 117
  literary tradition of, 60
  synagogue in, 118
Peter the Great, 117
Pevear, Richard, 32
phenomenology, 17, 38, 100, 102, 159n32
philo-Semitism, 44, 55
philosophy, 3, 5, 9
  Greek, 8–9
  idea-feelings and, 57
  poetry in tension with, 96–102
  study of experience, 10
  Western, 6
Pirozhkova, Antonina, 91, 153n23, 156n69
Plato, 96, 98, 158n22
Platonism, 36
*pochvenniki* intellectuals, 44
poetry, 12, 13, 93, 95
  ethics and, 132
  Judaic principle and, 94, 95, 130
  as "magic," 97, 106
  philosophy in tension with, 96–102
  as proximity, 104–5, 109
  as source of truth, 111
Poland, 39, 66, 70, 71
Poles, 60, 63, 65, 82, 86
Polish language, 74
politics, 5, 9, 12, 126, 138n7, 147n35
Pollak, Nancy, 93–94, 131, 164n85
postmodernism, 133
*Problems of Dostoevsky's Poetics*
  (Bakhtin), 15

prophecy, 34, 47, 61, 110, 115, 127
prose, 12, 88, 102, 132
prostitutes/prostitution, 68, 69, 74, 153n23
Proust, Marcel, 61, 152n3
proximity, 102–5, 106, 109, 110, 124
psychology, 50
psychotics, aestheticism of, 87
Pushkin, Aleksandr, 4, 111, 134, 163n71
Pyotr Stepanovich (*Demons*), 26, 29

Rashi, 116
Raskolnikov, Rodion (*CP*), 48–49, 61, 85
*raznochintsy* (people of indeterminate
  rank), 125, 126, 163n78
"Reality and Its Shadow" (Levinas), 96,
  97, 99, 101–3, 106
  aesthetic chaos and, 120
  anti-aesthetics of, 127
  condemnation of rhythm, 129
  poetic irresponsibility spurned in, 109
*Red Cavalry* (Babel), 12–13, 64–65
  "After the Battle," 63, 82
  "Argamak," 63
  "Church at Novograd," 113
  "Crossing the Zbruch," 65–66, 70–71,
    73, 89
  "Gedali," 76
  "In St. Valentine's Church," 113
  "A Letter," 76, 81–82, 155n47
  "The Life Story of Pavlichenko, Matvei
    Rodionych," 75, 85
  "My First Fee," 68, 71, 76, 86, 156n69
  "My First Goose," 63, 83, 88
  "Pan Apolek," 11, 71–74, 75, 113,
    156n69
  "Rebbe, The," 71, 76, 154n34
  "Rebbe's Son, The," 76, 154n31
  "Salt," 75, 80, 155n47
  "Sashka Christ," 11, 74
  "Story of a Horse, The," 80
  "Treason," 80
  "Zamost'e," 85–86
  *See also skaz* narratives
redemption, 32, 33, 45, 48–49, 115
religion, 16, 36
*Republic, The* (Plato), 36
responsibility, 7, 8, 23, 38
  asymmetrical, 99
  burden of, 50–51
  guilt and, 10
  Zosima's pledge of, 18

187

Index

# Index

# About the Author

VAL VINOKUR is a writer, a translator, and the director of Jewish studies and an assistant professor of comparative literature at Eugene Lang College/The New School, in New York. His essays have appeared in the *Boston Review, McSweeney's,* and *Common Knowledge,* among other publications, and his translation (with Rose Réjouis) of Patrick Chamoiseau's novel *Texaco* won the American Translators Association's award for best book in 1998. He is a 2008 Guggenheim Fellow.